This printed edition is published with the permission of Calico Pie Limited-

Printed by:

My History
5 Mexborough Business Centre
College Road
Mexborough
South Yorkshire
S64 9JP

Email: sales@my-history.co.uk
www.my-history.co.uk

ISBN 978-0-9572217-0-3

Contents

Contents

Contents

Contents

Contents

Contents

Introduction

Quick Start Guide   Chapters 1, 2 and 3 are designed to jointly constitute a *Quick Start Guide* for new users, and it is strongly recommended that all new users should work through these 3 chapters at least. It is not necessary to complete all 3 chapters before starting to use, or experiment with, Family Historian; but you will probably make quicker progress if you do.

GEDCOM   Occasionally in this document you will find references to *GEDCOM.* This is the name of the world-wide standard for sharing genealogical data. When you send or receive genealogical data from other people, using a computer, the most common way of doing this is to transfer the data in the form of a GEDCOM file – that is, a file in the GEDCOM format. Family Historian was designed from the start to be 100% GEDCOM-compatible, and 100% GEDCOM-complete – that is, it can load all GEDCOM (5.5) fields and can save all of its data to the GEDCOM format. In fact, Family Historian uses GEDCOM as the format that it saves data in.

Transferring Data into Family Historian   To learn how to transfer data into Family Historian, read the section *Create a New Project* at the end of Chapter 1. During project creation you will be given the opportunity to import data from a GEDCOM file, or directly from another genealogy program. If you want to merge the data into an existing project, use the **Merge/Compare** command on the **File** menu (see Chapter 15 for more on this).

Projects and Files   As we will see, the normal, recommended way of working with Family Historian is to create a *project* to store your genealogy research. You can have as many projects as you like, but it is quite common to have only one, and store all your data in that. You will be shown how to create a new project at the end of Chapter 1. When you create a new project, Family Historian will create a folder on your hard disk for your project, to manage all files relating to your project for you.

You can also use Family Historian to view and edit *GEDCOM files.* When a GEDCOM file is not part of a Family Historian project it is called a *standalone* GEDCOM file. Both approaches – working with projects and working with standalone GEDCOM files – are demonstrated in this book. Bear in mind that even when you are working on a Family Historian project, your data is still stored in a GEDCOM file, within the project folder.

Samples and Tutorials   Some chapters make reference to the pre-installed *Family Historian Sample Project* to illustrate the discussion. Chapters 6-17 are constructed in the form of tutorials that you can work through yourself if you wish. These chapters use pre-installed tutorial files. These tutorial files are all 'standalone' GEDCOM files – that is, they do not form part of a Family Historian project.

The sample project is installed in the default location for Family Historian Projects. If you have changed this location, you can reset it by clicking on the *Location* text link in the *Projects Window* (discussed in Chapter 1). A dropdown menu appears. Click on **Reset Location to Installation Default**. If you cannot see a project entitled "Family Historian Sample Project" in the list of projects in the Projects Window, click on the **More Tasks** button. A dropdown menu appears. Click on **Reset Sample Project** on the **Samples** submenu.

The same **Samples** submenu is also used for opening the tutorial files used in Chapters 6-17. Just click on the appropriate menu command to open the corresponding file.

If you make changes to the tutorial files, you can reset them to their original state at any time. You do this by clicking on **Reset Tutorial Files** on the **Samples** submenu. If you make changes to the Family Historian Sample Project, you can reset that project to its installation state at any time by clicking on **Reset Sample Project** on the same submenu.

The Help

Do not forget to use the Family Historian Help. If there isn't a **Help** button available, pressing **F1** will usually produce help which is relevant to the current context. The Family Historian Help is often the best place to go for *detailed* help. But it also contains more general information and tips, some of which is not available elsewhere.

The Help has a contents page, an index and a search facility, all of which can be reached by clicking on **Contents and Index**, in Family Historian's **Help** menu. You can also browse its contents, by clicking the browse buttons ('>>' and '<<'), which are available at the top of each page of the Help.

Terminology

Certain windows in Family Historian are called 'dialogs'. A *dialog* – also known as a *dialog box* – is a form-like window. Typically a dialog contains boxes (sometimes called *fields*) where you can enter data, or buttons you can press, or options you can tick.

Basic Windows Skills

Although aimed primarily at the relatively inexperienced Windows user, this book does assume a working knowledge of Windows, such as how to how to move and resize a window, how to use menus, etc.

1 Getting Started with the Focus Window

This chapter gives an introductory tour of some of the central features of Family Historian, based around the *Focus Window*. It ends by showing you how to create your first project.

The Project Window

Before looking at the Focus Window, we must first introduce another window: the *Project Window* – see Figure 1 below. This is the first window you will see when you first open Family Historian. The Project Window lists all of the Family Historian projects in the specified location. When you first install Family Historian there will only be one project: *Family Historian Sample Project*.

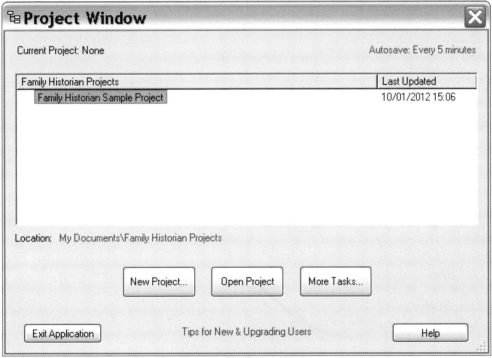

Figure 1– The Project Window

The Family Historian Sample Project

The Family Historian sample project is installed automatically when you install Family Historian. This book will make frequent reference to the Family Historian Sample Project. The people in the sample project are fictitious.

Select the sample project now by clicking on it and then clicking on **Open Project**. Alternatively, you can also open it by double-clicking on the name "Family Historian Sample Project" in the list. When you do this, the Project Window will close and you will see a screen like Figure 2 below.

3

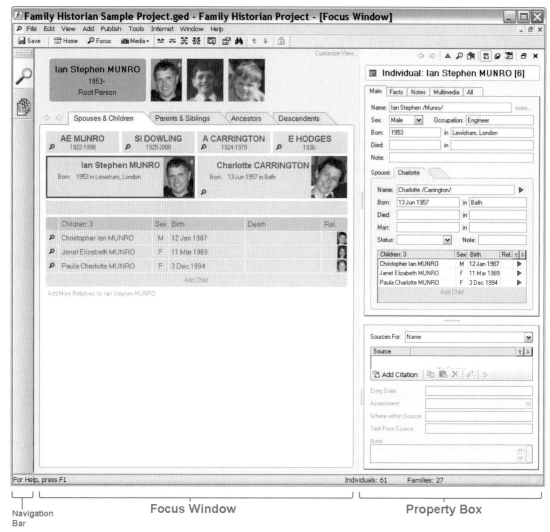

Figure 2 – The Sample Project, with three marked areas

The Navigation Bar

The main body of the window in Figure 2 (that is everything below the toolbar) is made up of 3 areas:

- The Navigation Bar
- The Focus Window
- The Property Box

Of these, the Navigation Bar is much the thinnest. It is the vertical grey bar on the left side. The top part of it is shown in Figure 3 on the right.

Subwindows

The Navigation Bar shows one icon for each open *subwindow* within the application. A 'subwindow' is a window within a window – in this case, within the Family Historian application window. The 'active' subwindow is highlighted. Click on any subwindow icon to make that window active – that is, to switch between windows.

Figure 3 – the Navigation Bar (top part only)

You can also right-click on any icon to see a menu of things you can do with it – this includes the **Close Window** menu command.

The first icon in
Figure 3 is the Magnifying Glass icon which represents the Focus Window. The
second icon (three overlapping sheets of paper) is the *Records Window* icon. The
Records Window is not yet open. This is the exception to the rule that the
Navigation Bar shows open windows. For convenience, the Records Window
always has an icon on the Navigation Bar, even if closed.

Later we will look at the Records Window, and also other subwindows, each of
which has their own distinctive icon in the Navigation Bar.

The Navigation Bar is similar to the task bar in Windows. The task bar is the bar at
the bottom of the screen, next to the **Start** button. Clicking on buttons on the task
bar lets you switch between open applications. Clicking on icons on the Navigation
bar lets you switch between open windows within the Family Historian application.

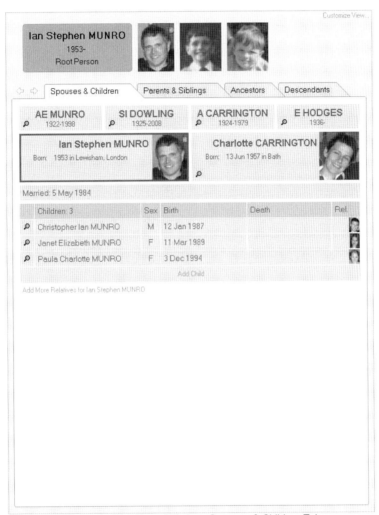

Figure 4 – The Focus Window: Spouses & Children Tab

The Focus Window The second of the marked areas in Figure 2 is the *Focus Window* – see Figure 4
above. The Focus Window shows information about a particular person, called the
focus person, shown at the top of the window. In this case, the focus person is Ian
Stephen Munro. There are three photos of Ian Munro, also shown at the top of the
window. You can show up to 9 photos here if you wish, and if there is space.
Don't confuse the term *focus person* with the term *root person*. As we will see
later, they don't mean the same thing.

In the area immediately below this you should be able to see 4 tabs.[1] These are *Spouses & Children*, *Parents & Siblings*, *Ancestors* and *Descendants*.

The Spouses & Children Tab
The *Spouses & Children* tab shows all of the focus person's spouses and children. In this particular case we can see that Ian Munro has one spouse only. If there were others, they would be shown. His wife is Charlotte Carrington, with whom he had 3 children: Christopher, Janet and Paula. Ian Munro himself also appears in the Spouses & Children tab, in the box next to Charlotte Carrington. His box has a dark blue border round it, to show that this person is the focus person.

As well as showing Ian Munro himself, his spouses and his children, this tab also shows both of Ian's parents, and his spouses' parents.

Select a Record
Within the Focus Window, you can select any record (any person) by simply clicking on the box or row that represents that person. The selected box is indicated by a darker than normal background colour. When you select a record, the Property Box changes to show you information about that person. We will be looking at the Property Box in the next chapter.

Set the Focus Person
You may have noticed that nearly all the boxes have a little picture of a magnifying glass in the bottom-left corner. Click on this magnifying glass to make that person the focus person – or just double-click on their box. Use either technique now to make Ian Munro's mother, Susan Dowling (S.I. Dowling in Figure 4) the focus person. When you do this, the Focus Window should change to look like Figure 5.

Multiple Spouse Families
Figure 5 shows what the Spouses & Children tab looks like when the Focus Person has more than one spouse. Susan Dowling married twice, so the window shows both of these families. She had three children, Judy, Ian and Sally, with her first husband, Anthony Munro. He died in 1998, and in 2001, she married Nigel Anderson. They had no children.

As can be seen by this example, the focus person gets his or her own box in each family, and each such box has a dark blue border. The boxes for his/her parents are also repeated. This way, each family is shown with all members present, including grandparents, and it is easy to see at a glance, who was married to whom, and, for any given child, who their parents and grandparents were.

Add Parents
You can see from Figure 5 that Susan Dowling's father was Richard Dowling. But her mother is not given. Instead there is just the words "Add Susan's Mother" in light-coloured text. This is a link. When you click on this link – the actual text, not just the box – a menu appears with two menu commands: **Create New Record** and **Link Existing Record**. If you choose the former, Family Historian will create a new record for you, and link this record to Susan as her mother. You can then type in the name of this person, and any other details about her, in the Property Box (we will be looking at the Property Box in more detail later). If you choose the latter, **Link Existing Record**, Family Historian will let you select from your existing records, and link the selected person as Susan's mother.

Actually, there are two boxes in this particular case, which have the text link "Add Susan's Mother" – one for each family. Both links work exactly the same way. It doesn't make any difference which you choose.

---

[1] The term 'tab' is used throughout this tutorial for 2 quite different things. You will frequently see it used to refer to **Tab** key – a key on the keyboard, usually positioned just above the **Caps Lock** key. In this usage, **Tab** is written with a Capital and emphasized in **bold**. The other use of the term is to refer to a tab in a tabbed dialog box, or tabbed window – such as the Focus Window. When used in the latter sense, tab is spelled in lower-case, and is not in bold.

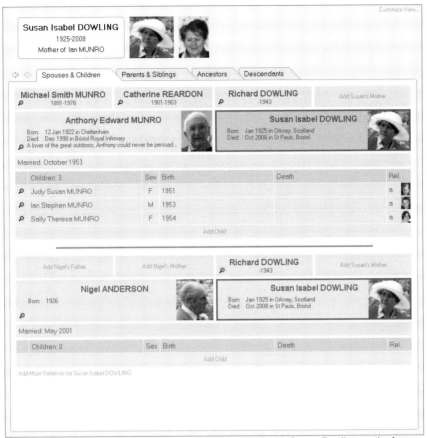

Figure 5 – The Focus Window (Spouses & Children tab) with Susan Dowling as the focus
person. She had two spouse families.

Undo/Redo   Try it now. Click on "Add Susan's Mother" (either box). Then choose **Create New Record**. Immediately, the text for Susan's mother's box changes to show "[unnamed person]". Notice that this changes in both boxes. Ordinarily you would go on to add a name for the new person in the Property Box, but we aren't ready to look at the Property Box yet, so instead of doing that, let's just undo what you just did. Click on the **Edit** menu. The first item on this menu is **Undo Create Parent [62]**. 62 is the record id that was allocated automatically to the new record you created. Click on this menu command now. When you do this, the new record you created for Susan's mother is removed and the box for Susan's mother reverts to showing the link "Add Susan's Mother".

Using the **Undo/Redo** commands on the **Edit** menu, you can undo and redo almost any change you make to your project data: creating new records, deleting records, and any edits you make to records – they can all be undone or redone. So don't be afraid to experiment!

The Focus Window doesn't just let you add parents for the focus person, you can also add parents for their spouses too. For example, you can add either father or mother for Nigel Anderson by clicking on the links "Add Nigel's father" or "Add Nigel's Mother".

Add Children   You've probably already guessed how to add children. If you want to add a child for Susan Dowling and Anthony Munro, click on the "Add Child" text link in the row immediately below their last child, Sally Munro. If you want to add a child for Susan Dowling and Nigel Anderson, click on the "Add Child" text link in the otherwise empty area where their children would be listed if they had any.

Whenever you click on a text link for adding any kind of relative, you will always

7

be given the choice of creating a new record for the new relative, or linking to an existing relative.

Add Spouses

Adding a person's first spouse in the Focus Window is always easy. They will always have a box next to them where the spouse should go and there will be a link you can click labelled "Add Husband/Parent" or "Add Wife/Partner". But what if the person already has a spouse? How do you add another one?

Add More Relatives

Below the last box in the Focus Window is another text link: "Add More Relatives for Susan Isabel Dowling". You can always click on this link to add relatives, if there isn't a handy box to click in. You can use it to add more spouses for the focus person.

You can also use it in other circumstances. Suppose, for example, that you wanted to add a child for Susan Dowling, but neither Anthony Munro nor Nigel Anderson were the father. In that case, you could use the "Add More Relatives" link, and it would let you pick the father – either an existing record or a new one.

Add More Sets of Parents

In Family Historian, a person doesn't have to have just one set of parents. They can have as many as you like. They might have birth parents, foster parents, adoptive parents, and so on. You can use the "Add More Relatives" link to add additional sets of parents.

Add Relatives Using the *Add* Menu

Another technique for adding relatives is to use the **Add** menu. You can always add relatives of any kind for anyone using the **Add** menu. Just remember to select the person who you want to add a relative to first.

If a person has more than one box in the Focus Window, which can happen whether or not they are the focus person, you can select them (select their record) by clicking on any of the boxes for them. It doesn't matter which one you choose.

Add Unrelated Person

When you add new people to a Family Historian project, most of the time you will be adding them as relatives of people that you have already added. But the people you add don't have to be relatives. If you want to add a person who is not related to anyone already in your project, click on the **Add** menu and then **Unrelated Individual**.

Add Grand-parents and Grand-children

There is no facility to add grandparents or grandchildren as such. There is no need for it. All relationships effectively reduce to combinations of parent-child and spouse-spouse relationships. So you don't need to enter a grandparent for a person. Simply add a parent, and then add a parent for that parent. Equally to add a grandchild, add a child, and then a child for that child.

Go Back & Go Forward Buttons

At this point, if you have been following everything carefully, Susan Dowling should still be the focus person, and the Focus Window should look like Figure 5 above. But suppose you accidentally clicked on the wrong person and made someone else the focus person by mistake? The Focus Window has its own **Go Back** and **Go Forward** buttons. These are in the top-left corner, just to the left of the 'Spouses & Children' tab. They are greyed when there is no-one to 'go back' or 'go forward' to. Try using them now. The left button is the 'go back' button and it should be ungreyed now. Click on it to 'go back' to the previous focus person. When you do this the right arrow becomes ungreyed. Click on this to 'go forward' again, to return to where you have just been.

The Home Button

A very useful button is the **Home** button. This is on the left side of the main application toolbar. Click it now to switch back to showing Ian Munro as focus person.

As we will see later, there are several other windows that you may be viewing, apart from just the Focus Window. Even if you have been viewing one of these other windows, the **Home** button will still be visible on the toolbar, and when you click it, it will jump you back to the Focus Window, with the *Root Person* as the focus person. So who or what is the *Root Person*?

The Root Person (the File Root)
In every Family Historian project, you can specify that one person is the *Root Person* or *File Root*. These two terms – 'Root Person' and 'File Root' – mean the same thing. There are various benefits to making someone the file root:

When Family Historian opens a project, it will always initially show the Focus Window with the file root as the focus person.
In the box at the top of the Focus Window, for the focus person, it will always show how the focus person is related to the file root (if they are related). If the focus person is the file root, it will just say 'Root Person'.
As we have seen, when you click the Home button, it jumps you back to the file root.

There are other benefits, but these will do for now.

Make File Root
You can change file root very easily at any time. When you're viewing the Focus Window, you just need to right-click[2] on any person and a menu appears. The first command on this menu is always **Make File Root**.

Ian Munro should be the current focus person. In the box for him at the top of the Window, it should have the text "Root Person". Right-click now on Ian's wife, Charlotte Carrington and make her the file root. When you do this, she doesn't become the focus person – that is still Ian Munro. But if you look at the box for him at the top of the window you should see that instead of "Root Person", it now says "Husband of Charlotte CARRINGTON". This is because Charlotte Carrington is now the file root.

To make Ian Munro the file root once again, you could just click on **Undo File Root Change** on the **Edit** menu. Or you could right-click on Ian Munro's box and click on the **Make File Root** command in the menu that appears. Choose either of these options now – whichever you like – and make Ian Munro the file root once again.

If you aren't using the Focus Window when you wish to make someone the file root, you don't have to switch to the Focus Window specially to do this. Simply select the person who you wish to make the file root, and click on the **Set as File Root** menu command. This menu command is on the **File Root** submenu, which is on the **Edit** menu.

The Focus Button

Another useful toolbar button is the **Focus** button. This button is just to the right of the **Home** button. If you select a person and click the **Focus** button, that will show the selected person as the focus person in the Focus Window. You may be wondering why that's useful. Why not just double-click on the person's box or click on their magnifying glass to make them the focus person? Bear in mind that those options are only available when you are viewing the Focus Window, and as we have already mentioned, there is much more to Family Historian than just the Focus Window.

You may also be wondering what the difference is between the Focus button, and the Focus Window icon (the magnifying glass) in the Navigation Bar (see Figure 3 above). The difference is this:

The Focus button only works when you have first selected a person. When you click on the Focus button, it activates the Focus Window and makes the selected person the focus person.

---

[2] In this document, whenever you see the phrase "right-click" this just means "click using the right mouse button".

No selection is required when you click on the Focus Window icon in the Navigation Bar. The Focus Window doesn't change at all when you click on this icon. It is merely *activated*. That is, if it is hidden because other windows are in front of, it is moved in front of those other windows – but that is all. So if you want to go back to the Focus Window *without changing its contents*, you need to click on the Focus Window icon. Another difference is that you can right-click on the Focus Window icon, as you can with any icon on the Navigation bar, and a menu will appear, showing you actions that you can take with the window in question. Right-clicking on toolbar buttons doesn't do anything.

Child is Adopted, Step, Fostered, etc

You should by now know how to make Ian Munro's mother, Susan Dowling, the focus person. Do so now.[3] The Focus Window should once again look like Figure 5 above. Look at the rows for the three children of Susan Dowling and Anthony Munro. The rightmost column is labelled "Rel." This is short for "Relationship to Parents". Normally this box will be blank (apart from a photo of the child, if any). But in this case, all three children have a letter 'a' in this column. This 'a' is short for 'adopted'.

Right-click on Judy Munro's row. When you do this a menu appears. The second item is a sub-menu titled 'Relationship to Parents'. You can change the value here or clear it. You can also remind yourself what a given letter signifies.

In some cases, a child may have different relations to each parent. In that case, choose **More Options** from the submenu. In the dialog box that appears you can specify the relationship to each parent separately. Click on the **Help** button in this dialog box for advice on when to use which value. Although 'Birth' (signified by the letter 'b') is a possible value, it is not usually needed. If no relationship type is specified, the relationship type is assumed to be Birth. You should only specify explicitly that a child's relationship is 'birth' if you have some specific reason to do so - e.g. to emphasize the nature of the relationship, in circumstances in which it might otherwise be doubted.

The **Clear** menu command can be used to clear the current setting.

The Marriage Box

Just below the boxes for Anthony Munro and Susan Dowling, there is a box with the text "Married: October 1953". This is the marriage box. It displays information about the couple's marriage if recorded. If they are divorced, it will show the date of divorce too, if that has been recorded. Later we will see how you can record this kind of information, using the Property Box. For now, right-click on the Marriage Box line and look at the **Marriage Status** submenu in the menu that appears.

Unmarried, Separated and Divorced Couples

In Family Historian, where you see 2 people listed as *Husband* and *Wife*, or as *Spouses*, this does not necessarily mean that they are or ever have been married. It means either that they are or were in some sense a couple (they may be married, but they don't have to be); or that they have had a child together – and this, of course, can happen without the parents ever having had a 'relationship' as such. There is no single term that covers these cases; so we use *Husband* and *Wife* as a convenient shorthand.

You can indicate that a couple are not married (or are divorced or separated) by selecting the appropriate value in the **Marriage Status** submenu. The default value is "Married (default)". If you choose any other value, the right side of the Marriage Box will show the chosen setting. Try this now. Use the technique described to mark Anthony Munro and Susan Dowling's marriage as having the status

---

[3] If you can't work out how to do it, here are some suggestions: if you can see her box, double-click on it, or click on the magnifying glass in the corner of the box. If you can't see her box, click the Home button which should take you back to Ian Munro as focus person, and she should be visible. Now double-click on her box.

"Divorced". Notice that the word 'Divorced' appears on the right side of the Marriage Box. Then click **Undo Change Marriage Status** on the **Edit** menu to undo this change.

Delete Record

Deleting a record in the Focus Window is easy. Right-click on the person in question and select **Delete Record** from the menu that appears.

Correct Relationship Mistakes

A more common requirement is not to delete the record but to *unlink it*. Suppose, for example, that you have added a child X of person Y. When you do this, two things are really happening: a record has been created for X, and X has been *linked* to Y as Y's child. You may over time acquire much information about X and record it all in his record. Later you discover that X was not the child of Y after all, but the child of someone else – Z, say. You don't want to delete X's record, with all the information it contains. You want to *unlink* him as a child of X and re-link him as a child of Z. One way of doing this is to use the Focus Window.

Unlink Record

If X has been linked as the child of Y, one way to unlink him is simply to make Y the focus person in the Focus Window, so that X is shown as Y's child in the *Spouses & Children* tab. Then right-click on X's box and choose **Unlink Record** from the menu that appears. Using this technique you can unlink anyone from their role in any family that they are linked into – either as child, spouse or parent.

You don't have to use the Focus Window to unlink records. You can select a record in any context and use the **Unlink From** submenu on the **Edit** menu to remove a relationship link.

Re-link Record

In our example, the next requirement, after unlinking X as a child of Y, was to re-link him as a child of Z. One way of doing this would be to make Z the focus person in the Focus Window. Then, in the *Spouses & Children* tab, you could use one of the various techniques described above to add a child for Z. If, for example, you click on the "Add Child" text link, a menu will be displayed with 2 menu commands: **Create New Record** and **Link Existing Record**. In this situation, because X's record still exists (you just unlinked it, you didn't delete it), you need the second command **Link Existing Record**. That will allow you to choose X's record from a selection dialog, and link him to Z as Z's child.

A similar technique can be used to link anyone not just as child, but also as spouse or parent.

Change Order of Children

If you have birth dates for children and marriage dates for spouses, Family Historian will ordinarily keep spouses and children in correct date order automatically. If you open a file in which the children or spouses are in the wrong order, Family Historian can correct any incorrect ordering, throughout the file, using these dates. To do this, run the **Re-order Out-of-Sequence Data** command on the **Tools** menu.

But what if you don't have these dates? Suppose, for example, that you don't know the dates for the children in a family, but you do know the order of their births, and the current order is wrong. You can re-order children in the Focus Window. Select the child you wish to move and click the **Move Up** or **Move Down** arrow buttons on the toolbar. Changing the order of spouses is best done using the Property Box, as we will see later.

The Parents & Siblings Tab

It may seem surprising that so far in this chapter we have only covered the first of the four tabs of the Focus Window. It is time to look at the second tab: the *Parents & Siblings* tab.

Click on the **Home** button on the toolbar, to make Ian Munro the focus person. The Focus Window should now look like Figure 4 above. Now click on the *Parents & Siblings* tab. The window should now look like Figure 6 below.

Your first thought when you see this tab is likely to be that it's very familiar – isn't it exactly the same as Figure 5?

Figure 6 – The Focus Window: Parents & Siblings Tab

Spouse Families & Parents Families In Family Historian, you will sometimes see references to *Spouse families* and sometimes to *Parent families*. Your *parents' family* is the family you grew up in. Your *spouse family* is the family you created with your spouse. But that means of course that from the point of view of your parents, what for you is a parents family, for them is their spouse family.

So when looking at Ian Munro's parent families, it should not be surprising that it looks a lot like his mother's spouse families. In fact the family we see in Figure 6 is exactly the same family as the first family shown in Figure 5. In Figure 5, the dark blue border was around Susan Dowling's box because she was the focus person – we were looking at her spouse families. This time the dark blue border is round Ian Munro's row, in the area listing the children of the family. This is because, this time he is the focus person, and we are seeing his parent families.

Why are we only seeing one family this time when in Figure 5 there were two? In Figure 5, we were looking at Susan Dowling's spouse families and she had two. This time we are looking at Ian Munro's parent families and he only has one parent family. He could have had more than one parent family, and if he had, they would have been shown. If he had had another parent family (if say he'd been adopted), this other parent family need not have included any of the members of the families shown in Figure 5.

So when viewing the Focus Window, always keep in mind who the focus person is and which tab you are looking at. If you don't, you may misinterpret the information you are being given.

Keyboard Shortcuts

Now is as good a time as any to point out that you don't always have to use the mouse! For example, instead of clicking on the *Parents & Siblings*, you can also switch tabs by pressing **Ctrl-Tab** (that is, press-and-hold the **Ctrl** key while pressing the **Tab** key). This will cycle you forwards through the various tabs. **Shift-Ctrl-Tab** will cycle you backwards through them. You can also use the arrow keys to change the selection in the Focus Window, and pressing the **Space bar** or **Enter** key makes the selected person the focus person. **Ctrl-Left Arrow** is equivalent to clicking on the **Go Back** button, and **Ctrl-Right Arrow** is **Go Forward**.

There are numerous keyboard shortcuts for the Focus Window and other windows in Family Historian. Some menu commands list their equivalent keyboard shortcut to the right of the menu command. For a complete list of keyboard shortcuts, see "Keyboard and Mouse Shortcuts" which is listed in the Contents pane of the Family Historian Help. The Family Historian Help can be accessed by clicking **Family Historian Help** on the **Help** menu.

Features of the Parents & Siblings Tab

We have covered the features of the Spouses & Children tab in some detail. There is no need to repeat this for the Parents & Siblings tab, because the features offered are the same. Such differences as there are, are there to remind you of which tab you are on. For example, in the Spouses & Children tab, the text link for adding children to a family was labelled "Add Child". The equivalent text link in Figure 6 says "Add Sibling for Ian". The link functions the same way in each case. It is labelled differently in each case, to remind you that in the first case you are adding a child to Ian's spouse family, and in the second case you are adding a child to Ian's parents' family.

The Ancestors Tab

Ian Munro should still be the focus person. Click now on the Ancestors tab to view his ancestors. It should look like something like Figure 7 below. Don't worry if the number of generations displayed isn't exactly the same when you do it. Family Historian will adjust the number of generations displayed, depending on how much space there is available.

The Ancestors tab shows the focus person in the leftmost position. Immediately to his right are his parents, then their parents, and so on.

Add Ancestors

Just like the links in the previous two tabs, there are links in the Ancestors tab for adding more ancestors too (labelled "Add Father" or "Add Mother"). And they work the same way. You can either click on the link or use the arrow keys to move the selection to them, and then press the **Enter** key. The arrow keys work here, just as they do in the other tabs. And the menu is the same too – with options to create a new record or link to an existing one.

Switch Focus

All boxes for ancestors have the little magnifying glass icon. So you can still make anyone the focus person by simply clicking on this icon. And the alternative of double-clicking on the person's box works too.

Right-Click Menu

Right-clicking on a box also works. Right-click now on Michael Smith Munro's box (Ian Munro's paternal grandfather). There are the familiar commands: **Make File Root**, **Delete Record** and **Unlink Record**. You should know what they all do by now, but try this anyway: click on **Unlink Record**. When you do this, not only does Michael Smith Munro disappear but so does the rest of that ancestral branch. Now click on **Undo Unlink Family Member** on the **Edit** menu to put Michael Smith back again. When you do so, the rest of the ancestral branch re-appears too. If you've understood how family linking works, there should be no surprises there.

Navigate up the Ancestral Tree

How would you view Arthur Munro's parents? One option would be to make him the focus person (e.g. click on his magnifying glass icon). This would show not just Arthur Munro's parents, but his ancestors stretching backwards (if recorded).

Suppose you just wanted to shift the whole diagram one generation to the left? To do that just click on Anthony Munro's magnifying glass icon (or double-click on his box). This will promote Anthony Munro to the focus person position, and move all generations as required. Of course you will also have discarded all the information about Susan Dowling's ancestry. If it was her line you were interested in, you could have made her the focus person instead. Either way, you can of course quickly return to the previous focus person by pressing the **Go Back** button.

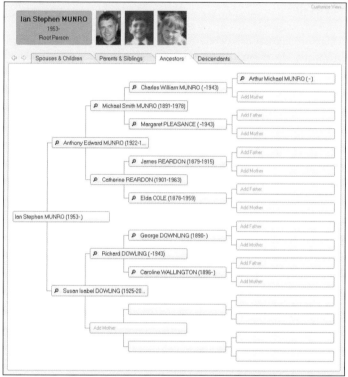

Figure 7 – The Focus Window: Ancestors Tab

Shift Focus in the Same Tab This illustrates another point which you may already have noticed. When you switch focus within the Focus Window, the current tab does not change. However, if you use a menu command or a toolbar button to switch the focus to someone, they will always be shown in the *Spouses & Children* tab. So, for example, if you click on the **Home** button, you will not only make Ian Munro the focus person, but you will also switch back to the *Spouses & Children* tab.

The Descendants Tab Finally, we turn to the fourth and last of the Focus Window tabs: the Descendants tab. If Ian Munro is still the focus person, when you click on the Descendants tab, the Focus Window should look like Figure 8 below.

Features of the Descendants Tab The descendants listing in Figure 8 is a very simple one. The focus person is shown in the top-left. His or her descendants are shown, indented below him to the right. Each descendant gets their own line. Any spouses of a descendant are shown on the descendant's line, to their right, in a lighter-coloured font, so that it is easy to visually distinguish them from descendants.

We can see that Ian Munro had 3 children and 2 grandchildren. He himself married once only (to Charlotte Carrington). Only one of his children married, and none of his grandchildren.

Once again, each person shown (except the focus person) has a little magnifying glass icon next to their name. You can make any displayed person the focus person, by either clicking on their magnifying glass icon, or by double-clicking on their name.

14

Right-clicking on any person's name also works as you would expect, and can be used to make any displayed person the File Root, or to delete or unlink a record. You can select any record by simply clicking on the person's name, and you can change selection using the arrow keys as you can on other tabs.

One small difference with other tabs is that there are no text links for adding relatives. But you can still do it. To add another child for Christopher Munro for example, you could click on his name to select his record, then click on the **Add** menu, and then click on **Child**.

Figure 8 – The Focus Window: Descendants Tab

More Features of Descendants Listings

To display all the features of the Descendants tab we need a more complex example than Ian Munro's simple listing. So instead we will look at a Descendants listing for Michael Smith Munro. To display this, click on the Ancestors tab. Michael Smith Munro is Ian Munro's grandfather. Make Michael Smith Munro the focus person, and then switch back to the Descendants tab. It should now look like Figure 9 below.

Although a little more complex than Figure 8, this is still quite simple. The focus person is again shown in the top-left corner. His descendants are laid out in columns, so picking out each generation visually is easy. Again, each descendant gets their own row. We can see that Michael had 4 children (Peter, Anthony, Amanda and Julia), and six grandchildren. All of Michael's children married and had children, except Amanda.

Only three generations are displayed by default (although as we will see shortly, you can change that); but you can click on the little expansion boxes ⊞ to expand these branches if you wish to find out about his great grandchildren, and more descendants below them. Clicking on the same boxes again closes the branch.

Space Bar vs. Enter Key

In all Focus Window tabs, pressing the **Space bar** when a record is selected, is one way of making that person the focus person. In all Focus Window tabs except this one, pressing **Enter** does the same thing. In the Descendants tab however, pressing **Enter** is the equivalent of clicking on the person's expansion box, to open or close that branch.

Figure 9 – The Focus Window: Descendants of Michael Smith Munro

Special Spouse Marking on Lines   You may also be wondering why three of the lines in the listing are overlaid with "(Susan)". The text in this case cannot be clicked on – or rather clicking on it doesn't do anything. Nor does right-clicking on it do anything. Think of the text in this case, as being a feature of the line – a visual embellishment of the line, if you like. The reason for it is this:

The descendants tab is designed to show not just all the descendants of the focus person, and their spouses, for a specified number of generations – it is also designed to show, for each descendant, who *both* of their parents were. If you look at Edmund and Emily Munro in Figure 9, it is easy to see who their parents were: Peter Munro and Helen Addison. But without the special marking on the lines for Judy, Ian and Sally Munro, you would have no way of knowing who their mother was. Their father married twice. The special marking is used to make it clear that their mother was Susan Dowling and not Julia Fish.

Spouse marking on lines is only used where it would otherwise be unclear who the children's parents are. Where there is no uncertainty – which is most of the time – it is not needed and is not used.

Customize Focus Window   So far we have just used the default settings for the Focus Window. But you can customize it to change it if you wish. Options for the Focus Window are specified in the Preferences dialog box, which is accessed from the **Tools** menu. A quick way to access the relevant options, though, is just to click on the "Customize View" link in the top-right corner of the Focus Window. When you do so, the Preferences dialog box opens at the tab for the Focus Window – see Figure 10 below.

Colours   Click the **Help** button for a detailed explanation of what all the options mean. You can change the colours of nearly all the elements that make up the Focus Window, so if there are some colours you don't like – just change them.

Tip: When changing colours using the colour selector dialog, always remember to select the item whose colour you wish to change, then pick the colour, and then click the **Select** button. The colour is not selected just by clicking on it. Also, don't be surprised if you see the colours of the Focus Window change in the background when you select a colour. This is done deliberately so that you can see what effect the colour change has. If you subsequently press **Cancel**, the colours will revert to

16

what they had been.

Text Size   As well as being able to change the colour, you can also change the text size, and the font, for the various elements of the Focus Window. So if the text is too small for you, make it bigger.

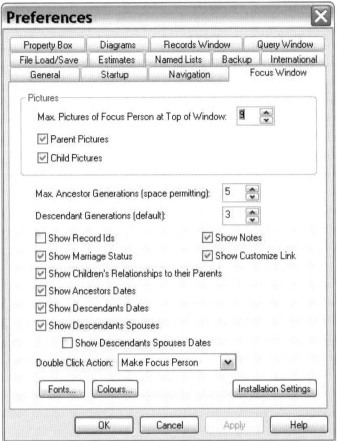

Figure 10 – Customize the Focus Window

Generations   As you can see from Figure 10, you can also change the default number of generations shown in the Descendants tab. The default is 3 generations, but anything up to 99 generations is allowed. This is possible because the Descendants tab has a scrollbar. If you choose to view a large number of generations, you may have to scroll to view them all.

The Ancestors tab has no scroll bar. You can specify a maximum number of generations to view, but this figure will only be honoured if space permits.

Other Options   Some people may prefer to not show children's relationships to their parents most of the time. You can opt to switch this off. You can also opt to show record identifiers and dates for various relatives.

If the Descendants tab seems too cluttered with spouse information, untick "Show Descendants Spouses" and unclutter it. Without the spouse information, it is a much simpler listing. Try it.

Don't be afraid to experiment. You can revert to the installation settings at any time by pressing the **Installation Settings** button.

Close Project   That concludes the tour of the Focus Window. In the next chapter, we will look at the Property Box. But before we do, we will quickly look at how you create your first project. But first close the sample project. To do that, click **Close Project** on the **File** menu. This will cause the project to be closed, and the Project Window of Figure 1 will be re-opened.

Tips for New & Upgrading Users

If you haven't already done so, you are recommended to click on the Project Window text link "Tips for New & Upgrading Users". If you are upgrading from an earlier version of Family Historian you are particularly recommended to read the section "Notes for Upgrading Users".

Autosave

Clicking on the **Help** button takes you to more general help on the Project Window, which explains all the things you can do with it. For now, you should at least take note that by default, Family Historian will autosave every 5 minutes. To change this setting, if you wish to do so, click on the Autosave text link.

Saving Changes to Projects

If you have unsaved changes when you close a project – which you may do, even if autosave is enabled – Family Historian will ask you if you want to save the changes. Unless you have some special reason not to, you should confirm that you do.

Create a New Project

When you are ready to do so, click on the **New Project** button in the Project Window to create your new project. There is usually no need to create more than one project. There is also unlikely to be any need to change the location for Family Historian projects. If you really need to, for whatever reason, you can always move your project folder at a later date.

Carefully read the instructions in the new project wizard that appears. If you wish to import a GEDCOM file into the new project you can do so. If you wish to import from a family tree file (such as a Family Historian project file, or a family tree file created by another genealogy program) click on "Import from other family tree file". If Family Historian does not recognise the family tree file you have, you should try to arrange to have the data exported as a GEDCOM file instead.

If you do not have any data to import, choose the option "Start a new project (no import"). You will be prompted to specify the name and sex (and parents if known) of the person who is to be the file root in your new project.

Then give your project a name and press **Finish** to create it. The Project Window will close, and the file root of your new project (or the first record, if you imported a file which has no file root) will be displayed as the focus person in the Focus Window.

2 Editing Records with the Property Box

The Property Box

The Property Box, which we encountered briefly in the last chapter, is used for viewing and editing record details. You can use it to edit record details for any kind of record. In the example in Figure 11 below, as the title shows, it is being used to display the record details for an Individual: Ian Stephen Munro.

By default the Property Box will usually display the record details for whichever record is selected. But if it isn't already open, you can open it to look at or edit a record, from anywhere in the program, by selecting the record and clicking on the Property Box icon on the main application toolbar:

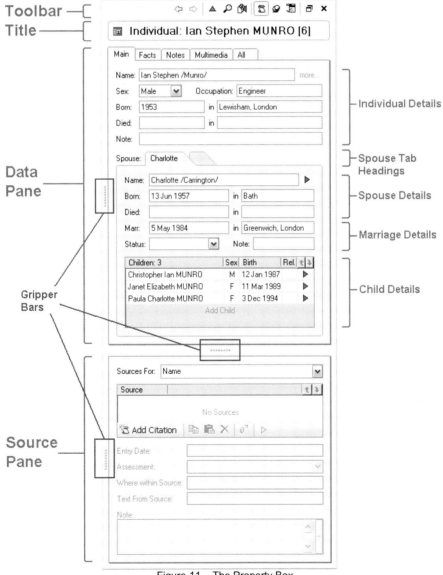

Figure 11 – The Property Box

19

The Data Pane and the Source Pane As you can see in Figure 11, the Property Box is made up of 2 panes: the Data Pane and the Source Pane. The Data Pane is where you will enter information of all kinds.

The Source Pane is used to record the *sources* for your information – where it came from. We will look at the Source Pane in more detail later. For now, you can hide it if you wish by unticking the Sources button on the Property Box toolbar: 🗞.

The Main Tab When showing Individual records, the Data Pane has 5 tabs: *Main*, *Facts*, *Notes*, *Multimedia* and *All*. We will start by looking at the *Main* tab (the selected tab in Figure 11). Later we will look at the other tabs. Later still we will look at how you can customize the Property Box, and even add additional tabs of your own if you wish.

Gripper Bars You can resize the Property Box in various ways. If you click-and-drag on any of the areas marked as "Gripper Bars" in Figure 11, you can change the size of the Property Box, or move the dividing area between the Data Pane and the Source Pane. Later when we look at other tabs of the Property Box, you will find that some of them have even more gripper bars.

Reveal Hidden Fields When you resize the Property Box, the fields will automatically be resized to fit the available space, if they can be. If there isn't room for some fields, they will be hidden and a dotted line, with the word 'more', will point to the missing fields:

Wherever you see a line like this, you can click on it to reveal the hidden fields.

Undo/Redo There is no **OK** button in the Property Box, and no **Cancel** button either. If you make a change to a field, the change is stored[4] as soon as you click or tab (press the **Tab** key) elsewhere. If you make a mistake, use the **Undo** command on the **Edit** menu to undo what you did. Or you can press **Ctrl-Z** for an 'instant undo' if you haven't even tabbed or clicked out of the field yet.

Entering Name Details The first field you are likely to use in the Property Box is the *Name* field. In fact there are two Name fields in Figure 11. One of the Name fields is in the area marked *Individual Details*, and the other is in the area marked *Spouse Details*. At this point, it is the *Individual Details* Name field that we are concerned with.

Whenever you create a new record for an Individual the new record will be selected and the Property Box will appear (if it had been closed), and the first thing you should do is type the name of the new person in the Name field.

Don't Use Capitals -Do Use Maiden Names When entering names genealogists traditionally enter surnames in CAPITALS. You can do this if you wish, but our recommendation would be that you enter the surname (and all other names) in Mixed Case. That way you will have recorded not only the letters of the surname, but also how it is capitalised, which may not always be obvious (e.g. McCracken). However you have entered them, you can always opt to display surnames in capitals in reports and diagrams (this is an option on the Preferences dialog).

It is also considered good practice to always use women's maiden names in this context. Later we will look at ways of recording their married name.

Use of the Tab Key When you enter a person's name, enter the whole thing (or as much of it as you know) and press the **Tab** key to move to the next field. Actually you don't have to

---

[4] Stored, but not saved to file. Changes are only saved to file when either an Auto-save occurs, or when you click on the toolbar **Save** button, or otherwise cause changes to be saved.

press the **Tab** key. You could click elsewhere with mouse, say. But in Windows, it is good practice to use the **Tab** key when you are changing data in a dialog box (a form-like window) to move from one field to the next. Use **Shift-Tab** to move back to the previous field.

Slashes Round Surnames
You will notice as soon as you tab out of the Name field that slashes have been put round the last word in the name. In Figure 11, for example, the name is given as "Ian Stephen /Munro/". The slashes mark the surname. If you don't specify otherwise, Family Historian will assume that the last name is the surname. If this is wrong – if for example the person has a double-barrelled surname – you should manually adjust the position of the slashes yourself.

If you only know the first names and not the surnames, enter '//' at the end of the name to show that the surname is not known.

Alternate Names, Titles, Nickname, etc
Family Historian allows you to record as many names, and titles, as you like for each person. To do so, click on the "more" text link to the right of the Name field. You can enter not only names and titles, but also other nicknames and name parts such as prefixes (e.g. 'Dr') and suffixes (e.g. 'Jr'). Click on the **Help** button in the Names/Titles dialog box for more information about the fields in this dialog box.

You can also add Titles (and supply more information about them) in the Facts tab of the Property Box. It doesn't matter whether the titles are added here or there. They will appear in both contexts either way.

No Mandatory Fields
There are no mandatory fields. If you have no data to enter for a given field – don't enter it. Leave it blank. You don't have to enter a person's name if you don't know it. You don't even have to enter a person's sex if you don't know it. The only exception is that you must enter their sex if you wish them to be a parent or spouse.

Same Sex Relation-ships
Family Historian supports same sex relationships. A couple can both be male or both female, and the parents in a family can be same sex too. Remember too that you can always change a person's sex after you have created their record, if you created the record with the wrong sex initially.

Birth & Death Details
If you want to enter facts about a person's life – e.g. their birth or death details, their occupation etc. – you could do this is on the *Facts* tab (which we will look at later). Purely as a matter of convenience, you can enter some key fact details on the *Main* tab too. If you do so, these facts will also appear in the *Facts* tab. It doesn't matter which way you do it – except that you can enter more details in the *Facts* tab than you can in the *Main* tab.

When entering birth and death details, put the date in the first box and the place in the second box, after 'in'.

Multiple Occupations, etc
If a person had multiple occupations, don't enter them all in the Occupations field on the Main tab. Enter each one as a separate fact in the Facts tab. For any given fact type (even *Birth* and *Death*!) you can have as many instances of them as you like.

Helper Dialogs
Many *fields* (boxes for entering data) have helper dialogs to help you enter data into them. You never *need* to use these Helper dialogs – it is always possible to enter any value without them. But they are there to make data entry easier. For example, date fields have a *Date Entry Assistant* dialog to help you enter complex date information. Place fields have a *Place List* dialog which you can use to select from a list of places that you have already entered (and much more besides). Other fields have similar helper dialogs. You can access the helper dialog for a given field, if there is one, by doing any one of the following:

Double-click on the field

Click or tab to the field and then press Ctrl-Spacebar
Click or tab to the field, or just move your mouse over it, and then click on the button with 3 dots that appears:

With most fields, the button with 3 dots only appears when you move the mouse over the field or click on the field. With large text fields, such as some Note fields however, the button with 3 dots may be long and thin, and always visible to the right of the field's scrollbar. Don't forget to make use of the Helper dialogs.

Each Helper Dialog has a **Help** button. Click on this button to learn how to use it.

Auto-Complete

Some fields auto-complete. For example, if you starting typing a place name into a place field, Family Historian will try to guess what name you're trying to type – based on other names already used in the same project – and will display its guesses as you type. If it guesses right, just press the **Tab** key to move to accept the suggested name, and move to the next field. If it guesses wrong, ignore it and keep typing.

How to Enter Simple Dates

When you enter a date into a date field, Family Historian will try to determine what date you mean. If it cannot do so, it will warn you that the date is invalid and ask you to correct the date information. It is important that Family Historian can determine which date you mean. It can use this information for a variety of purposes, such as filtering and sorting on dates, warning of improbable or inconsistent dates, offering alternative display formatting options, and calculating age information.

Family Historian tries to be as flexible as possible in allowing you to enter dates in a wide variety of styles. Entering dates using numbers only is fine (e.g. "3/12/1990" or "3.12.1990"). If your computer is configured to standard UK date settings, this will be interpreted as 3 December 1990. If your computer is configured to standard US date settings, this will be interpreted as 12 March 1990. You can change these settings in the Windows Control Panel.

Instead of specifying the month as a number, you can also specify it by name. Family Historian will accept "3 Dec 1910", "3 December 1910", "3rd Dec 1910", "Dec 3 1910", and many more variations. Always use 4 digits for years. "3 jul 89", for Family Historian, would be a date in the year 0089 A.D.

If you don't know the day of a date, simply omit it (e.g. "dec 1990" or "12 1990"). If you only know the year, just enter that.

Date Validation and Date Phrases

Dates are validated when you press the tab key or click elsewhere. If Family Historian does not recognise a date you entered it will prompt you to correct it. If you have mistyped the date, you can correct it now.

Sometimes you may want to enter a *date phrase* - that is, some text which isn't a date as such (like "Two weeks after his wife died"). Put double quotes round the text to show that it is a phrase. If you forget to put the quotes, Family Historian will warn you that it does not recognise the date. If you press OK at this point, Family Historian will allow you to save it as a date phrase, and put the quotes round it for you.

How to Enter Complex Dates

As well as simple dates, you can also enter date ranges, periods, quarter dates, date phrases and estimated dates in date fields. If you are not sure how to specify a particular date, use the Date Entry Assistant Dialog to help you enter the date. You can open this helper dialog by clicking on the button with 3 little dots at the right end of the date field (you may have to move your mouse over the field or click on it to see this button), or by double-clicking on the date field itself. However, when entering simple dates you should not need to use this dialog box.

If you frequently enter complex dates, you may prefer to use some of these shortcut techniques:

- Enter a '?' character, or the word 'approx' or '(approx)' or 'app' or '(app)' or 'about' or '(about)', either before or after a simple date, to show that the date is approximate. You can also enter 'circa' or 'c.' or 'c' before a date to show that it is approximate.
- Enter a '~' character, or the word 'est' or '(est)' or 'estimated' or '(estimated)', either before or after a simple date, to show that the date has been estimated.
- Enter the word 'cal' or '(cal)' or 'calculated or '(calculated)', either before or after a simple date, to show that the date has been calculated.
- 2 dates with a hyphen between them (e.g. "Jan 1910 - May 1914" or "1921-1923") will be interpreted as a date range (between ... and ...). You can also prefix the 2 dates with 'btw', 'bet' or 'between', or separate them with 'and' instead of the hyphen (e.g. "btw 1910 and 1920").
- 2 dates with a hyphen between them, but preceded by the word 'from' will be interpreted as a period (from ... to ...). You can also prefix the 2 dates with 'frm', or separate them with 'to' instead of the hyphen (e.g. "from 1910 to 1920").
- A single date preceded by 'from' or 'frm' will be interpreted as a period ('from ...').
- A single date preceded by 'to' will be interpreted as a period ('to ...').
- A single date preceded by 'bef' will be interpreted as a date range ('before ...')
- A single date preceded by 'aft' will be interpreted as a date range ('after ...')
- The letter 'q' followed by 1, 2, 3 or 4, and then a year will be interpreted as the 1st, 2nd, 3rd or 4th quarter of that year (e.g. "q4 1910")

Improbable Date Warnings   If you enter a date which is valid, but improbable for whatever reason, Family Historian will warn you that the date looks wrong. For example, if you entered Ian Munro's date of death as 1951, a 'balloon' tip would be displayed looking like this:

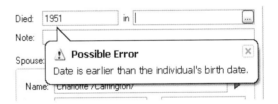

You can close this balloon by clicking anywhere on it (you don't have to click specifically on the little cross button in the top right corner of the balloon, but that also works). Or press the Esc key. Or click or tab back to the field that the balloon is pointing to.

You can disable the 'balloon' tip warnings in Preferences if you wish.

Spouse Tabs   The *Main* tab of the Data Pane is divided into 2 areas: The top part is the Individual Details area (marked on the right in Figure 11). Below that are the *spouse tabs*. There is one spouse tab for each of the Individual's spouses, plus one blank one which is used if you wish to add more spouse families.

In the example in Figure 11, Ian Stephen Munro has one spouse, 'Charlotte', and her tab is the currently selected one (see the area marked 'Spouse Tab Headings' in Figure 11).

Each spouse tab displays (in order) spouse details, marriage details, and child details (all marked on the right in Figure 11). So you can view and edit the basic details for each spouse and for the marriage (if any). And you can view and edit the children in the spouse family.

Add Child   In the example in Figure 11, Ian Munro has 3 children with his wife, Charlotte

Carrington. You can edit their names here if you wish, as well as their sexes, birth dates, and relationship to their parents (remember to leave this last blank if theirs is a default 'birth' relationship).

You can also add more children using the Property Box. To do so, click on the faint "Add Child" text link which appears below the last child in the child listing. If there are numerous children in the list, you may sometimes have to scroll to see them all, and to see the "Add Child" link.

When you click on this link, the familiar menu appears, giving you the choice to **Create New Record** or **Link Existing Record**.

If you add a child here, they will appear in the Focus Window and vice versa. So it doesn't matter which technique you use to add relatives. Just use whichever method is most convenient to you at the time.

Change Order of Children

Changing the order of children is also something that can be done in the Property Box. To move a particular child up or down in the list of children, click on their name, or any other field in their row, in the *child grid* (the small table that shows *Child Details* – see Figure 11). When you do so, either or both of the arrow keys in the top right corner of the child grid will become enabled (see Figure 12 below).

Click on the **Up** arrow to move the child up the list. Click on the **Down** arrow to move the child down the list.

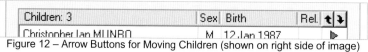

Figure 12 – Arrow Buttons for Moving Children (shown on right side of image)

Change Order of Spouses

You can also change the order of spouses in the Property Box. If a person has more than one spouse, two buttons will appear to the right of the Spouse Tab Headings. They don't show in Figure 11 because Ian Munro has only one spouse in that case. The buttons can be seen in Figure 13 below, which shows the spouse tab headings of the Property Box for a person who had 3 spouses: Anthony, Nigel and Brian.

Click on the **Up** arrow to move the current spouse (Nigel in this case) up the list. Click on the **Down** arrow to move the current spouse down the list.

Figure 13 – Arrow Buttons for Moving Spouses (shown on right side of image)

Add Spouse

If you click on the blank spouse tab, it looks like Figure 14 below. This is the blank tab for Ian Munro of Figure 11. He already has one spouse called 'Charlotte'.

Click on the text link "Add Spouse/Partner" to add a new spouse. Click on the text link "Add Child" in the child grid, to add a child. As always, it doesn't matter whether you add spouses in the Property Box, or in the Focus Window – or elsewhere. Choose whichever method suits you and is most convenient.

Add Children of Unknown Parent

You don't have to add a spouse before you can add a child. In the example in Figure 11, Ian Munro had 3 children with Charlotte Carrington. Suppose you knew that he also had a fourth child, Michael. All you know about the mother is that she wasn't Charlotte Carrington. In that case, do not add Michael as a child on Charlotte's spouse tab. That would imply that Charlotte was Michael's mother. Instead, click on the blank tab and add Michael as a child there.

If at a later date you learn who Michael's mother was, you could add her by clicking on the "Add Spouse" link on this tab.

In general, make sure that you add children to the correct spouse tab. There is no limit to the number of children you can add for each spouse; and no limit to the number of spouses either.

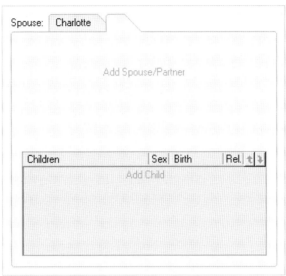

Figure 14 – The Blank Spouse Tab

Go To Buttons

You have probably noticed that there are blue triangles at the right end of the row for each child in the child grid. These are **Go To** buttons: ▶ . Click on any of these buttons to make the Property Box switch to showing that child's record details.

There is also a **Go To** Button to the right of the Name field for the spouse, in the *Spouse Details* area (see Figure 11). As you might expect, clicking on this button will show the spouse's details in the Property Box.

The *Up* Button (Go To Parents)
▲

In the Property Box toolbar, there is also an **Up** button ▲ , which switches the Property Box to showing record details for the person's father or mother.

This button only has a function if the record being viewed in the Property Box is an Individual. With records of all other types it is always greyed.

Go Back/Go Forward Buttons
⇦ ⇨

Like the Focus Window, the Property Box has its own Go Back and Go Forward buttons. Click on **Go Back** ⇦ to go back to the previous record you were viewing in the Property Box. Click on **Go Forward** ⇨ to undo the effect of clicking **Go Back**.

Display in Focus Window
🔍

If you wish to make the current Individual the focus person in the Focus Window, click on the **Display in Focus Window** button 🔍 .

Like the **Up** button, this only has a function if the record being viewed in the Property Box is an Individual. With records of all other types it is always greyed.

Go to Record

We haven't looked at the Records Window yet – we will look at it in a later chapter. If you want to look at the current record's entry in the Records Window, click on the **Go To Record** button:

Show Sources This button was mentioned at the start of this chapter. Use it to hide or show the Source pane (see Figure 11 above).

Sync with Selection It was mentioned at the start of this chapter that every time you change the selection in the main part of the application, the Property Box will automatically show the details for the selected Individual/record. If you don't want it to do that, untick **Sync with Selection** pin button. When you do that, the button will appear unpinned, like this: 🔲. Click it again to re-enable **Sync with Selection**. When you do so, the button once again looks like this: 🔲.

The Property Box Menu 🔲 The next button on the Property Box toolbar is the **Menu** button. When you click on this, a dropdown menu appears, with menu commands **Text Size** (a submenu), **Sort Family Events in Date Order**, **Customize** and **Options**.

Setting the Text Size and Font The **Text Size** submenu lets you choose the size of text in the Property Box. If none of the standard sizes (**Small**, **Medium**, **Large** or **Very Large**) are suitable for your needs, or if you want to change not just the text size, but the font too, click on **Custom**.

Sort Family & Events in Date Order Ordinarily, Family Historian will keep spouses, children and events in date order automatically. But you can override this. If you notice that spouses, children or events are not in date order in the current record, click on this menu command to sort them automatically.

*Tip: You can re-sequence all spouses, children and events throughout the project, in date order, using the **Re-Order Out-of-Sequence Data** command on the **Tools** menu.*

Customize the Property Box The Property Box can be extensively customized to suit your requirements. For example, suppose you wanted to add *Baptism* and *Burial* to the Main tab of the Property Box – or perhaps even have them instead of *Birth* and *Death* – you can do that. Remember that you can always add Birth, Death, Baptism and Burial details on the *Facts* tab – and much more besides. But you may find it convenient to put fields that you use all the time on the *Main* tab. Click the **Customize** menu command to open the Customize Property Box dialog – see Figure 15 below.

The Property Box can be separately customized for each record type. Not only can you specify which fields you wish to appear on the Main tab, you can also create new custom tabs – as many as you like, for each record type – and add fields to them. If you wanted, you could, for example, have an entire tab devoted to occupations – showing all the occupations a person had at different times. Or you could have a tab devoted to all their residences and addresses. Or you could have a tab for record flags (not yet covered in this book) or a tab with a mixture of fields of all types. It's up to you.

To add items to a given tab, simply select each item you wish to add in the 'Available Items' list on the left side, and click the 🔲 button to add it to the list on the right side ('Selected Items'). To remove an item, select in the 'Selected Items' list and click the 🔲 button to remove it.

Figure 15 – The Customize Property Box dialog

Version 3 Compatibility
The Property Box changed significantly between versions 3 and 4. In version 3, for example, there was an extra tab called 'Detail'. If you would like that tab back, just click on the **Version 3 Compatibility** button and it will be re-created. Even if you don't want this tab, it is worth trying it out anyway, just to see an example of what can be done. After pressing **Version 3 Compatibility**, press **OK** to close the Customize Property Box dialog and click on the new *Detail* tab in the Property Box to view it. To get rid of it again, and revert to default settings, re-open the Customize Property Box dialog and press the **Installation Settings** button. Then press **OK** to close the dialog.

To learn more about customizing the Property Box, click the **Help** button within the Customize Property Box dialog.

Property Box Options
The last menu command on the Property Box menu is the **Options** command which is a quick shortcut to the Property Box tab of the Preferences dialog (which can also be reached via the **Tools** menu).

Float/Dock Property Box
By default, the Property Box is *docked* (i.e. fixed) to the right side of the Focus Window. But it doesn't have to be. You can, if you prefer, let it *float* in front of the Focus Window – or any other Family Historian window – by clicking on the Float Property Box button. When you do this, the Property Box is displayed in a dialog box with a caption instead of the Title field. You can resize it, or move it, like any other dialog box, but it will stay in front of other Family Historian windows.

If you want to 'dock' it again, click on the Dock Property Box button which is now at the rightmost position in the Property Box toolbar.

Auto-Docking and Auto-Positioning
When you switch from one subwindow to another (when, for example, you open a diagram) Family Historian tries to anticipate what your requirements for the Property Box are likely to be: do you want it to be opened or closed? Do you want it to be docked or floating? You can specify what you want, for these and other issues, in **Property Box Options**.

If you would prefer Family Historian to leave the Property Box alone when you switch subwindows, just set all the **Property Box Options for Subwindows** to

None.

Close Property Box

When the Property Box is *floating*, the **Close** button is the usual one at the right end of the caption bar. Its appearance will depend on your version of Windows. In some versions it looks like this: . When the Property Box is *docked*, there is no caption bar, so a **Close** button is added to the right end of the Property Box toolbar instead. This **Close** button looks like this: ✕.

How to Open the Property Box

How do you get the Property Box back if you close it? Select a record that you wish to view in the Property Box (e.g. by clicking on a box in the Focus Window, or by clicking on a box in the Diagram Window) and click on the Property Box 📑 on the main application toolbar.

There are numerous shortcut ways of opening the Property Box. In the Diagram Window and the Records Window, for example, you can simply double-click on a record/box to open the Property Box for that record. In the Focus Window, double-clicking on a box doesn't (by default) open the Property Box (because by default, it will open anyway). But even in the Focus Window, you can right-click on any box and click on the **Properties** menu command to open the Property Box, if it's closed.

You Never Have to Close the Property Box

The Property Box is designed to be used in conjunction with other Family Historian windows. *You never have to close it* – and this is true both when it is docked and when it is floating. Anything you could do when it is closed can also be done when it is open. This is very useful because the dialog box provides immediate access to the full record details for whichever record you have selected in the current window. It is an application-wide resource which you can access and use from anywhere in the program. Of course, you might want to close it if it's taking up too much space, and in the way. But you never have to.

Help for the Property Box (F1)

There is a great deal of Help for the Property Box. Press the **F1** key, when using the Property Box, to get help which is relevant to the current context. The **F1** works similarly with subwindows, and dialog boxes too.

3 Introduction to Diagrams

Some of the Things You Can Do with Diagrams

This chapter will introduce the Diagram Window and the most common standard diagrams. Family Historian diagrams are *interactive* – for example, you can click-and-drag to add relatives. They are also *dynamic* – that is, they update immediately to reflect a change, even if that change is made elsewhere in the program. They can be scaled to any size. They can have any horizontal or vertical orientation you want. They can contain multiple trees of different types and orientation, and you can insert additional elements of your own such as pictures, lines, arrows, rectangles, text boxes, and so on. You can move and resize boxes and branches, and the trees – known as 'Smart Trees' – will automatically adjust as you do so. The boxes can be configured to show just about any information you want, and their appearance, style and layout are also ultra-configurable. Diagrams can be instantly created on-demand or saved as charts, to be worked on, and improved, over time (or saved in 11 different image formats, including PDF).

There is, in short, a great deal that can be done with diagrams. This chapter is just an introduction to the basics.

View Ancestors

Open the Family Historian Sample Project and confirm that Ian Munro is selected in the Focus Window. If he isn't, select him. Then click on the **View Ancestors** button on the main application toolbar. When you do this a window – called the *Diagram Window* – opens to display the ancestors of Ian Munro. See Figure 16 below.

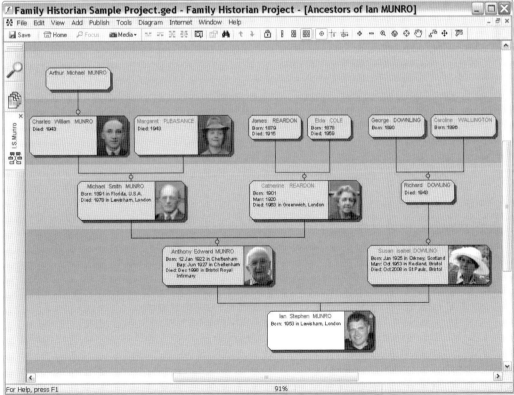

Figure 16 – the Diagram Window: Ancestors Diagram

Navigation Bar Icon for Diagram Windows

When the Diagram Window is opened, a new icon is added to the Navigation Bar – this is the green and yellow icon shown on the left, with the text "I.S.Munro" displayed vertically above it (see image right). The Focus Window was not closed. It is still there now, hidden behind the Diagram Window. Click on the Focus Window icon (the magnifying glass) on the Navigation Bar now, to bring it to the front. Now click back on the Diagram Window icon to bring the Diagram Window back to the front. Notice that the *active* subwindow[5] (the one that is in front of the other application windows if any) always has an orange background in the Navigation bar.

About Subwindows

There are 7 types of subwindows in Family Historian. As well as the Focus Window and the Diagram Window there is also the Multimedia Window, the Records Window, the Reports Window, the Book Window and the Query Window. Each type of subwindow has its own distinctive icon. You can see at a glance which subwindows you have open because each open window's icon is displayed in the Navigation Bar.

A common mistake is to think you have to close one subwindow before you can 'go back' to another. You never have to do that. You can switch easily between any subwindows, whenever you want, by just clicking on icons on the Navigation bar.

Later we will see how you can also have open more than one subwindow of the same type. You can have several Diagram Windows open at the same time if you wish, for example.

How To Close Subwindows

Although you don't *need* to close subwindows, you will want to sometimes. You won't want your application to become unnecessarily cluttered with windows when you are no longer using them. There are several ways to close subwindows:

You can click on the little Close button ☒ just above the icon on the right, in the Navigation bar. Only the 'non-essential' windows (which usually means all subwindows except for the Focus Window and the Records Window) have these close buttons. If an icon is not selected, the Close button won't appear until you move your mouse over it.

You can right-click on the icon in the Navigation bar and choose **Close Window** from the menu that appears.

Each subwindow also has another close button near the top right corner of the main application window. The only trick about this is to make sure you are clicking on the correct close button. In Figure 16 there are two **Close** buttons. These are shown in close-up in Figure 17 below.

Figure 17 – Window Buttons

The red one ☒ is the **Close** button for the application. The small grey one ☒ is the subwindow **Close** button (in this case, the **Close** button for the Diagram Window). If the Property Box is docked on the right hand side, its Close button will be just a little way below the subwindow close button. Try not to confuse them. Finally, if you want to close *all* subwindows except the Focus Window, click on **Close All Non-essential Windows** on the Window menu.

---

[5] You may remember from Chapter 1 that a 'subwindow' is just a window-within-a-window – i.e. in this case, a window within the Family Historian main window.

The Focus Window is unusual in that, unlike all other subwindows, if you close the Focus Window the current project is also closed. As we saw earlier, the Record Window is also a little special in that by default it always has an icon in the Navigation Bar, even if closed.

The Diagram Menu and Toolbar

You may have noticed that when the **Diagram Window** appears, a new toolbar also appears. This is the *Diagram Toolbar* – see Figure 18 below. As well as the toolbar, you may also notice that there is a new menu, **Diagram**, that has appeared just to the right of the **Tools** menu.

Both the **Diagram Menu** and the **Diagram Toolbar** are only displayed when the active subwindow is a **Diagram Window**.

Figure 18 – the Diagram Toolbar

Zooming In and Out

Locate the Zoom In and Zoom Out buttons on the **Diagram Toolbar**. Click on each of them in turn a few times to familiarise yourself with them.

If you want to zoom a long way quickly, in or out, clicking these buttons repeatedly is a very slow way to do it. A better alternative is to use the – (minus) and + (plus) keys on the *numeric keypad*. The advantage of these keys over the buttons is that you can press and hold the key, and the diagram will zoom in or out, until you release the key, so you can do the entire zoom in one action. The **Diagram Window** must be the *active* window when you do this.

If you are using a laptop, you may find it more convenient to use Ctrl-K and Ctrl-L instead of Num+ and Num-.

There are various techniques for zooming in and out, and we shall look at all of them. None of them affect the size of the diagram when printed. Various techniques for setting the size of a diagram when printed are discussed in Chapter 10.

View Whole Diagram

At any time, you can jump to a view of the whole diagram, by clicking on the *View Whole Diagram* button: (its supposed to look like the globe). Click on this button now. You should be able to see the whole diagram without having to scroll.

Diagram Options

In the rest of the chapter, you will be frequently asked to set particular diagram options, so it is worth learning now how to open the **Diagram Options** dialog box. One way is to click on **Options** on the **Diagram** menu. A second, sometimes slightly faster way, is to right-click on the *background* of any diagram and click on **Diagram Options** in the dropdown menu that appears.

Specify Number of Generations

Now that you have opened the Diagram Options dialog, you can specify the number of generations that you wish to see in your diagram (without expanding branches). This is set in the first tab (the 'General' tab) of the Diagram Options dialog. Set **Generations Up** value to the number of generations you wish to see. If you want to see all generations, select 'All' from the dropdown list . Press **OK**. Click on the **View Whole Diagram** button to get the best view of the diagram.

31

Select View

You can select the exact part of the diagram that you wish to view. In this example, we will zoom in on the boxes for Charles Munro and Margaret Pleasance.

Steps

1. Change diagram options so you are viewing all generations and click on **View Whole Diagram** to zoom back so you can see the whole thing.
2. Click on the **Select View** button ⊕ on the diagram toolbar.
3. The button remains selected. Now move the mouse over the **Diagram Window**. Notice that the cursor's shape has changed and now looks similar to the **Select View** button (it's supposed to look like a magnifying glass).
4. Click just above and to the left of Charles Munro's box on the diagram. Keeping the mouse button depressed, drag down and to the right. A stretchy box should appear. Drag in such a way that the stretchy box surrounds the diagram boxes for both Charles Munro and Margaret Pleasance; then release the mouse button.
5. The *Diagram Window* view changes to show a close-up view of the selected area. The **Select View** button is no longer depressed.

Tip: Select View works well in conjunction with View Whole Diagram. Use the latter to get an overall view. Then use the former to pick the precise area you want to look at.

Centre Diagram

The *Centre Diagram* command does not zoom in or out. It re-centres the diagram on the individual or individuals who are the root, or roots, of the diagram (as we will see later, diagrams can be based around a couple, as well as on a single individual).

When showing ancestors (at least in top-down orientation) the root individual or couple will be centred at the bottom of the **Diagram Window**. When showing descendants, they will be centred at the top of the **Diagram Window**. For other diagrams they will be moved to the horizontal and vertical centre of the window.

The Grabber

The *Grabber* also does not zoom in or out. Rather it is a convenient alternative to clicking on scrollbars, if you want to reposition the diagram.

Steps

1. Click on the **Grabber** button 🖑 on the diagram toolbar. The button stays depressed.
2. Move the mouse over the **Diagram Window**. Notice that the cursor's shape has changed and now looks similar to the **Grabber** button (it's supposed to look like a hand).
3. Click anywhere on the diagram and, keeping the mouse button depressed, move the mouse up and down, left and right. Notice that when you do this, you reposition the whole diagram.
4. Click once again on the **Grabber** button, to end this mode.

Tip: A quick way to switch temporarily to 'grabbing' mode is to simply press-and-hold the spacebar. You can then click-and-drag anywhere on the diagram to move it. When you release the space bar, the diagram will revert to its previous mode. This is a very useful technique which is well worth remembering.

*Tip: A quick way to end 'grabbing' mode is to click with the Right Mouse button. Another way to end it (which also works with the **Select View** mode) is to press the Escape key (**Esc**).*

Expansion Buttons

You should at this point still be viewing Ian Munro's ancestors. Change the number of generations to 3. Locate the ***Expansion Buttons*** button ⊕ on the diagram toolbar. Click it a few times and observe the effect on the diagram. When pressed in, some of the lines should have circles in them. When pressed out, the circles disappear. These circles are *expansion buttons*.

Ensuring that the **Expansion Buttons** button is pressed in, click on the expansion button above Anthony Munro. His parents disappear. Click it again. They re-appear.

The expansion button above Catherine Reardon (amongst others) has a cross over it. This shows that she has at least one ancestor, but the diagram isn't showing it. The reason that his ancestors are not being shown is because we set the number of generations to 3. Nevertheless, click on her expansion button. Her parents now appear. When you specify the number of generations, you only specify the *initial* number of generations to display. It does not prevent you exploring further generations, using the expansion buttons.

Using the expansion buttons you use diagrams to explore and browse family trees, following branches when they interest you, and closing off other branches as needed.

*Tip: If you want to expand all levels of a branch, to show all ancestors of a given person, right-click on their box and then click on **Expand Branch (all levels)** on the dropdown menu that appears.*

*Tip: An alternative to clicking on an expansion button is to press the **Enter** key when the relevant box is selected. If you press one of the arrow keys the selection will change appropriately from one box to another. Using the arrow keys to move, in combination with the Enter key to expand or hide boxes, is a convenient and easy way to move around a diagram.*

The Property Box & the Diagram Window

In Family Historian, diagrams are not just for printing. They are also for editing and for browsing. In both of these latter roles, the **Diagram Window** is designed to be used in conjunction with the **Property Box**. You should still be viewing an Ancestors diagram for Ian Munro at this point.

Steps

1. Double-click on the box for Anthony Munro. The **Property Box** appears showing his details. If you like you can dock the **Property Box** at the side of the window. It doesn't make any difference whether it is docked or floating.
2. Now single click on other boxes in the diagram in turn. Notice that the **Property Box** updates itself to show details for each one (if it doesn't, make sure the **Sync with Selection** button on the Property Box toolbar is pushed in so that it looks like this: 🗨 and not like this: 📌).
3. Now repeat steps 1-3, but choose the **Facts** tab of the Property Box. Notice that you can easily see all the events and attributes for each Individual in turn. Whichever Property Box tab you pick, you can see the relevant details for whichever diagram box you select.

Diagrams are *Dynamic*

Diagrams in Family Historian are *dynamic*. That is, they keep themselves up-to-date, and always reflect the latest changes. To illustrate this, select Anthony Munro. The Property Box shows his details. Using the **Name** field of the Property Box (Main tab) change his name from 'Anthony Edward Munro' to 'Tony Munro'. Press **Tab**. Notice that the diagram updates immediately to use the new name. Click on **Undo Individual [1] Name Edit** on the **Edit** menu. The name reverts back to what it had been both in the Property Box and on the diagram.

View
Descendants

You should still be viewing the ancestors of Ian Munro. Locate his great grandmother, Margaret Pleasance, expanding branches if necessary. Click on Margaret's box to select it. We are going to view her descendants. Notice that you don't have to select her record in the **Focus Window**. Any selection in any window is just as good as any other, for any command which requires a selected record.

Click on the **View Descendants** button on the toolbar. A diagram of Margaret Pleasance's descendants is displayed (confirm that the window title either is, or ends with, "Descendants of Margaret Pleasance").

Multiple
Diagram
Windows

At this point there should be four icons in the Navigation Bar, including two sets of Diagram Window icons looking like this:

The selected Diagram Window – the one you are viewing now – has "M.Pleasa..." (the name is too long to fit in the space) displayed vertically above its icon. The other Diagram Window (with I.S.Munro above its icon), is the one you were viewing before, showing Ancestors of Ian Munro. Click on each icon in turn to switch between them, effectively bringing the clicked-on window to the front. Satisfy that yourself that you can switch between diagrams at will. Then switch back to viewing the Diagram Window displaying the descendants of Margaret Pleasance.

Spouse
Display
Options

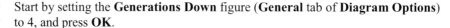

Start by setting the **Generations Down** figure (**General** tab of **Diagram Options**) to 4, and press **OK**.

When viewing a person's descendants, how do you display information about the *spouses* of descendants? Family Historian provides 4 different ways of handling spouses. When working through the examples, don't forget that you can click on **View Whole Diagram** at any time, to get the best view of the diagram.

Steps

1. Click on the **No Spouse Info** button ⊟ on the **Diagram** menu. Notice that the diagram displays 1 child for Margaret, 4 grandchildren and 6 great grandchildren. Including her own box, there should be 12 boxes in all. So far, there is no information about spouses.

2. Now click on **One Box Per Marriage** ⊞. An extra box appears. Unlike the others it is pink, and linked to Anthony Munro's original box by a zigzag line (called a *stretchy* line). This box is a *remarriage* box for Anthony Munro. When *One Box Per Marriage* is selected any descendant that is married more than once will get one extra box for each extra marriage. At this point, each box contains the name of the descendant's spouse, if any. We can now see that Anthony had 2 wives: Julia Fish and Susan Dowling. Judy, Ian and Sally Munro are the children of Anthony Munro and Susan Dowling.

3. Click on **Spouses in Own Box** ⊟⊟. This time, 9 new brown boxes have appeared, and the pink remarriage box has gone, making a net increase of 8 boxes. The brown boxes represent *spouses* – one for Margaret's spouse, and one for each of her descendants' spouses.

4. The 4th option is rarely used. If you want you can have *both* spouses *and* remarriage boxes. This can only be set from the **Spouse display options** section of the Diagram Options dialog.

Box Types

This example shows that the *Descendants* diagram is a little more complicated than the *Ancestors* diagram. Whereas the boxes in the Ancestors diagram are all of the same type, and all display the same information, the Descendants diagram can contain up to 3 different types of box: normal descendant boxes, remarriage boxes, and spouse boxes. These boxes can, and usually will, display slightly different information. You may have noticed that Anthony Munro's date-of-birth was not repeated in his remarriage box, for example.

As we will see later, you don't have to accept the default colours for boxes. You don't even have to base their colouring on the box type. You have almost complete control over this, and other aspects of the box appearance.

The Diagram Root
With the sole exception of the **Everyone** diagram, all diagrams have a *root*, called the Diagram Root or Chart Root. Don't confuse this with the *File Root* of Chapter 1. The *diagram root* is the person whose ancestors, descendants or relatives you are viewing in the diagram. Although the diagram *root* box is coloured differently from other boxes (white, in this diagram), it shouldn't be thought of as another type of box. In descendant diagrams the root box will always display the same information as normal descendant boxes, and is therefore referred to as a descendant box. In an ancestor diagram it is treated like an ancestor box.

Pause a while to make sure you have a good understanding of the Descendants diagram, before moving on. Switch backwards and forwards between all 3 spouse options, until you are clear about what they do. Notice that a given box type may display different information in different circumstances. Descendant boxes only display spouse information if spouse boxes are not being displayed, for example. Notice that you can switch spouse option at *any* time, even if you have expanded and hidden branches, and made other changes to the diagram.

Text Schemes
The text that is displayed in a box is determined by the *Text Scheme*. Up to now, unless you changed it, you will have been using the default text scheme: *Birth, Marr, Death*. However, there are numerous standard ones for you to use:

Steps

1. Bring up the Diagram Options Dialog (click on Diagram > Options).
2. Select the **Text** tab.
3. Select the text scheme "Name Only" from the list. Press **OK**.
4. Notice how the text has changed. Repeat this exercise selecting in turn: "Name Only (Compact)", "Name, Dates, How Related to Chart Root" and any other text scheme you wish to try. Try pressing the **Apply** button instead of the **OK** button. Notice that the diagram changes behind the Diagram Options dialog when you do this. **Apply** applies changes to the current diagram exactly as **OK** does, but the Diagram Options dialog doesn't close, which can be more convenient if you are experimenting.

Some text schemes may appear identical because the differences between them are only manifested when you have more data.

The *Box Types* scheme is a useful one if you are at all unclear about which type a given box belongs to. With this scheme, each box displays its own box type in capital letters (Ancestor, Descendant, Spouse, Remarriage or Proxy[6]). Try using it, while changing the *Spouse Display Options* (see previous). It should help to clarify what they do.

Later we will look at how you can change text schemes, and create your own.

View Ancestors and Descendants
The *Ancestors and Descendants* diagram is sometimes referred to as an Hourglass Diagram, for obvious reasons. Locate Ian Munro. Select his box and click on the **View Ancestors and Descendants** button ⌘. Another Diagram Window is displayed showing an *Ancestors and Descendants Diagram* for Ian Munro. If you

---

[6] We haven't encountered 'Proxy' boxes yet. They are a special type of box, only used in *All Relatives* trees.

have been following the instructions in this chapter precisely, you should now have three DiagramWindows open (count the diagram icons in the Navigation Bar). If you look at the **Diagram Options** you will see that you specify both the number of **Generations Up** and **Generations Down** separately, for this diagram. Set both the **Generations Up** and **Generations Down** fields to 'All'. Click on **View Whole Diagram** to see it all.

The *Ancestors and Descendants* diagram is not hard to understand, but it is worth pausing to get a good grasp of it before moving on, if only because it will help to make sense of the *All Relatives* diagram.

You should be able to see that the *Ancestors and Descendants* diagram is simply the grafting of an *Ancestors* diagram on top of a *Descendants* diagram. Ancestors are displayed in the top part, descendants in the bottom. The *Spouse Display Option* buttons all work with this diagram, but only affect the lower, descendant portion of the diagram. They have no effect on the display of ancestors.

Try selecting *Box Types* as the text scheme. Depending on which *Spouse Display Options* you use, you should be able to see 3 different types of boxes: *Ancestor*, *Descendant*, and *Spouse*.

View All Relatives

We will now use the *All Relatives* diagram to show all the relatives of Ian Munro.

Select Ian Munro and click on the **View All Relatives** button to display the *All Relatives* Diagram in yet another Diagram Window[7]. This **Diagram Window**'s title reads 'Relatives of Ian Munro'. See Figure 19 below. In that example, the 'Box Types' text scheme is used. If you use a different text scheme, this will not only affect the contents of each box, but also the box sizes and shape, which in turn will affect the shape of the overall tree to some extent.

Ian Munro's direct ancestors are all coloured in green. This is just the style of the default diagram. You can use other colouring schemes (see the **Box** tab of the Diagram Options dialog).

Interpreting the *All Relatives* Tree

Large *All Relatives* trees can be complex. If you zoom in on a small part of an All Relatives tree, containing a large number of boxes, you may wonder if you click on an expansion button, which part will disappear: the area above the expansion button or the area below it? It is easy to get confused about what you are looking at.

A few key points may help. Remember that all trees, including the *All Relatives* trees 'extend out' from a root. It is true that trees can have a couple (i.e. of individuals) as their root, but the couple will always be side-by-side. So it remains the case, even then, that all trees are anchored in a starting point, and that all lines extend out from there. In a tree with top-down orientation, Descendant trees extend out downwards. Ancestor trees extend out upwards. Ancestor and Descendant trees extend out both upwards and downwards. And All Relatives trees extend out both downwards, and upwards-and-then-downwards. But they don't extend out downwards-and-then-upwards (this is because your descendants' ancestors are not *per se* your relatives, but your ancestors' descendants are).

Trees show you how individuals are related to the root. Clicking on expansion branches hides outermost branches of the tree. The branch area leading back to the root is not hidden. When, as with the *All Relatives* tree, you get lines crossing over themselves and 'outer' branches that fold back on themselves so that the tips are physically close to the root, it's easy to get confused.

---

[7] If you would prefer Family Historian to re-use an open Diagram Window rather than creating a new one, each time you open a diagram, you can specify this in the Navigation tab of Preferences.

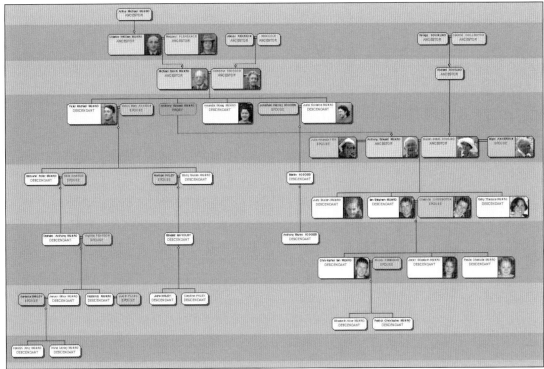

Figure 19 – A 'Layered' All Relatives Diagram showing relatives of Ian Munro

Basic Diagram Options
Open **Diagram Options** now and look at the *General* tab. The **Tree** field takes 4 values: *Ancestors, Descendants, Ancestors and Descendants* or *All Relatives*. Click on each of these in turn and observe the effect on the diagram options. Fields that are not applicable for a given diagram type are hidden or disabled.

The initial size of an *Ancestors* diagram is determined by **Generations Up**. For a *Descendants* diagram, the equivalent field is **Generations Down**. For an *Ancestors and Descendants* diagram, both fields must be specified. For an *All Relatives* diagram, the **Generations Down** field either specifies the number of generations down from each ancestor (the diagram root isn't his own ancestor, but counts as one for this purpose), or specifies the number of generations down from the diagram root, depending on the value of the **...counting down from** field.

Generation Stripes
You will have noticed that by default the *All Relatives* diagram has a striped background. Each stripe corresponds to a generation. Belonging to a generation has nothing to do with age. You can have an uncle who is younger than you; but he is still a member of the previous generation. A person's generation is relative to a relationship, and is determined by how many generations back you have to go to find either them or a common ancestor; and then (if they aren't an ancestor) how many steps back down you have to go to reach them from the common ancestor. Your uncle is 2 steps back to a common ancestor (your grandparents) and one step down from them (he is their child). So, in terms of generations, he is one step back from you.

The *All Relatives* diagram in Figure 19 above is showing 8 generations.

Relationship Descriptions
Any diagram can have labels for each row describing the relationship of individuals in that row to the diagram root. To see this, set **Relationship Descriptions** to any value other than *None*.

You can change the font (including font style and colour) for Relationship Descriptions by clicking the **Font** button to the right of the **Relationships Descriptions** field in the Diagram Options dialog.

By default, the row in which the root appears is labelled 'root & siblings'. You can change this in the **Diagrams** tab of the **Preferences** dialog, which is available from the **Tools** menu.

'Layered' vs. 'Flat' All Relatives Trees

In the *All Relatives* diagram in Figure 19 above the parents of the tree root are not aligned with their siblings. If the other ancestors had siblings, they too would not be aligned with their siblings. In this 'layered' layout, you can get more than one row of boxes per generation. Also, in a layered tree, each row corresponds to a different relationship type. For example, all first cousins twice removed will be grouped together in a row of their own. Look at the relationship descriptions for each row of a layered *All Relatives* tree to confirm this.

To try the alternative 'flat' layout, set the **Style** field to 'Flat' in the **General** tab of **Diagram Options**. The 'Flat' version of the *All Relatives* diagram in Figure 19 looks like Figure 20 below. In this version, you only get one row per generation.

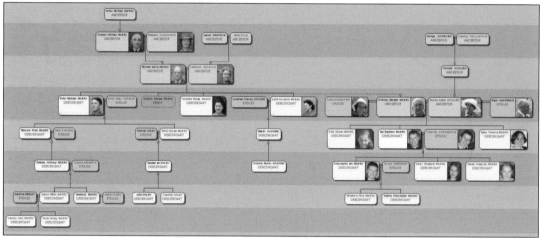

Figure 20 – A 'Flat' All Relatives Diagram

Close the Diagram Windows

You may have as many as six icons in your Navigation Bar at this point, including four diagram icons representing four open Diagram Windows. If you can't remember how to close the Diagram Windows, review the section *How to Close Subwindows* above.

Use the Help

There are many more features of diagrams than we have covered so far. More information is available in the Family Historian Help. This can be accessed from the **Help** menu, or by clicking a **Help** button if you see one (e.g. in **Diagram Options**) or often by pressing the **F1** key.

4 Pictures & Multimedia Part 1: The Property Box

In this chapter we will look at how to work with pictures and other multimedia (video, sound, etc). You will learn how to associate pictures and other multimedia with Individuals, Families and Source records – and also with Individual and Family events such as christenings or weddings. You will learn how to link Individuals not just to each picture in which they appear, but *even to their face in each picture in which they appear*. Later you will learn how to make use of these pictures (and faces) in reports, books, charts, websites and family tree CDs or DVDs.

Two Ways of Adding Pictures and Other Multimedia

There are two ways of working with pictures and other multimedia in Family Historian: you can either start from the perspective of a particular record and add pictures or multimedia to the record. Or you can start from the point of view of the picture or multimedia, and add it into your project, and then link it to the records associated with it (that is, to the Individuals, Families or Sources that it displays). The difference is purely one of convenience.

If you are approaching the issue of pictures from the point of view of the record you want to add them to, you probably should to use the Property Box to add pictures or multimedia. If your focus is more on the picture/multimedia itself, you are more likely to want to use the Multimedia Window. The two approaches are not mutually exclusive. You can switch between them at any time. Nor does it make any difference to the outcome. In this chapter ("Part 1") we will look at how you use the Multimedia tab of the Property Box. In the next chapter ("Part 2") we will look at how you use the Multimedia Window.

Video, Sound Files, and Other 'Media'

Most of the discussion in this chapter applies not just to pictures, but also to other multimedia – such as video and sound files. In fact, Family Historian lets you treat *any* kind of file (even including GEDCOM files!) as multimedia. However, for reasons of stylistic convenience we will mainly just refer to 'pictures'. Please remember that in most cases, the discussion applies to all forms of multimedia and not just pictures. Where we do refer to other forms of multimedia, we will often abbreviate the term to simply 'media' as is done in the program itself.

Add Pictures in the Property Box

We will start by looking at how you can use the Property Box to add pictures. Open the Family Historian Sample Project and select Ian Munro's record in the Focus Window. When you do this, the Property Box will automatically show his record details. Click on the *Multimedia* tab of the Property Box. If you hide the Source Pane, the Property Box should now look something like Figure 21 below. There are already 3 pictures of Ian Munro, displayed in date order.

Add Media
🔖 Add Media

Suppose you wanted to add another picture of Ian Munro (there is no limit to the number of pictures each person can have). To do this you click on the **Add Media** button.

When you do so, a dropdown menu appears with two menu commands: **Insert from File** and **Link to Existing Multimedia Record**. Family Historian automatically creates a Multimedia record for each picture you insert. This means that you can view and search pictures without needing to think about which records they're linked to. It also means that you can link the same picture to as many Individuals (or other records) as you like.

If you wanted to link an existing picture to Ian Munro – one that already had been inserted into your project – you would choose the **Link to Existing Multimedia Record** menu command. To add a picture that is completely new to your project, click on **Insert from File**.

Insert Video, Sound Files, Etc

When you click on **Insert from File**, a selector dialog is displayed to let you choose the file to insert. By default it shows image files. If you want to insert video, sound files, or other multimedia, change the **Files of type** setting appropriately in this dialog box. Remember, you can treat *any* external file as a multimedia file. Family Historian does not have to have any built-in knowledge of the type of file type you insert. If necessary, set the file type to 'All Files', to find the file you wish to insert.

Insert Multiple Pictures

You can insert as many pictures as you like in one go, as long as they are all in the same folder. You just need to select them all and click on the button to insert them. There are various standard Windows techniques for selecting multiple items in lists of this kind. If the items are contiguous, click on the first, and then press-and-hold the **Shift** key while clicking on the last, to select them all. Another technique is to press-and-hold the **Ctrl** key while clicking on individual items that you want to add or remove from the selection. Yet another technique is to click-and-drag on the background of the list, to form a stretchy box to 'lasso' the items you wish to select.

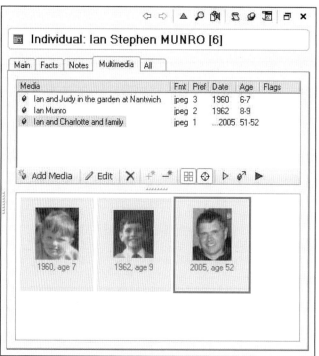

Figure 21 - The Property Box, Multimedia Tab

Copy Files into Project

When you have chosen the file or files you wish to insert, you will be asked if you wish to copy the files into the current project – see Figure 22 below. You don't have to do this, but it is recommended.

Organizing Your Multimedia Files

Some users like to organise multimedia files in a structured way. You can do this, even if you choose to let Family Historian copy your multimedia files into the project folder. Multimedia files will be kept in a folder called 'Media' within the project folder. But within that folder, you can have whatever kind of folder structure you want to store your multimedia files. If you wish to do this, be sure to set the **Destination folder (if copying)** field to "Let me choose". If this is not a concern for you, just leave the value as "Default". Either way, if at some later date you decide you want to re-organize the way that multimedia files are stored, you can do so using the **Work with External File Links** tool, on the **Tools** menu.

Figure 22 – The *Copy Media Files* Prompt

Why You Should Link to Faces   At this point, any new pictures you have inserted will have been added to the list of pictures in the Multimedia tab of the Property Box. If you are adding pictures of an Individual though, there is a further step you may wish to take.

In our example, we imagined that we were adding a picture of Ian Munro. There may be several people in the picture - which is Ian Munro?

One bad solution to this problem is to use an image-editing tool to 'crop' the picture, to only show Ian Munro. This is a bad solution because in cropping the picture, you are losing what is best about it. The best and most interesting pictures are the ones that show groups of people – especially family members – in interesting, and evocative contexts. Often (as in the example in figure below), the picture may even say something about family relationships and dynamics. You won't get any of that if you crop out each person!

In practice, we have found that even if you have a picture with only one person in it, it is still a good idea to link the person to their face. The reason is that for many purposes – in diagram boxes, in individual-related sections in reports and books, and in similar contexts within websites and elsewhere – a tight close-up on a face is exactly what you want. But even when it's just one person, you still don't want to lose the rest of the picture. If you have a picture of a man wearing a military uniform, say, you want both the close-up of his face, but also the whole picture shot of him in his uniform.

In some cases, such as the Family Group Sheet report, you will be able to choose to show *both* a whole picture (e.g. of the family) and close-ups taken from the same picture.

Note: You can if you wish use the link-to-face capability of Family Historian to link to items that are not faces. In the Multimedia Window, it is not unusual to link a note to any item of interest in a picture for example.

How to Link to Faces   To link people to their face in a picture, from within the Multimedia tab of the Property Box, you need to use the **Edit Media Item** dialog box (see Figure 23 below). If you insert a single picture in the Multimedia tab of the Property Box, this dialog box will automatically be opened for you when the picture is inserted. If you insert multiple pictures, it won't – you will need to select each picture in turn and click on the **Edit** button on the Multimedia toolbar (see Figure 25 below) to edit it.

Edit Media Item   In the example in Figure 23, a picture of Ian Munro and his family has just been inserted. To link a person to their face, the next step would be to click on the **Link to Face** button and then move the cursor over the picture. You should notice when you do this, that the cursor looks like a cross. You click-and-drag on the picture to draw a stretchy box round Ian Munro's face. When you release the button, he should have a rectangle round his face with 8 little white boxes on the sides and corners. You can click-and-drag inside the rectangle to move it, or click-and-drag on any of the white boxes to resize the box. Once you are satisfied, you can press **OK** to save changes. And that's it.

Figure 23 – *The Edit Media Item* Dialog Box

Link Other Faces   Of course you may be immediately wondering – what about all the other people in the picture? How would I link the picture to them? You can do this in much the same way that you linked the picture to Ian Munro. First, for each of the people, you would add this media item to their record. Then link to their face. The only difference would be that when you click on the **Add Media** button to add the picture to their record, instead of choosing the **Insert From File** menu command, you should choose the **Link to Existing Multimedia Record** command.

The alternative approach would be to do all the linking in the Multimedia Window. We will look at this in the next chapter.

Updating & Deleting Frames   If at some later stage, you wish to adjust the position or size of the frame round a person's face (Ian Munro's say) re-open this dialog box and click on the **Select Frame** button. When you do this the 8 white boxes are once again shown round the rectangle that frames Ian Munro's face, and you can size and move the frame as before. If you wish to delete the frame altogether, simply press the **Delete** key after selecting the frame.

Edit Picture Details   The fields above the picture in the **Edit Media Item** dialog box, are all about the picture itself. By default, the picture will be given a **Title** based on the file name. But if the file name is not very meaningful (as it isn't in the example in Figure 23) it would be a good idea to change the title to something more useful. If you want to add a note about the picture as a whole, you do so using the **Picture Note field** at

42

the top. If it's a long note you wish to add, use the helper dialog[8] for it.

If possible, it's a very good idea to specify a date for each picture. If you don't know the exact date, you can give just a month and year, or even just a year. Family Historian can automatically calculate each person's age and show this information in picture captions. But it can only do so if knows both the birth date of the people in the picture and the date of the picture itself.

Keywords It is a good idea to associate each picture with keywords that you might later want to use later for searching and filtering (in the Multimedia Window – see below). There's no need to use keywords for the Individuals in the picture if you link the picture to all the people in it. But you might want to use keywords for other topics that are of importance to you – e.g. 'holiday', 'occupation', 'family group', etc. Each picture can have as many keywords as you want. They should be entered as a simple comma-separated list, such as this:

Picture, Family Group, Holiday, Ireland

The **Keyword** field has a helper dialog. So if you prefer, you can also use that to choose from a list of previously-used keywords. As well as keywords you create yourself, Family Historian will automatically allocate one keyword to each multimedia item, based on the type of item it is – in this case, a *picture*.

The *Links* Field To the right of the **Keywords** field is the **Links** field. You can't edit this. It shows you how many records the picture is linked to. In Figure 23 this value is 1. The picture, in the example, has just been inserted and so far is only linked to Ian Munro. You can view the same picture in the Family Historian Sample Project. It is listed under the name "Ian and Charlotte and family" in the Multimedia tab of the Property Box, for Ian Munro. Select that picture and press the **Edit** button. You will notice that the number of links is 5. This is because within the sample project, the picture has already been linked to all the people in it.

Edit Link Details Whereas the fields above the picture are all about the picture itself, the fields below the picture are all about the *link* between the current person (or record) and the picture. In the example in Figure 23, they are about the link between Ian Munro and this picture.

Attach a Note to a Link Suppose, for example, you wanted to write a note about Ian Munro *in relation to this picture* you should do so in the unlabelled large white box below the picture. Such a note might say something like "Usually wears spectacles but took them off for this photo" (say).

Exclude From Diagrams & Reports Sometimes you may want to link a person to a picture but not use that picture as a picture of them, in diagrams and/or reports. This might be because they weren't actually in it (you might link them to the picture if, say, they *took* the picture), or because they don't look good in it, or whatever. In such cases, you should tick **Exclude from Diagrams** or **Exclude from Reports** or both. If a picture is excluded from diagrams, it won't be used in the Focus Window either. If a picture is excluded from reports, it won't be used in books, web-pages or family tree CDs or DVDs.

Use Note as Caption By default, Family Historian will generate captions for pictures for you, in reports. The only exception to this is if the picture is a picture of an event or attribute (we will look at this case shortly). When generating a caption, Family Historian will usually give the person's name, date, and their age at the time of the picture. If you prefer however, you can use your own caption. To do this, enter the caption in unlabelled white box below the picture and tick **Use Note as Caption**.

---

[8] 'Helper dialogs' are explained in Chapter 2.

The Edit Media Item Toolbar

Immediately below the picture is the Edit Media Item toolbar – see Figure 24 below below. The first two buttons ( ) are for zooming in and out. And the current percentage zoom is displayed next to them. The **Autosize** button , if checked, sizes the picture to fit within the available space (you can resize the dialog box to make it bigger if it's too small). The **Full Size** button resets the picture to 'actual size' (100% zoom). The **Grabber** button is useful when the picture is too large for its frame, so you need to scroll to see it all. In that case, check the **Grabber** button and click-and-drag on the picture to scroll it.

The **View in Multimedia Window** button will close the **Edit Media Item** dialog box and display the media item in the Multimedia Window instead. As we will see shortly, depending on what you're trying to do, there can be advantages in using the Multimedia Window, instead of the Multimedia Tab of the Property Box, to work with pictures. The main advantage is that in the Multimedia Window, it's easier to link a picture to *all* the people in it, rather than just one.

Finally the **Open Editor/Player** button allows you to open the media item in an external program – whichever program is configured on your PC as the application of choice to use for playing/editing multimedia of that kind.

Figure 24 – The toolbar for the *Edit Media Item* Dialog Box

Multimedia Tab of the Property Box

We looked briefly earlier at the Multimedia tab of the Property Box, but it is now time to look in more detail at this tab. Look once again at the Multimedia tab of the Property Box for Ian Munro. It should look like Figure 21 above.

The top part of the tab lists all the multimedia items for the person. The columns show the title of each item, its format, preference ordering (to be explained shortly), date, age (that is, the age of the Individual at the time when the picture was taken), and flags associated with the item. Click on any column heading to sort the list on that heading.

The flags column shows whether the item has been flagged to be excluded from diagrams ( ) or excluded from reports ( ), or if the note is to be used as a caption ( ); or any combination of all three.

Multimedia Tab Toolbar

Below the listing is the Multimedia Tab Toolbar (see Figure 25). We have already looked at the **Add Media** button (for adding new multimedia for the current record) and the **Edit** button (which opens the **Edit Media** Item dialog box).

Figure 25 – The Property Box Multimedia Tab toolbar

Unlink or Delete

The **Unlink** button can be used either to unlink the current record from the picture (from its Multimedia record) or it can be used to delete the multimedia record altogether. You will be given the choice.

Preference Ordering of Pictures

The pictures in Figure 21 are listed in the default order, which is date order. But in some contexts (such as the top of the Focus Window) Family Historian will display pictures in your order of preference. Click on the **Higher Preference** or **Lower Preference** buttons to adjust the preference ordering for pictures. The picture with the highest preference ordering will have '1' in the 'Pref' column of the listing above the toolbar. The next highest will be '2', and so on.

Thumbnails

Click the **Thumbnails** button ▦ to toggle between viewing thumbnails of the pictures, or one-picture-at-a-time. Thumbnails if displayed with follow the same ordering as the list above. The current selection will have a blue border around it.

If you display one-picture-at-a-time, the picture displayed is the selected picture in the list above, or none if there is no selection.

Show Face

Click on the **Show Face** button ⊕ to toggle between showing complete pictures and just showing the person's face in the picture. When displaying thumbnails, the caption will include the date of the picture, the person's age at the time, and any note associated with this person in relation to this picture.

Go To Record
▷

We discussed earlier, that when you insert a picture into Family Historian, a Multimedia Record is automatically created to represent that picture in the program. When you add a title, picture note, or date for a picture, these details are stored in the picture's Multimedia Record. Records of any type can be viewed in the Property Box – and that includes Multimedia records. Click on the **Go To Record** button ▷ to view the currently selected picture's Multimedia record in the Property Box. Of course you can press the Property Box's **Go Back** button ◁ – on the main Property Box toolbar – to then return.

View in Multimedia Window
⌗

We have already encountered the **View in Multimedia Window** button ◪ in the toolbar for the **Edit Media Item** dialog box (see Figure 24 above). It does the same thing here that it did there. It allows you to view the current person's multimedia in the Multimedia Window.

Open Editor/ Player
▶

The **Open Editor/Player** button ▶ was also present on the **Edit Media Item** dialog box toolbar, and does the same thing here that it did there – namely, it allows you to open the picture (or sound file, video, document, or other multimedia item) in an external program – whichever program is configured on your PC as the application of choice to use for playing/editing multimedia of that kind.

Pictures of Families

So far, we have looked at the Multimedia tab in the Property Box, with respect to records for *Individuals*. The example we used was Ian Munro. But if you look at a *Family* record in the Property Box, you will find that it has a Multimedia tab too. The same is true if you look at a *Source* record in the Multimedia tab. Families can have pictures linked to them, and so too can Source records. And most of what we have discussed in this chapter, still applies in these cases too.

Pictures of Source Records

Pictures of sources are typically scanned images of documents – such as birth certificates or census returns – but they could also be pictures of grave stones, say. If your source is an interview, the multimedia item could be an audio recording of the interview, or a video of it.

Pictures of Events and Attributes

So you can have pictures of Individuals, Sources and Families. Each Individual, Source or Family record can have as many pictures as you like, and each picture can be shared between as many records as you like. But what about pictures of events – such as a wedding or a christening? Or what about a picture of a place that your father came from, or a house your parents used to live in? Suppose your grandfather was a craftsman and you found some great photos of the kinds of tools that he would almost certainly have used? What do you do with these photographs?

In the next chapter we will be looking at how you can use the Property Box to record *events* in the lives of people and families, and also to record their *attributes* – occupation, residence, and so on. All such information is – or can be – recorded in the *Facts* tab of the Property Box. You will see there that each event or attribute that you record can have associated with it an unlimited number of pictures or other multimedia. As you will see, you view, add to, or edit the list of multimedia items linked to an event or attribute by clicking on the **Show Media** button ▣ on the *Facts* tab toolbar.

As you will see, you add and edit pictures and media items for events and attributes, in the same way that you add and edit pictures and multimedia for Individuals, Families and Sources. And it can be the same pictures and multimedia in each case.

How to Show Pictures in Reports

As you will find when you look at reports, Family Historian reports are very configurable. They are configured in the **Report Options** dialog. Most reports have a tab, within Report Options, for configuring pictures. Typically you will specify the maximum number of pictures to be included – for Individuals, for family members of all types, for Sources, and so on. Pictures of events and attributes will be counted towards these maximum figures. So if you have 3 pictures of Ian Munro, say, and 2 pictures of events involving him, you will need to set the Max Pics value to 5 or more, if you wish to see all of them in a report.

Bear in mind that too that depending on the report type, Family events and attributes may be treated differently from Individual events and attributes.

The same issue applies to books, web-pages and family tree CDs and DVDs, all of which use either report option dialogs, or similar dialogs, to allow you to specify picture options.

5 Pictures & Multimedia Part 2: The Multimedia Window

The Multimedia Window

In the last chapter we looked at how you can add, and work with, pictures and multimedia in the Property Box. In this chapter, we will look at how you can add and work with pictures and multimedia in the Multimedia Window.

The Multimedia Window is another subwindow like the Focus Window and the Diagram Window. Like both of those windows, it has own **Navigation Bar** icon – shown on the left.

Add Picture

Shortly we will look at how you can use the Multimedia Window to link pictures to Individuals, and even to link people to their faces in pictures; but before you can do that you must be viewing the picture in the Multimedia Window. How do you get it there?

If your picture is a physical photograph on your desk, or a picture in a book, you need to find a way of getting the image into digital format (typically jpeg, png, tiff, bmp, or gif). The normal way to do that is to use a scanner. If the picture was taken by a digital camera, you just need to transfer the image onto your PC. But either way, you need to end up with a file on your computer that holds the picture in a format Family Historian recognises. Once you have this file, click on Family Historian's **Add** menu and then choose **Pictures**. As discussed in the previous chapter, you can select multiple pictures and insert them all in one go. You can also choose whether or not to copy the pictures files into the project folder (which is recommended) and, if so, whether or not you wish to organise exactly where in the project folder they go.

When you do this, the Multimedia Window will be opened, if it wasn't already opened, and the new Multimedia Records will be listed in it.

Add Video, Sound Files, and Other Multimedia

Of course you could equally be adding video, sound files, or other multimedia. Adding any of these is much the same as adding pictures, except that you click on the **Add** menu and then choose **Other Multimedia** (or **Document** or **OLE Object**, depending on what kind of Multimedia item you want to add). Again, you can choose whether or not to copy the files into the project folder, and if so, whether or not you wish to organise where the files go.

Remember that Family Historian allows you to treat *any* kind of file as a Multimedia item, and link it to your project.

As with the last chapter, most of the discussion in this chapter applies not just to pictures, but also to other multimedia – such as video and sound files. Once again, for reasons of stylistic convenience, we will mainly just refer to 'pictures'. Again – please remember that in most cases, the discussion applies to all forms of multimedia and not just pictures.

Multimedia Records

As we saw in the previous chapter, when you insert a picture, sound, video, document, or any other kind of multimedia object into your project, a Multimedia *record* is automatically created for each one, to represent that multimedia object.

The View Multimedia Button

Of course it may be that you don't want to add any new pictures (or other Multimedia) to your project. You just want to open the Multimedia Window to view Multimedia records that are already in it.

To do this click on the **View Multimedia** button on the main application toolbar. When you click on this button, a dropdown menu gives you a choice of **View All Media**, or **View Media for Selected Records**. If in doubt, use the **View All Media** command. This will list all Multimedia records in the current project, in the Multimedia Window. As we see shortly, you can then use various filtering techniques within the Multimedia Window itself to filter this list, if you need to.

If you use the **View Media for Selected Records** command when you have a single person (or record) selected, the Multimedia Window will be displayed showing just Multimedia that is linked to that person or record. If you use the same command when you have more than one record selected, the Multimedia Window will be displayed showing all multimedia linked to any or all of the selected records. Suppose, for example, you are viewing a diagram. It is quite easy to select all the boxes in a diagram: zoom right back, and then click-and-drag on the background of the diagram, to draw a stretchy box to 'lasso' all the boxes in the diagram. Then if you click on **View Media for Selected Records** the Multimedia Window will be displayed showing all the Multimedia for all the people in the diagram.

Open the Sample Project

We will use the *Family Historian Sample Project* again to demonstrate the features of the Multimedia Window. Open this project, select Ian Munro and click on the **View Multimedia** button on the main application toolbar. Then click on **View Media for Selected Records**. When you do this, the Multimedia Window will be displayed looking something like Figure 26 below, except that you will probably be viewing thumbnails in the pane in the bottom right, rather than a single picture.

The Multimedia Menu and Toolbar

Like the Diagram Window, the *Multimedia Window* has its own menu (the **Multimedia** menu) and its own toolbar, both of which only appear when the **Multimedia Window** is open and active.

Elements of the Multimedia Window

The **Multimedia Window** has 2 areas, separated by a vertical dividing line (see Figure 26 below). The area on the left is called the *Context Pane*. The **Context Pane**, is further sub-divided into 4 areas, all marked in Figure 26. These are:

- The Filter Pane
- The Multimedia Records List
- The Linked Records List
- The Note Box

The area on the right consists of the **Title Pane** at the top, and, underneath it, the **Display Pane** (also marked in Figure 26).

The partition lines between the Context Pane and the right side of the Multimedia Window, and between the bottom 3 areas within the Context Pane, can all be moved. Move your cursor over any of these partition lines and click-and-drag to reposition them.

The Multimedia Records List

The **Multimedia Records List** displays a list of Multimedia records – three in this case. These are the three Multimedia records that are linked to Ian Munro.

The Multimedia record that is selected in the **Multimedia Records List** is the one that is displayed in the **Display Pane**. Further details for this Multimedia Record are displayed (and can be edited) in the **Title Pane** above.

If you are currently viewing thumbnails double-click now on the particular thumbnail labelled "Ian and Charlotte and family". What you are seeing should now look much like Figure 26.

Now click on the background of the **Multimedia Records List** so that no Multimedia record is selected. You should find that the **Display Pane** goes white, and the **Title Pane**, **Linked Records List** and **Note Box** are all greyed. Now click once again on "Ian and Charlotte and family" in the **Multimedia Records List**, so that the screen looks like Figure 26 once more.

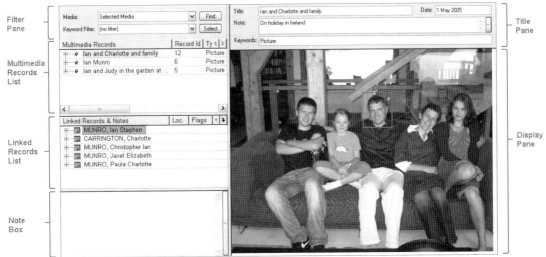

Figure 26 – the Multimedia Window

The Linked Records List

Why does the **Linked Records List** now list 5 records? Because it lists all records that the current multimedia object is linked to. Click on each record in the Linked Records List in turn. As you do so, a rectangle will appear round the corresponding face in the picture in the **Display Pane**. Now try it the other way. Click on each face in turn. This time notice that the selection in the Linked Records List changes accordingly. So you can either look at the list, and find out which person in the picture is corresponds to a name in the list. Or you can start from the picture and find out which name in the list is linked to a given face.

Despite the name, the **Linked Records List** doesn't just show linked records. It is possible to attach as many notes as you like to any picture – and even to link these notes to faces (and other areas too!) within the picture. These notes are not linked records, but they are nevertheless included in the Linked Records List (which is why the main column heading is "Linked Records & Notes").

View Property Box for Linked Record

Now double-click on one of the faces in the picture. This time the Property Box opens to show you the record details for the person in question. If you leave the Property Box open and single click on each face in turn, it will update to show you the record details for that person. Of course you could equally have simply selected a person, by clicking on their face, and then opened a diagram or report to display information about them, if you preferred.

Double-clicking on a linked record in the **Linked Records List** also works.

Add Link to Face

We saw in the last chapter how you can link a given individual to their specific face in a picture, using the Property Box. When you link a face within a picture to a person, in the Multimedia Window, you will usually link the picture to the person and to their face in a single step (in the Property Box, these are effectively two steps). To do this, click on the **Add Link to Face** button and then move the cursor down over the picture. You should notice that the cursor now looks like a cross. Click-and-drag on the picture to draw a stretchy box round the face in question. Don't worry if the box isn't quite right – you can correct it in a moment. When you release the button a dialog box will appear entitled "Create Link" (see Figure 27 below). Confirm that "an Individual" is selected and press **OK**. A dialog appears with the title "Select Record", showing a list of Individual records. Select the person in question and press **OK**.

Repeat these steps to link the picture to all the people in it.

Figure 27 – the Create Link dialog box

Add Simple Link

Sometimes you will want to link a person to a picture, but not link them to their face in the picture (perhaps because they aren't actually in it – maybe they took it, say). In that case, click on the **Add Simple Link** button. In this case the *Create Link* dialog box is displayed immediately, letting you select the record to link to. There is no need to draw a stretchy box round a face.

Attach a Note to a Link

You may remember in the previous chapter, that you could *attach a note to a link*. In the example, we imagined that you might want to say about Ian Munro that he "Usually wears spectacles but took them off for this photo". You can add, edit or view that note here too. That is what the **Note Box** is for (see Figure 26 above). To add a note to Ian Munro's link to this picture, just select Ian Munro in Linked Records List and then type your note into the **Note Box**. The **Note Box** always displays whatever note is associated with the selected row in the **Linked Records List**.

Exclude Picture From Diagrams & Reports ✖ ☒

If you don't want a particular picture of a person to be used in diagrams and reports, right-click on their row in the **Linked Records List**. In the dropdown menu that appears, you can choose the level of exclusion that you want. Excluding a picture from reports and web-pages will also exclude it from books and family tree CDs and DVDs.

The appropriate symbol (see left) will be displayed in the Flags column.

Use Note as Caption

By default, Family Historian will generate captions for pictures for you, in reports. The only exception to this is if the picture is a picture of an event or attribute (see previous chapter). When generating a caption, Family Historian will usually give the person's name, date, and their age at the time of the picture. If you prefer however, you can use your own caption. To do this, select the relevant link in the **Linked Records List** and enter the caption you want in the **Note Box**. Then right-click on the relevant row in the **Linked Records List** and check **Use Note as Caption** in the dropdown menu that appears. The appropriate symbol (see left) will be displayed in the Flags column.

Title, Date, Note and Keywords

You can add or edit the picture title, date, note and keywords in the **Title Pane**. The fields here are the same ones that appeared above the picture in the Edit Media Item dialog box, discussed in the previous chapter. The issues are exactly as discussed there, so we won't repeat that discussion, except to say that providing a date for all discussions is a very good idea if possible, and keywords too can be very useful. See the previous chapter for more on both topics.

How to Annotate Picture Details

If you want to write a note about a picture as a whole, you should use the **Note** field in the Title Pane. And if you want to add a note about one of the linked people (or records) in the picture, we've seen how you can attach a note to a link. But there is another, very useful, kind of note you might also want to attach to a picture.

Imagine that you have a photograph of a couple, sitting in front of a table, and on the table is a wooden box. You happen to know that that box is a very early hearing aid, used by the woman. It would be nice to include a note about the hearing aid. You could mention it in the main note for the picture in the **Title Pane** ("the box on the table is an early hearing aid"), but that might not work well in practice. A better options would be to draw a stretchy box round the hearing aid and link that to a note. To do this, just follow the directions for how to **Add Link to Face** above, but when the **Create Link** dialog box appears (see Figure 27), instead of selecting "an Individual", choose "Nothing (note only)" instead. That will create a link to the thing you drew your stretchy box around. This link will be included in the Linked Records List (although not a link to a record). Select this link and type the note into the **Note Box** below.

You can also add a simple link for a note if you wish.

Delete Link

To delete a link, simply select the link in the **Linked Records List** and press the **Delete** key. You will be asked to confirm that you want to delete it.

Delete Multimedia Record

To delete a Multimedia record, simply select the record in the **Multimedia Records List** and press the **Delete** key. You will be asked to confirm that you want to delete it.

If you are displaying thumbnails, you can equally select the record by clicking on the appropriate thumbnail. This works just as well.

View Multimedia Record in Property Box

The Property Box is the window of choice for viewing record details. And Multimedia records are records. So how do you view a Multimedia record in the Property Box? Here are 3 techniques:

- Double-click on the record in the Multimedia Records List
- Select the Multimedia record (either in the list or as a thumbnail) and click on the **Property Box** button [image] on the main application toolbar
- Right click on the picture (or on the thumbnail if viewing thumbnails) and choose "Multimedia Record" from the menu that appears.

The Multimedia Window Toolbar

The Multimedia Window toolbar (see Figure 28 below) is similar in many respects to the toolbar in the **Edit Media Item** dialog box, discussed in the previous chapter. The **Context Pane** button [image] is used to toggle between hiding or showing the Context Pane. The **View Thumbnails** button [image] is used to toggle between showing thumbnails (or just showing one picture at a time). The **Previous** and **Next** buttons ([image] and [image]) are used for stepping through the list of Multimedia records (most useful when viewing one picture at a time).

We have already looked at how to use the **Add Link to Face** button and the **Add Simple Link** button.

Figure 28 – the Multimedia Window Toolbar

Convert Simple Link to Face Link

The **Convert Simple Link to Face Link** button is useful if you have a 'simple' record link (not linked to a face) that you want to convert to be a 'face' link. Select the link in question in the **Linked Records List**, and click on the button. When you move the cursor over the picture it will turn into a cross, and you can click-and-drag to draw a stretchy box frame round the relevant face.

Select Frame

If you want to change the size, shape or position of a frame (the rectangle that defines a person's face) click on the face so that the frame is visible, and then click on the **Select Frame** button to select it. Eight white buttons will appear round the frame. At this point you can click on any of these white buttons to resize the box, or you can click-and-drag inside the frame to move it. Click anywhere else in the picture to cancel the selection.

More Toolbar Buttons

The remaining buttons are all the same as the buttons in the **Edit Media Item** dialog box toolbar, discussed in the last chapter. The two buttons ( ) are for zooming in and out. And the current percentage zoom is displayed next to them. The **Autosize** button , if checked, sizes the picture to fit within the available space. The **Full Size** button resets the picture to 'actual size' (100% zoom).

The **Grabber** button is useful when the picture is too large for its frame, so you need to scroll to see it all. In that case, check the **Grabber** button and click-and-drag on the picture to scroll it.

Finally the **Open Editor/Player** button allows you to open the picture (or sound file, video, document, or other multimedia item) in an external program – whichever program is configured on your PC as the application of choice to use for playing/editing multimedia of that kind.

Keyword Filtering

We saw in the last chapter that you can add a comma-separated list of keywords for each Multimedia record (and indeed that the **Keyword** field as a helper dialog to help you pick them). The **Keyword Filter** field in the **Filter Pane** (see Figure 26 above) is a dropdown list containing all used and standard keywords. Pick one to filter on that keyword. This filter applies to whatever the current 'set' of Multimedia records is. So, for example, if you want to see all the sound files in the current project, you should first set the **Media** field to 'All Media' and then set the **Keyword Filter** to Audio'.

If you want to filter using a combination of keywords, or none, click on the **Select** button to the right of the **Keyword Filter** field.

Searching

Whether or not you use the **Keyword Filter**, you can also use various means of finding Multimedia records using the **Media** field (just above the Keyword Filter in the **Filter Pane)**. This too is a dropdown list. You can choose to view 'All Media' or media linked to records of various types. You can also choose to view 'New/Unlinked Media'.

Clicking on the **Find** button produces a dropdown menu which includes these options as menu commands, as well as others. The **Search Text** menu command allows you to search for Multimedia by specifying text to search for. You are given the choice of searching in the Title only, or in all text fields.

Find Using Query

The **Find Using Query** command on this menu, allows you to search using a query. If the query is a Multimedia record query type, the records returned will be displayed in the **Multimedia Records List**. If the query is any other type of query, the **Multimedia Records List** will display the Multimedia records that are linked to the records returned by the query.

Select Records
Finally, the **Select** menu command allows you to use **the Select Records** dialog box to choose the records you wish to view. This dialog box has 3 tabs (including a *Thumbnails* tab and a *Named Lists* tab) and provides various ways of selecting and finding the records you want.

As with most lists in Family Historian, you can sort the lists in the **Select Records** dialog by clicking on the appropriate column heading.

File Links and Record Links
As we have explained before, a Multimedia record is created for each picture (or other Multimedia object) that is inserted into your project. The actual multimedia file itself is copied into the project folder, or left where it was, depending on what you chose to do. Either way, the multimedia file itself is not actually embedded into your GEDCOM file[9]. What happens is that each Multimedia record stores a link to an 'external' file in a field called **Linked File**. You can view (and edit – though it's not usually recommended) this field in the *Main* tab of the Property Box, when viewing any Multimedia record in the Property Box.

Incidentally, 'External' in this case means 'external to the GEDCOM file'. It doesn't (necessarily) mean 'external to the project'.

Don't confuse *file* links with *record* links incidentally. These are quite different.

Work with External File Links
You can see all of the external file links in your Family Historian file, organised in a hierarchical folder structure, in the **Work with External File Links Dialog** – see figure 35 below. This can be accessed by clicking on **Work with External File Links** on the **Tools** menu.

This dialog effectively allows you to update the **Linked File** field in all your Multimedia records. If you always keep all your multimedia files within the project folder, you may never need to do this. But what if you don't? Suppose, for example, you kept all your pictures in a folder called C:\Pics and you decided to move them into a folder called C:\Family Historian\Pics. You would first move the files using Windows Explorer. You would then open your Family Historian file, and open the **Work with External File Links Dialog**. The listing would show the files in the C:\Pics directory (with a cross through each file, to show that it wasn't really there). You would click on the *Pics* folder and click **Re-Map**. A dialog with a listing like Windows Explorer, of all the folders on your computer, would appear. You would select C:\Family Historian, and press **OK**. If you pressed **OK** again to close the **Work with External File Links Dialog**, all your file links would be updated appropriately.

The **Work with External File Links Dialog** cannot be used to move or copy external files. It is simply for maintaining file *links*. It can be used for maintaining links to files both inside and outside the current project folder.

For more information about how to use it, click on the **Help** button within the dialog.

---

[9] It is possible to do that, using Family Historian, though it is not usually recommended because files containing embedded multimedia tend to become large and slow. If you open a 'standalone' GEDCOM file (i.e. one that is not part of a project) the Multimedia menu will have two additional menu commands to allow you to 'absorb' (embed) or 'expel' (make linked) Multimedia objects. There is an advanced Preferences option to enable these menu commands with projects too – but again that is not recommended.

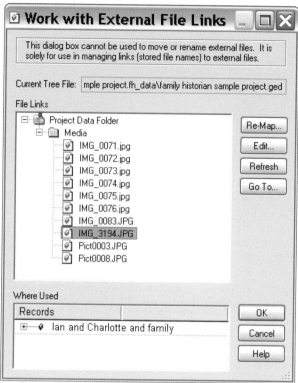

Figure 29 – the *Work with External File Links* Dialog Box

Working with Multiple Multimedia Windows

Like the **Diagram Window** (and unlike the **Focus Window** and the **Records Window**) you can have multiple **Multimedia Windows** open if you want to. But unlike Diagram Windows, Family Historian will not open a new Multimedia Window each time by default when you make a new request to view multimedia. So to open a 2nd **Multimedia Window** when you already have one open, click on the **Lock Window (prevent reuse)** button 🔒 on the main application toolbar, to lock the active **Multimedia Window.** Another way to do the same thing is to right-click on the Multimedia Window's icon in the Navigation Bar, and select the **Lock Window (prevent reuse)** command. Either way, if you then click on the **View Multimedia** button 📷 Media ▾ on the main application toolbar, instead of the current Multimedia Window being 're-used', another Multimedia Window will be opened.

If you want to prevent Family Historian reusing open Multimedia Windows, you can configure this in the Navigation tab of Preferences (accessible from the Tools menu).

6 Events, Attributes & Notes in the Property Box

Unlike previous chapters, this chapter is constructed as a tutorial. To work through the tutorial, you will need to use a special tutorial file, "Tutorial – Chapter 06", that was installed onto your computer when you installed Family Historian. To learn more about the tutorial files (and how to reset them and discard changes if you ever wish to do so), see the discussion of "Samples and Tutorials" in the Introduction.

The tutorial file contains details about a fictitious person called Cameron Peabody and his relatives. In this chapter you will add more details about these people. The new data will illustrate how to use all but one of the as yet unexplored tabs on the **Property Box**.

You will begin by changing the details about Jean Clare Anderson (Cameron's 2nd wife) to record the fact that she was always known not as 'Jean' but as 'Jean Clare'.

You will record the fact that Richard Peabody was Sir Richard Peabody, and that Norman Prentice Salt was Lord Dalhousie.

You will then record the following facts about Cameron Peabody: Cameron Peabody was always known as 'Ron' to his friends. He was tall and slim. He lived in Lewisham, London from 1906 to 1922, and then in Durban, South Africa from 1922 to 1926. He and Sarah Watts took up residence in Cape Town after their marriage and lived there until they divorced in 1935, when Cameron was 34. The divorce was an amicable one, and no third parties were involved. Between 1907 and 1911 Cameron attended a boy's school, Clarence House, in Lewisham, London. He worked as a printer for 3 years, between 1923 and 1926 in Durban. His hobby was watch-repairing. Cameron Peabody died sometime in the 1970s (exact date not known) of a stroke.

You will add the following note about Cameron: "A quiet, introverted individual, he read widely, and struggled hard to make up for the fact that he had had little formal education as a child".

You will add the following note about Cameron's marriage to Jean Clare: "Jean Clare and Cameron were a devoted couple who, from the day of their marriage, never spent a night apart".

You will also create the following note "The Prentice Salt family may be related to the Salts of Cornwall.", and link this note to all Prentice Salts.

Open Tutorial File

Start by opening the file "Tutorial – Chapter 06"

From the **Project Window**, click on the **More Tasks** button, and then in the dropdown menu click on **Samples**, and finally **Tutorial – Chapter 06**. The file opens and Cameron Peabody is displayed as the focus person in the Focus Window. There are no pictures.

Given Name Used

Locate Jean Clare Anderson's box (she's Cameron's second wife) and select it to display her record in the **Property Box**. Now record the fact that she was always known as 'Jean Clare'.

Steps

1. Click on the **more...** text link to the right of the **Name** field in the *Main* tab. The **Names/Titles** dialog box opens.
2. Enter 'Jean Clare' in the **Given Name Used** field
3. Click **Close** to close the **Names/Titles** dialog box. The text link now reads 'more (+)'. The plus sign indicates that additional information has been entered.

Sometimes people are known by their middle names. Had Jean Clare Anderson been known as 'Clare', for example, you would enter 'Clare' as **Given Name Used**. Where a person is known by his or her first name, you should leave **Given Name Used** blank.

Figure 30 – the Names/Titles Dialog Box. Jean Clare Anderson's *Given Name Used* has been set to 'Jean Clare'

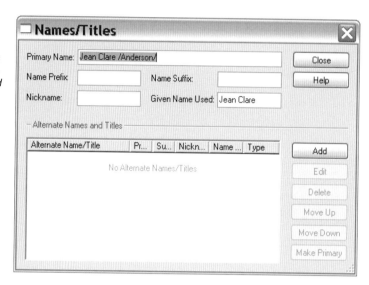

Nicknames   Now open Cameron Peabody's record in the Property Box. Notice, on the **Main** tab, that the spouse tab for Jean Clare Anderson is now labelled 'Jean Clare'. Click on the **more...** link to the right of the **Name** field. In the **Names/Titles** dialog box, enter "Ron" in the **Nickname** field and close the dialog box.

Titles, Name Prefixes, Name Suffixes   Now add titles for Richard Peabody and Norman Prentice Salt.

Steps

1. Navigate to Richard Peabody's record (he was Cameron's paternal grandfather) and click on the **more...** link to open the **Names/Titles** dialog box for him.
2. In the **Name Prefix** field, enter "Sir", and close the Names/Titles dialog box again.
3. Navigate to Norman Prentice Salt's record (he was Cameron's maternal grandfather) and open the **Names/Titles** dialog box for him. Click on the **Add** button and choose **Title** from the menu that appears. In the **Title** field, enter "Lord Dalhousie" and press **OK**. Press **Close** to close the **Names/Titles** dialog box.

Do not enter name prefixes such as 'Sir', 'Mr', 'Dr', 'Lt. Cmndr.' etc. in the **Title** field. They should all go in the **Name Prefix** field. The **Title** field should be used to store complete titles of nobility or royalty, such as "Lord Dalhousie".

The **Name Suffix** field is used for any text that should be appended to a person's name. For example, 'Jr.' could be a name suffix, as in 'Sammy Davis Jr.'

The Facts Tab   Navigate back to Cameron Peabody's record, and click on the *Facts* tab of the **Property Box**.

In Family Historian, the word 'Fact' is often used as shorthand for 'Event or Attribute'. The *Facts* tab shows events and attributes.

Everyone should know what an *event* is: **Birth**, **Death**, **Christening** ... are examples of events.

An *attribute* is anything that is associated with a value. For example, **Occupation** is an attribute, the value for which would be 'printer' in Cameron Peabody's case. Another example is **Marriage Count**. In Cameron's case, the value for this attribute would be '2'.

In a sense, **Name** and **Sex** are both attributes too; but in Family Historian (and GEDCOM), you will not see name and sex information listed under 'Attributes'. If you like you can think of them as attributes which are too important to be listed with the other attributes.

The top half of the **Facts** tab (the *Events/Attributes List*) shows birth and marriage details that could have been entered previously either on this tab or on the *Main* tab. Some events and attributes such as these can be displayed (or entered) on more than one tab of the Property Box (actually, if you customize the Property Box to do so, they all can).

Figure 31 – Property Box, Facts Tab. The fields in the bottom half of the dialog show details about the fact selected in the list. In this case they are showing details of Cameron's birth.

Add Facts   We will now add a description of Cameron, and record details of his divorce and his death.

Steps

1. Click on the **Add Fact** button on the ⚹ Add Fact Facts tab toolbar.
2. The **Event/Attribute List** appears. In the bottom left corner is a field **Close Dialog After Adding**. If this field is ticked, untick it now. That way you can add several facts without having to re-open the dialog each time.

57

3. Select 'Physical Description' in the list and click **Add**.
4. Select 'Divorce' and click **Add**. A dialog will ask you to confirm which family this event applies to. Select "...of Cameron Peabody and Sarah Marie Watts" and click **OK**.
5. Select 'Death' and click Add. Optionally tick **Close Dialog After Adding** once again, and then click **Close**.
6. In the Facts tab, select the row with "Desc:" in the Fact column. Set the Physical Description field (below the list) to "Tall, Slim"
7. Select the 'Died' row and in the **Cause**: field below the list (only available for some events and attributes) enter 'Stroke' (i.e. this was his cause of death).

*Tip: In the **Event/Attribute** List you can add items by simply double-clicking on them.*

*Tip: The **Event/Attribute List** may contain events or attributes that you never use. If so, you can hide them to make it easier to find the ones you do use. Click on the **More >>** button when viewing the Event/Attribute List; then select the events or attributes you are not likely to need and click the **Hide** button. You can always unhide them again later if you change your mind. Click the **Help** button for instructions on how to do this.*

Tip: A quick way to scroll down to the 'Ds' in the list is to click on any item in the list, and then press the D key. This technique works for most lists in Family Historian if sorted in alphabetical order.

Date Ranges   We will now set Cameron's date of death as being sometime in the 1970s

Steps

1. Select his death event in the list and open the helper dialog for the **Date** field. You should remember from earlier chapters that you can open a helper dialog, for a field that has one, by double-clicking on the field itself, by moving the cursor to the field and click on the button with 3 dots that appears at its right end, or by moving the cursor to the field and pressing **Ctrl-Spacebar**. The **Date Entry Assistant Dialog** appears.
2. Click on the **Range** tab and select *Between* as **Specifier** (see left hand side of dialog)
3. Leave the **Calendar** values as 'Gregorian' (this is the calendar used in the Western world today). Enter '1970' in the top row **Year** field, and '1979' in the bottom row **Year** field. The dialog should look like Figure 32 below. Press **OK**. The **Date** field displays "btw 1970 and 1979" (you could of course perfectly well just have typed that in – but the intention was to illustrate use of the **Date Entry Assistant Dialog**).

For more information on date ranges, and other types of date, see the box *Advanced Date Types and the Date Entry Assistant Dialog* below.

Divorce   We will now enter details of the divorce between Cameron and Sarah Watts.

Steps

1. Select "Divorce from Sarah" in the Facts list.
2. In the **Date** field, type '1935' and press **Tab**.
3. In the **Age** field, type '34' (Cameron's age at the time) and press **Tab**.
4. In the **Notes** field, type "The divorce was an amicable one, and no third parties were involved" (double-click on the Notes field to open a separate Note window to type the note into, if you prefer).

Figure 32 – the Range tab of the Date Entry Assistant Dialog

Two Types: Individual & Family
There are fundamentally two kinds of events in Family Historian: *Individual* events and *Family* events. In Individual events, one individual only is the principal participant (examples would be **Birth**, **Christening**, **Death**, etc). In Family events, it is a couple who are the joint primary participants (examples would be **Marriage** and **Divorce**). Family events are effectively shared between the two primary participants.

Exactly the same distinction applies to attributes. All of the *standard* attributes that Family Historian provides are Individual attributes, but as we shall see later, when you create *custom* attributes, you can create custom attributes for families too.

You can tell at a glance whether a listed event or attribute is an Individual one or a Family one. Individual events or attributes have a blue circle next to them: ● . Family events and attributes have a red circle next to them: ● .

As we saw, **Divorce** is a family event. This means that both Cameron Peabody and Sarah share this event equally. To confirm this, navigate to Sarah Watts record, and then click on the **Facts** tab to view her events and attributes. Notice that she too now has a **Divorce** event ('Divorce from Cameron'). Select it (by clicking on the date in the first column). Notice that the **Date** for this event is '1935' and that the **Note** is as you entered it. If you had specified a **Place** and a **Cause**, they too would have appeared, as you had entered them. The only field for this event which does *not* appear as you entered it, is **Age**.

Age
Even with Family events, when you specify a value for **Age,** you are always specifying the age of the Individual whose record you are looking at, at the time of the event. Cameron was 34 when he was divorced. Sarah's age at the time is not known. In the Events/Attributes List, her age (right-most column) is given as "(27-28)". The brackets are there to show that this is data that Family Historian has computed for you – which it will only do if no actual age has been entered.

If your sources of information do not include the age of a participant in an event, you should not enter anything in the age field – even if you think you can work out what it must have been. Family Historian, after all, does that for you anyway.

If you do enter an **Age** value, Family Historian will display it as entered. However, it will add "(!)" after the value, if it thinks that this value cannot be correct (or at least, that the **Age** value, the event date and the individual's recorded **Birth** date cannot all be correct). Try this now. Enter the values of 27, 28 and 29, in turn, for Sarah's age at the time of the divorce (press **Tab** or click elsewhere, between entering each number, to get Family Historian to 'register' each value). Notice that '27' and '28' display as entered (because both are possibly correct), but when you

59

enter '29', the listing actually displays '29 (!)'.

Now clear the **Age** field, and navigate back to Cameron Peabody's record (hint: one quick way would be to click on the **Go Back** button).

Add Residence

Cameron lived in Lewisham, London from 1906 to 1922, and then in Durban, South Africa from 1922 to 1926. Add that information now. You should be looking at the **Facts** tab for his record at this point.

Steps

1. Click on the **Add Fact** button ⏣ Add Fact on the toolbar.
2. Select **Residence** and click **Add** (or just double-click on **Residence**).
3. In the **Date** field, enter "From 1906 to 1922" and press **Tab**.
4. The 'value' of a Residence attribute is a *place*. So enter the value "Lewisham, London" in the **Place** field now and press **Tab**.
5. Repeat Steps 1-4 to add another residence, only this time enter "From 1922 to 1926" as the **Date**, and enter "Durban, South Africa" in the **Place** field.

Auto-Complete

When you started typing "Durban, South Africa" did you notice that Family Historian guessed that this was what you were going to type after the first 'D'? This is because there is already a "Durban, South Africa" as a place in the current file. If Family Historian guesses correctly, just click tab to accept its suggestion. If Family Historian's guess is wrong, just ignore it and keep typing.

Place List Helper Dialog

Place fields have helper dialogs. Double-click on any **Place** field (or click on the little button with 3 dots ⊡ at the end of the place field) to view a complete list of all places that have been entered into the program. You can click on an item in the list and press **Select** to select one. Or, if you click on the **More >>** button, you can find more options. Using this powerful dialog you can even spot and correct misspellings and inconsistencies in place names throughout the file. Click the **Help** button for more details.

Custom Attributes

Cameron and his first wife Sarah were both resident in Cape Town between 1926 and 1935.

In GEDCOM, **Residence** is always an Individual attribute. Obviously one could enter the same attribute for Sarah and Cameron, to show that they both lived in Cape Town during this period. But that would be consistent with them living in separate houses. What we really want is a similar attribute that applies to couples. GEDCOM doesn't provide one, but you can make up your own custom attributes; so that is what we shall do.

You should still be looking at the **Facts** tab for Cameron Peabody's record at this point.

Steps

1. Click on the **Add Fact** button ⏣ Add Fact on the toolbar.
2. Click on the **More >>** button in the **Event/Attribute List** dialog
3. Click on the **New...** button.
4. Enter "Co-residence" as the **Fact Name**. Change the **Fact Type** to "Attribute". Change the **Record Type** to "Family". Leave the **Fact Set** name as "Custom". Click on the **Create** button.
5. The **Fact Definition** dialog box appears. Leave the **Label** as 'Co-residence'. Add 'Resident' as the **Abbreviation**. Change the **Template** to read as follows:

   {date} {couple} lived {place}

The template determines how facts about **Co-residence** will appear in Narrative reports.

6. We have created Co-residence as an attribute which means that we will specify the place as the attribute value. We won't need a Place field for this attribute. If we did we would have two different boxes to record the place in. So untick 'Place' in the Fields Required area. Leave all other fields at their default values and press **OK**.

7. You should now be viewing the **Event/Attribute List** dialog. Confirm that there is a new attribute, **Co-residence**, in the list (with a red dot to show that it is a family attribute). Select it and click on the **Add** button.

8. Another dialog appears titled "Select Family". Select the Family Record "...of Cameron PEABODY and Sarah Marie Watts" and press **OK**. The dialog closes and the event is added to the events list.

9. Enter "Cape Town, South Africa" in the **Co-residence** field. Press **Tab**.

10. In the **Date** field, enter "From 1926 to 1935" and press **Tab**.

For every event and attribute, Family Historian allows you to enter a number of 'subfields': date, age, place, address and note. In some cases, these fields may not be appropriate - just as a separate Place field was not needed with our new Co-resident field. You can hide any subfields that you don't need, using the Fact Definition dialog.

Married Names

Family Historian does not provide a standard attribute for married names. If you wish to store married names for women, you should create a Custom Attribute (for an Individual), called "Married Name", and use that. This is not illustrated in this tutorial.

Custom Events

The procedure for entering custom events is not significantly different from the procedure for entering custom attributes - see *Custom Attributes* above.

Occasionally it may happen that you want to enter some data about something that isn't really quite an event or an attribute. For example, suppose you wanted to record the fact that a person X was *alive* in 1986. Being alive is not an event, in any usual sense of the term (it is really a *state*), but you shouldn't let that put you off entering it as an event - a custom event[10]. As with most labels in Family Historian, do not feel obliged to interpret them too literally.

More Attributes

Between 1907 and 1911 Cameron attended a boy's school, Clarence House, in Lewisham, London. He worked as a printer for 3 years, between 1923 and 1926 in Durban. His hobby was watch-repairing. Education and Occupation are both standard attributes for Individuals.

Hobby: Another Custom Attribute

Hobby is not a standard attribute. We shall first enter it as a custom attribute.

Steps

1. Click on the **Add Fact** button [Add Fact] on the toolbar.
2. Click on the **More >>** button in the **Event/Attribute List** dialog
3. Click on the **New...** button.
4. Enter "Hobby" as the **Fact Name**. Change the **Fact Type** to "Attribute". Leave the **Record Type** as "Individual". Leave the **Fact Set** name as "Custom". Click on the **Create** button.
5. The **Fact Definition** dialog box appears. Leave everything as it is except change the **Template** to read as follows:

   {individual's} hobby was {value} {date} {place} {age}

---

[10] If you're not averse to Latin, some genealogists use 'Floruit' as a kind of event, to mean 'was alive at...', or (more literally) 'flourished at ...'.

Enter this exactly as specified here. If you forget the apostrophe in the first word, or add extra spaces, it won't work! You can use the << **Insert Code** button if you wish to help you build up this sentence. To get the first code "{individual's}" select "Name of Individual (or His/Her)" from the menu that appears when you click on << **Insert Code**.

6. Press **OK**. You should now be viewing the **Event/Attribute List** dialog. Confirm that there is a new attribute, **Hobby**, in the list (with a blue dot to show that it is an individual attribute).

Quick Ways to Enter Multiple Events and Attribute

We've already looked at one technique for adding multiple facts in one go: unticking the **Close Dialog After Adding** tick box. Adding events and attributes to records is something you should expect to do often; so it is well worth taking the time to learn more techniques for making it easier and quicker. If you know that you are going to add several events and/or attributes to add, it makes sense to save time by adding them all in one go. Here's how you can do this.

Steps

1. Click on **Education**.
2. Press-and-hold the Ctrl key, and click on **Occupation** (you may have to scroll to find it).
3. Press-and-hold the Ctrl key, and click on **Hobby** (our new custom attribute – again you may have to scroll to find it).
4. Click **Add**. All 3 attributes are added in one go.

Tip: Like many dialogs in Family Historian, the Event/Attribute List dialog is resizable. Click-and-drag on any corner to make it the best size and shape for your needs. It will remember its size and position throughout the session.

Supply Missing Details

We have now added 3 attributes to Cameron's list. We will now supply more details about each of them. You should still be in the *Facts* tab of the Property Box.

Steps

1. Select 'Educ.' The fields below the list change to show education details.
2. Enter "Clarence House" into the **Education** field.
3. Enter "from 1907 to 1911" into the **Date** field.
4. Enter "Lewisham, London" into the **Place** field.
5. Select 'Hobby' and enter "Watch-repairing" in the **Hobby** field. Press **Tab**.
6. Select 'Occup' and enter "Printer" into the **Occupation** field.
7. Enter "from 1923 to 1926" into the **Date** field.

Dateless Attributes

It will frequently happen that events and attributes have no date. Wherever an event or attribute has no associated date, the Date column of the Event/Attribute listing will contain a line. You should not interpret this line as implying that your data is in any sense incomplete! In the case of some attributes, a date may not even be meaningful or relevant.

Multiple Instances

You can have as many instances as you like of any attribute or event - custom or standard. If, for example, Cameron had been educated in 2 schools and a university, you should enter 3 **Education** attributes: one for each. Likewise with **Occupation**. You should be aware, however, that whereas the *Facts* tab will show all instances of all the attributes (and events) that you enter, the *Main* tab, by contrast will only show one **Occupation** attribute.

The **Occupation** attribute displayed in the *Main* tab is actually the *first* instance of an **Occupation** attribute for the given record. This is not necessarily the occupation which has the earliest date – it is first in the order in which the attributes are stored in the record. You can see this order by looking at the attributes in the **All** tab of the **Property Box**. Attributes are initially stored in the order that they are created, but as you will see in a moment, you can change this ordering.

Of course many individuals will only have one **Occupation** attribute or one **Religion** attribute. The other reason why some of these attributes are included on the *Main* tab is just convenience. You can enter and edit their values there, rather than having to switch to another tab (although, of course, if you want to include further details of dates, places, addresses and notes with the attribute, you can only do that on the *Facts* tab).

Advanced Date Types and the Date Entry Assistant Dialog

We have already looked briefly at the Helper Dialog for **Date** fields – this is the *Date Entry Assistant Dialog*. Find any **Date** field (e.g. the one in the Facts tab of the Property Box) and double-click on it, or more your mouse over it, and then click on the button with 3 dots that appears at the right ⬜. The dialog that appears is the *Date Entry Assistant Dialog*. Figure 32 above shows the *Range* tab of this dialog. If you click on the various tabs of this dialog, you will see that Family Historian (and GEDCOM) supports multiple calendars, simple dates, date ranges, date phrases (interpreted or not), periods and quarter dates. The **Date Entry Assistant Dialog** makes it easy to specify all these different kinds of date values. Simply choose the date type that you want, enter the details into the dialog, and press OK. The **Date Entry Assistant Dialog** will then put the appropriate text into the Date field.

The difference between a *period* and a *range* is this: a date *period* is used for something that occurred over a period of time (e.g. **Residence**). A date *range* is used for something that occurred on a specific date, but you are not sure what it is. For example, we know that Cameron Peabody died some time in the 1970s. This is a date range, between 1970 and 1979. Don't use date ranges if all you know is that an event occurred in a particular year. Just enter the year without specifying the month or day. Equally you if you know the year and month but not the day, just omit the day.

The *Date Phrase* option is very useful for cases where you don't know the date but you have a textual clue as to when it occurred (e.g. "5 weeks after his wife died"). You should enter the text as a *Date Phrase*. If you think you know what the corresponding date is, you can specify that too.

If you enter a date in a date field in a format that Family Historian does not recognise, it will always assume that you have entered a *Date Phrase*, and put double-quotes round the text to show this.

There is no need to stick too literally to the intended role of this date type. If you want to include a note with a date, you could use a Date Phrase and add the date as the 'interpretation'.

Automatic Ordering of Events and Attributes

Family Historian will, by default, store all events and attributes in date order – but only if you enter them or edit them using the Property Box (*All* tab excepted). If you use 'low-level editing' (see Chapter 2) in the Records Window (or use the *All* tab of the Property Box) to enter or edit event or attribute dates, Family Historian will not automatically re-order them for you.

If you want to check that an Individual's events and attributes (and spouses and children) are in correct date order, click on the Menu button 📇 on the Property Box toolbar, and choose the **Sort Family & Events in Date Order** menu command. If any items are not in date order, Family Historian will offer to re-order them for you.

If you are not already viewing an Individual in the Property Box, you can simply select that Individual and click on **Re-order Events by Date** on the **Edit** menu.

Manual Ordering of Events and Attributes

The Events and Attributes displayed in the *Facts* tab are displayed by default in date order, which (thanks to automatic ordering) is usually also the order in which they are stored. But it might not be. If you opened a GEDCOM file created elsewhere, or if you have used low-level editing, the events and attributes could be out of sequence. Even if you have used automatic ordering, some events and attributes have no dates to order them by. You can manually order events in the Facts tab of the Property Box. Before doing so, however, you must first ensure that they are displayed in the order that they are stored. To do this, click on the **List in Record Order** button ⊞ on the *Facts* tab toolbar. The order of the items listed changes to be the order in which they are stored. Thereafter the **Move Up** ↑ and **Move Down** ↓ buttons on the toolbar will be ungreyed and you can click on them to change the order as you wish. Family events/attributes can only be re-ordered relative to other family events/ attributes.

Manual Ordering of All Fields

The technique just described only applies to Events and Attributes. There is another technique that can be used to manually order any fields that you wish to be re-ordered (as long as this is permitted – not all fields can be re-ordered).

Click on the *All* tab. You should be looking at the record for Cameron Peabody. There should be a row "Residence from 1906 to 1922 in Lewisham, London". Somewhere below this should be another row "Residence from 1922 to 1926 in Durban, South Africa". Click on the first of these rows.

There are 2 little buttons near the top-right of the dialog: ↑↓. Click the right button (the *Move Field Down* button) now. Notice that the **Residence** field swaps position with the next field. Now click the left (*Move Field Up*) button to return it to its original position.

You can use these buttons to re-order any fields that are instances of a similar *type* – for example, you can re-order any 2 events or attributes or any 2 name fields. But you cannot move a name field after an event or attribute field.

Sorting

By default, events and attributes are listed in date order in the *Facts* tab of the Property Box. When you add events or attributes, however, they will appear at the bottom of the list. Click on the **Date** column heading to sort the list by date. Click on the other 2 headings to sort alphabetically or by age.

You may be wondering what the difference is between *Sorting* and *Ordering* (or *Re-ordering)*. In Family Historian, when you *sort*, you affect the order in which items are displayed; but you do *not* affect the underlying order in which the items are stored. When you *order* (or *re-order)* items, by contrast, you *are* changing the order in which they are stored.

Re-order Out-of-Sequence Data

If you want to be sure that *all* events and attributes in a file are ordered sequentially, you can use the **Re-order Out-of-Sequence Data** command on the **Tools** menu, to re-order an entire file in one go. As well as Events and Attributes, you can also use this command to re-order Spouses, Children and LDS Ordinances (religious ordinances associated with the LDS Church).

Child Events

In addition to Individual and Family events, there is one extra category of events: *Child* events. Actually *Child* events are really Individual events. You can only edit or view Child events for individuals who are already linked to you as your children. The only two Child events that you can edit or view are **Birth** and **Adoption** events. If you see a **Birth of Child** event, for a given child, you will find that same event in their own listing as a **Birth** event. Likewise for **Adoption of Child** events.

If you don't wish to include these events in the listing, click on the **Menu** button ⊞ on the *Facts* tab toolbar and uncheck **Show Birth/Adoption of Children** in the dropdown menu that appears.

Copy and Paste Events & Attributes

Before leaving the Facts tab, one final thing to notice is that you can copy events and attributes by clicking on the **Copy Fact(s)** button on the Events tab toolbar, and you can paste them using the **Paste Fact(s)** button: . You can select multiple events and attributes (by clicking on the first, and then pressing-and-holding the **Ctrl** key while clicking on others) and copy them all, and then paste them all, in one go. This can be a useful technique if you have repetitive data. When you do this, all details relating to each event or attribute (even including source citations if any – see Chapter 12) are included in the copy. The only restriction is that you can only copy events or attributes that are local to the record you are looking at. So, for example, you cannot copy family events and attributes if you are viewing them in the context of an Individual record. If you try to, you will be told that you can't.

Copy and Paste Any Field

In Chapter 12, we will see how as well as being able to copy and paste events and attributes, you can also copy and paste source citations. In fact, if you are using *low-level editing* (see Chapter 7) and looking at a record in the Records Window or in the *All* tab of the Property Box, you can copy and paste *any* field.

You can only paste data into contexts in which that data is valid. You can't paste a date field into a place field context, or vice versa, for example.

Copy and Paste Text

Wherever you can see any editable text (in any field where you can type characters) you can copy and paste text. To copy it, select it and press **Ctrl-C** (press-and-hold the Ctrl key while pressing the C key on your keyboard). To paste previously copied text, press **Ctrl-V**.

Copy and Paste Records As Text

If you select a record in the Records Window (covered in Chapter 7) you can even copy the entire record. But when you do this, you only copy it as text. You can paste the text into a word-processor, or some other text context. But whereas you can paste a field as a field – e.g. an event is still an event when you've pasted it in the *Facts* tab, say – you cannot paste a record as a record. You can only paste it as text, in a context which accepts text.

The *Notes* Tab

You should still be viewing the record for Cameron Peabody (check the title of the Property Box if in doubt – it should say "Individual: Cameron Peabody"). Click on the *Notes* tab now. You should see a large white box occupying the top part of the tab. In the bottom part of the tab there should be a large grey box. The top box is the *Notes Listing*. The grey box shows the contents of the selected note in the Notes Listing (none at present). We will call this the *Note Contents Box*.

We have already seen that notes can be associated with events or attributes. However, frequently you will want to associate a note with a person as a whole.

Add Local Note

First, enter a note about Cameron, as an Individual.

Steps

1. Click on the **Add Note** button on the *Notes* tab toolbar.
2. In the dialog that appears, confirm that **Create local note** is checked, and press **OK**.
3. The dialog disappears. A row has been added to the Notes Listing. The first column should be selected and should say "<No text>". The second column should say 'Local'.
4. In the **Notes Contents Box**, type the following: "A quiet, introverted individual, he read widely, and struggled hard to make up for the fact that he had had little formal education as a child". Press **Tab**.

A Local Note is an Individual Note if you are entering it into an Individual record.

If you were entering data into a Family record directly (not covered in this tutorial, but you can do it if you want to), a Local Note would be a Family Note. It just means: a Note that will be stored in the current record.

There is no limit to the number of notes you can enter (of whatever kind).

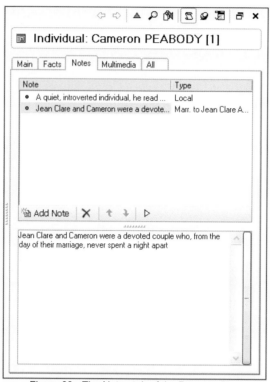

Figure 33 - The Notes tab of the Property Box
for Cameron after adding a Local Note and a Family Note

Add Family Note   It often happens, once a person is married, that you will want to enter notes that are just as applicable to their spouse as to them. Rather than having to make the difficult decision about which of them to enter the note for (or worse, make 2 copies - one for each of them), it is much better to allow them to share a note. We have seen how couples can share family events and family attributes. They can just as easily share notes.

Steps

1. Click on the **Add Note** button ![Add Note] on the toolbar.
2. In the dialog that appears, check **Create family note**. In the **Family** field which becomes ungreyed when you do this, select "Jean Clare Anderson". Then click on the **OK** button.
3. The dialog disappears. A second row has been added to the Notes Listing. The first column should be selected and should say "<No text>". The second column should say 'Marr. to Jean Clare ANDERSON'.[11]
4. In the Notes Contents Box, type the following: "Jean Clare and Cameron were a devoted couple who, from the day of their marriage, never spent a night apart". Press **Tab**.

You will remember from earlier that in the **Events** tab listing, Individual attributes or events have a blue circle next to them: • . Family attributes or events have a red circle next to them: • . The same is true here. Individual notes have a blue circle

---

[11] You probably won't be able to see all of the text of the second column. To see it all, click and drag the left edge of the column heading to the left. Then click and drag the right edge of the same column heading to the right.

next to them. Family notes have a red circle next to them.

Navigate to Jean Clare Anderson's record in the **Property Box** and confirm that she too now has a red-dotted note: "Jean Clare and Cameron were a devoted couple who, from the day of their marriage, never spent a night apart "

*Tip: the first Local Note for an Individual is displayed in the **Main** tab. The first Family Note for a couple is also visible in the **Main** tab (it is one of the Marr. fields). It may be often more convenient to enter these notes there. If you need a larger window to enter details into, you can click on the 3-dots button* ⬚ *to the right of the Note field, or double-click on the Note field itself, to open a larger window to work in.*

Add Note Record

Sometimes you will want to enter a note that is relevant not just to one individual, or even to a couple, but to many individuals. To do this, you must create a Note Record and link it to all the individuals, to whom it is applicable.

Steps

1. Navigate to Naomi Prentice Salt's record (she was Cameron's mother) and display the *Notes* tab for her. Her *Notes List* should be empty.
2. Click on the **Add Note** button ⬚ Add Note on the toolbar.
3. In the dialog that appears, check **Add link to Note Record...** and press **OK**.
4. Another dialog will appear showing an empty list of Note Records. Click on **New...**
5. The dialog disappears. An entry has been added to the Notes Listing. The first column should be selected and should say "<No text>". The second column should say 'Note Record (1 link)'.
6. In the Notes Contents Box, type the following: "The Prentice Salt family may be related to the Salts of Cornwall.". Press **Tab**.

Link to Existing Note Record

Now select the record for Norman Prentice Salt, Naomi's father, and again choose the *Notes* tab.

Steps

1. Click on the **Add Note** button ⬚ Add Note on the toolbar.
2. In the dialog that appears, check **Add link to Note Record...** and press **OK**.
3. Another dialog will appear showing a single Note Record – the one you created in the previous section. Select it now and press **OK**.
4. The dialog disappears. An entry has been added to the Notes Listing. The first column should be selected and should say "The Prentice Salt family may be related to the...". The second column should say 'Note Record (2 links)'.
5. Now click on Sally Prentice Salts record in the Focus Window (Sally was Norman Prentice Salt's daughter). The Property Box updates to show her (empty) list of notes. Repeat steps 1-4. Notice that in step 4, the second column now says 'Note Record (3 links).

Save Changes
⬚ Save

Now save the work that you have done. From the **File** menu, click on **Save** (or click on the **Save** button on the toolbar).

Fact Sets

We saw in this chapter how easy it is to create custom events and custom attributes. When we did this we had to specify a 'fact set' name. We set this to 'custom'. In fact we could have used any name we like as the fact set name, except 'Standard' which is reserved. Fact Sets are simply convenient groupings of related fact types. For example, suppose you have an interest in medical history. You could create custom events and attributes relating to medical history and give them all the same fact set name: 'Medical History'.

Importing and Exporting Fact Sets

Now suppose that somebody else decides that they also are interested in medical history. They would like to use the same set of events and attributes (the same fact set) that you have created. All you have to do is click on **File** > **Import/Export** > **Export** > **Fact Set**, and then pick the fact set you wish to export. This fact set will then be saved as a file (you will specify where to save it). Then you just give the file to your friend (email is fine). They can then install the fact set by importing the fact set file into their version of Family Historian. They click on **File** > **Import/Export** > **Import** > **Fact Set** and choose the file you sent them.

Examples of Possible Fact Sets

If you are constructing a fact set, especially if you think that it might be of interest to others, give it a meaningful name that clearly evokes what it is about, and try to only include events and attributes that are relevant to its intended function. Here are some possible examples of fact sets that people might want to create:

- Medical history
- Military History
- A fact set for a given occupation (e.g. sailor, farmer) storing events and attributes that are relevant to that occupation.
- A fact set for each of the major religions

The Benefits of Installable Fact Sets

One obvious benefit of installable fact sets is that it saves effort for the recipient. They don't have to reinvent the wheel. But the benefit is potentially wider than that. When you define an installable fact set you potentially are creating a new *standard* for how data of that type can be stored.

Learn More About Creating Fact Sets

To learn more about fact sets, and how to create them, click on **Work with Fact Sets** on the **Tools** menu. This opens the **Event/Attribute List Dialog**. Click on the **Help** button to learn more.

7 Browsing, Searching & Editing in the Records Window

This chapter introduces the **Records Window**, and shows you how to use it for browsing and searching. It also introduces some low-level techniques for editing records. These techniques are applicable both to the Records Window and to the *All* tab of the Property Box.

Open Tutorial File

Start by opening the file "Tutorial – Chapter 07". From the **Project Window**, click on the **More Tasks** button, and then in the dropdown menu click on **Samples**, and finally **Tutorial – Chapter 07**. The file opens and Cameron Peabody is displayed as the focus person in the Focus Window. There are no pictures.

The Records Window

We briefly encountered the Records Window in Chapter 1. In the **Navigation Bar** on the left side of the main application window, you should see an icon for the Records Window looking like the 3 sheets of overlapping paper (see left). Click on this icon now. The Records Window should look like Figure 34 below.

The Records Window is another Family Historian *subwindow*. Other subwindows we have already looked at include the *Focus Window*, the *Diagram Window*, and the *Multimedia Window*. Subwindows – and the Navigation Bar which is used to switch between them – were discussed in Chapter 1.

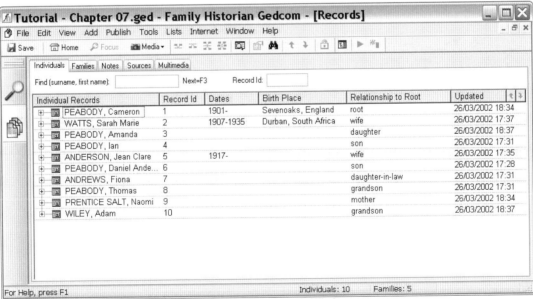

Figure 34 – The Records Window

The Individuals Tab

Make sure that you are viewing the **Individuals** tab of the Records Window now. Within the **Individuals** tab, the Record Window displays all the records for individuals in the file. Each Individual record has a little picture (called an *icon*) next to it: ▦. It is supposed to resemble an identity card. Wherever you see this icon, it always represents an Individual record.

Columns in the Individuals Tab   There should be 10 records in the **Individuals** tab of the **Records Window** (there should be a pane with the text 'Individuals: 10' in the status bar). The rows are divided into 6 columns: *Individual Records*, *Record Id*, *Dates*, *Birth Place*, *Relationship to Root* and *Updated*. As you will see later, different record types (in different tabs of the **Records Window**) will have different columns. But they all have *Record Id* and *Updated*.

Each record is assigned a unique id by Family Historian. *Dates* shows the dates of birth and death, if known, or possibly other dates if not. *Updated* shows the date and time at which the record was last updated.

Configure Columns   You can configure the columns in the Records Window to show whatever you want. Right-click on any column heading and select **Configure Columns** from the menu that appears. The Configure Columns dialog box appears – see Figure 35 below.

Select any column in the list on the right side and click on this button [>] to add the item to the list of columns on the right. Use the **Move Up** and **Move Down** arrow buttons [↑][↓] to re-order items within the right-side list.

You can remove any column you don't want by selecting it, and clicking on the [<] button. Don't be afraid to experiment and try things out. You can reset the list back to the installation settings at any time, by clicking on the **Installation Settings** button.

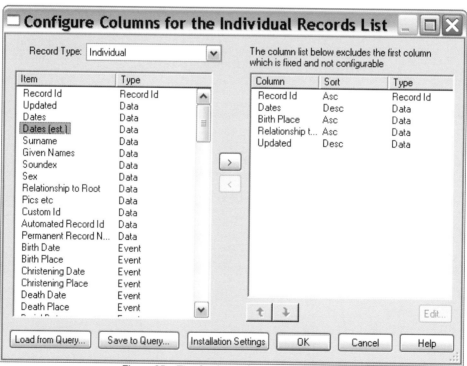

Figure 35 – The Configure Columns Dialog Box

Estimated Dates   As an example of what you can do, select the item "Dates(est.)" in the list on the left-side, and click the [>] button to add it to the list on the right. Select the new column in the right side list and use the arrow keys below the list to move the "Dates (est.)" column to just below the existing "Dates" column. Then press **OK**.

The Records List now has a new column "Dates (est.)". If you can't see the whole thing, click and drag on the line separating the "Dates (est.)" column heading from the column heading immediately to its right. All columns can be resized in this way.

You should see that whereas only 3 rows have dates in the "Dates" column, 9 rows have dates in the "Dates (est.)" column. The "Dates (est.)" column displays estimated dates. Or rather, it shows estimated dates if there are no recorded dates it can show instead. Recorded dates are always displayed if there are any. If there aren't, Family Historian generates its own estimates, based on any dates it can find – such as other event dates in the life of the person, and their near relatives. Dates that Family Historian has generated as estimates always have a tilde (~) character in front of them, so you won't confuse them with definite dates.

Reset Columns

You can, if you wish, use estimated dates either in addition to, or instead of, the ordinary dates column. For now, however, re-open the **Configure Columns** dialog box and click on the **Installation Settings** button to reset columns to their default state. Then press **OK** to close the **Configure Columns** dialog once again.

Sort Records

Click on any column heading to sort the records in the order of that column. If you click on the first column, records will be sorted alphabetically. If you click on *Birth Place*, they will be sorted by place of birth (records with no place of birth will come first; so you may need to scroll down, if you are working with a large file, to see the effect of this). If you click on *Updated*, records will be sorted in update order – with the most recently-updated records first.

If you press the **Alt** key while clicking on a column heading, the records will be sorted in reverse order.

Clicking on *Dates* will sort the records by date-of-birth. If a date-of-death has been supplied, but no date-of-birth, Family Historian will estimate the date-of-birth as 50 years earlier than the date-of-death, for sorting purposes; however, this value can be changed in the **Preferences** dialog (available from the **Tools** menu) if you wish.

Quick Search Tips

A quick way to search for an Individual is to enter all or part of their name (surname, first name) in the **Name** field at the top of the Record Window. This is a fast way of searching for the first record that matches the entered data. Press **F3** to find other matches.

This quick searches technique often works best if you have first sorted the list alphabetically (by clicking on the column heading for the first column). If you press **Ctrl+Shift+D** Family Historian will automatically sort the first column heading for you and position the cursor in the **Name** field. Alternatively, pressing **Ctrl+D** moves the cursor to the Name field but does not sort the list.

If the list is already in order, simply pressing any letter key will jump you to the first record matching that letter. This works with many lists in Family Historian.

Finally, if you know the record id, you can also enter that in the **Record Id** field at the top of the Records Window, as a fast way of finding a given record.

We will look at more techniques for doing more complex searches for records shortly.

View Property Box

Unless you have changed the Property Box options, the Property Box will have closed when you opened the Record Window. But it's very easy to re-open it. Just double-click on any record in the list; or select any record and click on the **Property Box** button on the toolbar; or right-click on a record and select 'Properties' from the dropdown menu that appears.

Browse Records by Expanding Branches

When you enter data in the **Property Box** the data is actually stored by Family Historian in a hierarchical field structure. You can browse this field structure in the **Records Window** in the same kind of way that you can browse files and folders using Windows Explorer[12].

If the records are not sorted alphabetically, sort them now by clicking on the *Individual Records* column heading. The first record entry should read: "Anderson, Jean Clare". The next should be "Andrews, Fiona". Each record has an *expansion button* next to it ⊞, similar to those in Windows Explorer, which you can click on to show or hide details. Click on the expansion button for Cameron Peabody's record now. You should be able to see 6 rows of record details for Cameron Peabody. The 3rd line of Cameron Peabody's record should say "Born 3 January 1901 in Sevenoaks, England", and it too should have an expansion button. Click on this now. You should see 2 further lines, showing the date and place (of his birth) as separate items.

You can expand an entire record by in one go by pressing the **Alt** key while double-clicking on the text (for all branches *within* the record itself, you don't even have to press the **Alt** key). Repeat the same action to hide the branch. The significant advantage of this is that it means you can see at a glance, all the information you have in a given record.

Individual Records and Family Records

Now expand Amanda Peabody's record. Her record shows that her parent's family is the family '... of Cameron Peabody and Sarah Marie Watts'. There is a little icon next to the text: 🏠 (its supposed to look a bit like a family tree diagram). This represents a *Family record*, just as the identity card icon 🆔 represents an *Individual record*. You may be a bit confused by this. Where did these *family* records come from? And where are they kept?

The answer to the first question is that the Family records were created for you by Family Historian. Family records are used to record family relationships between Individuals (primarily).

The question about where a record *is*, is always a moot one in any computer program. Suffice it to say that they can be displayed in the **Records Window** exactly like Individual records, in a separate **Family** tab of their own. But right now the **Family** tab is hidden (unless you have already changed your **Records Window** options to show it).

In general, you rarely have to do anything very much with family records. If they are needed, they will be created for you. It doesn't hurt to understand that they are there though.

View Linked Records

Back to Amanda's record. Next to the family record icon 🏠 for the family '...of Cameron Peabody and Sarah Marie Watts' is an empty white box ☐ called the *View Linked Record* box. Click in the *View Linked Record* box now.

When you do this, the View Linked Record box becomes checked, and the **Records Window** expands to show you the details of Amanda's parents' Family record, 'nested' within the context of her own Individual record, as though her parents' Family record were part of her own Individual record. Amanda's father, mother and brother are listed, as well as Amanda herself. Notice that they all have the Individual icon 🆔 next to their names to show that they represent Individual records. Amanda's entry is in grey, both as a reminder that it is *her* parents' family that you are looking at, and to make it easy to see where she fits in.

---

[12] Windows Explorer is a standard accessory program that comes with all versions of Windows. It is a powerful and very useful tool for exploring, and working with, all the files and folders on your computer.

To look at Amanda's father's (i.e. Cameron's) Individual record, click on the *View Linked Record* box next to his name. Now the **Records Window** expands again. This time it shows Amanda's father nested in the context of his Family record (which, in turn, is nested within the context of Amanda's Individual record). Click the box again to hide Cameron's details.

You can keep on expanding records within records in this way, indefinitely.

Go To Record

Although it is useful to be able to see one record nested within another, it gets confusing if you nest them too deeply. Rather than viewing Cameron's record in the context of Amanda's record, you might prefer to view it on its own. Almost always, when you can see a reference to a record, you can jump straight to that record's main entry in the Records Window – each record has one. For example:

Steps

1. Within Amanda's parents family record, click on the text 'Cameron PEABODY', next to the Individual Record icon now.
2. Click on the **View** menu then **Go To**, then **Go to Record**. The record for Cameron Peabody is located and selected.

When the list of records is short, there is little benefit in this. However, with a long list it becomes a much more useful feature.

*If you select a record in its 'main entry' location (i.e. not nested within another record) and click on **Go to Record**, don't be surprised that nothing happens. You are trying to get to the place you have already reached!*

Find Record

In the previous example, you had already found a link to a record and wanted to go straight to it. But frequently you will want to find a record without having previously found any references to it. If you know the name of the record, one option is to sort the records in alphabetical order (if they aren't already in alphabetical order) and scroll to find it – or use some of the Quick Search techniques described. But what if you only know part of a name, say, and want to search using that? In this example, we will search for the record for Naomi Prentice Salt:

Steps

1. Click on the **Find Record** button on the toolbar: 🔍. The **Find Dialog** appears.
2. Confirm that the **Record Type** is the default value: 'Individuals', and that the **Search Type** is the default value: 'Name/Title Search'.
3. In the **Search For** field, type 'Naomi Prentice Salt'. Press **Find First**. The record for Naomi Prentice Salt is located and selected.
4. Now press **Find Next**. The message 'End of file reached' is displayed to show that there aren't any other matches.

You don't have to type a full name. If you typed 'Naomi' on its own, this would have worked equally well, because there is only one record containing the name Naomi. If you typed 'Sal' on its own, this would find any record that contained 'Sal' as part of the name; so all the Prentice Salts would have been found.

The order of the names does not matter. 'Pren Salt' and 'Salt Pren' will both match all the Prentice Salts.

Tip: If you want to search for a particular surname, put it between slash characters. For example, the search text "/Anderson/" will match Jean Clare Anderson's record, but not Daniel Anderson Peabody's record. This has to be an exact match. "/And/", for example, will not match anything. However, "/And", will match any record where the surname begins with the letters 'And' – i.e. it will match Jean Clare Anderson and Fiona Andrews – and 'son/' will match any record where the surname ends with the letters 'son'.

Delete Record

Deleting a record in the **Records Window** is easy. Simply select the record and press the **Delete** key, or click on **Delete** on the **Edit** menu. A warning dialog will ask you to confirm that you definitely want to delete the record.

Experiment with this now if you wish to, but remember to undo any deletions you perform, using the **Undo** command on the **Edit** menu.

Tip: Although you can select multiple records in the Records Window, Family Historian will not let you delete more than one in one go. If you have a large number of records you wish to delete, you should use a Named List to do this. You can delete all records in a Named List if you wish. See the chapter on Named Lists below, for more information. Other techniques for deleting a large number of records include using the Split Tree Helper feature (on the File menu), or using a Query. Both of these options are discussed in later chapters.

Select Record

Many of the menu and toolbar commands in Family Historian require a record to be selected. The behaviour of the **Property Box** too can depend on the current record selection. It is worth being clear about what it means to "select a record" in the **Records Window**.

So far, you have encountered 2 types of records: *Individual* Records (with the identity card icon: 🟦); and *Family* records (with the family tree diagram icon: 🟦). Later you will encounter more record types. There are 9 in total, although several of them are not used much. Each record types has its own distinctive record icon.

At its simplest, wherever you see a record icon, of whatever type, in the **Records Window**, you can select a record by clicking on the text next to the icon. Clicking on the text 'Cameron Peabody' in the first column, where it appears next to the record icon, 🟦, is an example of one way to select Cameron Peabody's record. However, we saw earlier that when you expand a record, you may see links to other records too. By clicking on the text next to the record icon in the *right-hand* column (the number of columns effectively reduces to 2 in the expanded portion of an expanded record) you can select these records too. This was how we selected Cameron Peabody's record in the *Go To Record* section above, while viewing linked records.

Cells Type and Field Icons

As we have seen, when you expand a record in the **Records Window** by clicking on its expansion button, the record is displayed in two columns. What would normally be the second and subsequent columns are all collapsed into one single column effectively at this level. These two columns divide each row into two areas called *cells*. Only unindented cells in the left column represent records. All other left-column cells represent fields (or *tags* as they are called in GEDCOM). Remember that in GEDCOM, fields are hierarchical and can contain sub-fields. Just as records are always represented by a record icon, fields are always represented by a field icon. Field icons are always little coloured circles. *Individual fields* (fields in Individual records) have a blue circle: ●. *Family fields* (fields in Family records) have a red circle: ●.

Edit Field

Where the left column cell contains a field, the right column cell contains the value of that field. For example, the left column cell might contain the label 'Sex' and the right column might contain the value 'Male'. If you click in the right-cell you will find that, in most cases, it is editable. For example, if you click on the text 'Male', you will find that a drop-down list appears and you can select a different sex if you want to.

Where a field stores a link to another record, you can edit the link by right-clicking on the text in the right cell. A menu will appear to show you what options are available to you.

Although you can edit fields in the Records Window, you rarely need to. Ordinarily, you will do all editing in the Property Box, which is much easier to work with.

Add Field   Not only can you edit cells in the **Records Window**, if you want to, you can also *add* them. This is an advanced topic, and you will rarely want to do it, but exceptionally you can add fields to a record directly within the Records Window if you want to. To do this, click on any left-hand cell with the right mouse button. A context menu appears listing all the 'sub-fields' that can be added to the chosen field. For example, if you right-click on the word 'Name' in the left cell, you will find a list of sub-fields that can be added, to qualify a Name field.

*Again, it should be emphasised that you will rarely need to add fields directly in the **Records Window**. Instead, you should simply enter data into the **Property Box** which will automatically create any fields that you need for you.*

Delete Field   Whereas you rarely need or want to add or edit fields in the **Records Window**, you are more likely to occasionally want to *delete* fields in the Records Window (or in the *All* tab of the **Property Box** – see below).

We have already seen how you can delete records in the Records Window. The technique for deleting a field is the same, except that instead of selecting a record, you select a field, and then press the **Delete** key – or click on **Delete** on the **Edit** menu. You select a field by clicking in the left-hand column (remember that indented rows represent fields, and unindented rows represent records). Family Historian will always warn you of what you are about to do, and give you a chance to cancel, before it will let you delete any data.

When you delete a field, any sub-fields in the same record are also deleted.

The *All* Tab of the Properties Box   Open Cameron Peabody's record in the Property Box, and select the *All* tab. The *All* tab is the last tab. As you can see, the record is laid out in the *All* tab in exactly the same way that it is laid out in the **Records Window**. So here too, you can see at a glance, all the information you have stored in a given record.

You can browse a record in the *All* tab, exactly as you can in the **Records Window**, and you can view linked records in exactly the same way. You can even edit fields, add fields, delete fields and unlink records in the *All* tab – in exactly the same way that, as we have seen, you can in the **Records Window**.

Unlink From Parents or Spouse   The easy way to unlink any child from its parents, or to unlink a parent from his family or one spouse from another is to select the record in the Records Window and use the **Unlink From** command on the **Edit** menu. This is easy and convenient but only works for unlinking family relationships. You cannot use this technique to remove other kinds of links between records.

Remove Any Links   You can remove any record links in the *All* tab of the Property Box if you wish to. When a record is linked to another record, it has a field which stores this link. So to unlink 2 records you merely need to delete the field that links them together. For example, to unlink Cameron Peabody from his marriage to Jean Clare Anderson, you could simply select the second occurrence of *Spouse family* in the left-hand column of his record, and press the **Delete** key. Then press **OK** when warned that 'The selected field will be deleted'.

You can use the same technique, of course, in the Records Window.

Low-level Editing   Ultimately there is very little in the way of editing, that cannot be done in either the **Records Window** or in the *All* tab of the **Property Box**. If you experiment, you will find that there are even ways of creating records directly in the Records Window (one way to do this is simply to right-click on an unused area of the Records Window – a menu will appear that will give you the option to create a record of the current record type). However, editing in the Records Window (and in the *All* tab of the Property Box) is mainly 'low-level' and not appropriate for most purposes. You should think of editing in the Records Window, and in the *All* tab of the Property Box, as a *fallback* – only to be used if what you want to do cannot be done any other way.

This is not to say that all editing must be done in the other tabs of the **Property Box**. On the contrary, as we will see later, Family Historian supports diagram-based editing, as well as other editing techniques.

Close the Current File   To close the file, click Close on the File menu. The file is closed, and the Project Window is re-displayed.

8 Diagram-based Editing

In Chapter 1 we looked at how you can add relatives in the Focus Window. In Chapter 2 we saw that you can also add relatives in the Property Box. In this chapter, we look at yet another, and often better, way of doing it – using the **Diagram Window** *interactively*. This is called *Diagram-based Editing*. The advantage of doing it this way is that you can see visually what you have done, and you can, literally, see a bigger picture. In the *Main* tab of the **Property Box**, at any given time, you can see one person, their spouses, and their children by one of their spouses. In the Focus Window you can see more. But in the **Diagram Window**, at any given time, you can see as many relatives as you can comfortably fit onto the screen. This makes it easier to spot gaps and mistakes.

The reason that we did not start first with Diagram-based Editing is that, although it is not at all difficult to add relatives by clicking-and-dragging in a diagram, you do need first to understand the diagrams, and what they are showing you. Also, Diagram-based Editing makes use of the ***Property Box*** too, and can be combined in any way you like with the techniques we have already learned.

In this chapter we will use a tutorial file similar to ones we have used in other chapters, and add some new relatives using Diagram-based Editing. We will add two spouses for Daniel Peabody: Pamela Jean Winters and Isabel Thompson. We will add three children for Daniel and Pamela (Michael, Anthony and Robin Peabody), and a fourth for Daniel and Isabel (Charles Peabody). We will change the order of Daniel's spouses. We will make Sally Prentice Salt the older sister of Naomi Prentice Salt. We will add a father, Thomas Andrews, for Fiona Andrews.

Automatic Source Citations

It is a good idea to record the sources for all your data. Sources and source citations will not be covered till Chapter 10; but it is worth mentioning automatic source citations now as this is an important feature which works well with Diagram-based Editing. When you set an automatic source citation, you specify a source and citation details, and all new data will get that citation until you cancel it. For now, the important thing to realise is that this works just as well with Diagram-based Editing as it does with any other kind of editing. So you can use Diagram-based Editing and still fully document your sources easily.

See "Set Automatic Source Citations" in Chapter 12 for more details.

Open Tutorial File

Start by opening the file "Tutorial – Chapter 08". From the **Project Window**, click on the **More Tasks** button, and then in the dropdown menu click on **Samples**, and finally **Tutorial – Chapter 08**. The file opens and Cameron Peabody is displayed as the focus person in the Focus Window. There are no pictures.

Trees vs. Diagrams

Up to now, we have not clearly distinguished diagrams from trees. But henceforth they will need to be distinguished properly.

In Family Historian, a *diagram* is everything that can be displayed in the *Diagram Window*. A *tree* however has a more specific meaning. A *tree* is an arrangement of lines and boxes within a diagram. There are four types of tree, corresponding to the four types of diagram: *Ancestor, Descendant, Ancestor & Descendant,* and *All Relatives*. When you first create a new diagram it contains a single tree. But you can insert additional trees of any type, into any diagram – as many as you like.

If the Tree Will Show It, You Can Add It You can use *any* Family Historian diagram for Diagram-based Editing – not just the four default diagram types but also all pre-configured standard and custom diagrams. You can also use any type of *tree* for Diagram-Based Editing. However, there is one golden rule: *you can only add a relative to a tree if, when added, that relative would be displayed in that tree.* For example, if you are viewing an *Ancestor* tree, you cannot add a child or a spouse to the tree root because that type of tree does not display children or spouses of the root. But you can add parents (if not already there), or add parents to the parents, etc, because these will be displayed.

Note that this rule applies to *trees*, and not to diagrams.

What is a Relative? You might be tempted to think that in the *All Relatives* tree, you must be able to add anything, but that is not correct: even an *All Relatives* tree only shows relatives of the tree root – it doesn't show *everyone*.

Family Historian defines a 'relative' of yours as any ancestor of yours, any descendant of yours, any descendant of any ancestor of yours, and any spouse of any of these people. In addition anyone who is a relative of any spouse of yours, by this definition, also counts as your relative.

Fiona Andrews is Cameron Peabody's daughter-in-law. By our definition of *relative* Fiona Andrews is Cameron Peabody's relative by marriage. But her *father* isn't a relative of Cameron Peabody's – not even a relative by marriage. So although you may be able to see Fiona Andrews in an *All Relatives* diagram for Cameron Peabody, you still can't add a parent for her by clicking-and-dragging on her box. [13]

Installation Settings We will start by adding two spouses for Daniel Peabody: Pamela Jean Winters and Amanda Thompson. As we have seen, any diagram will do which displays all spouses for Daniel Peabody – i.e. any diagram type, except *Ancestor* diagrams. We will use the *All Relatives* diagram with Cameron Peabody as the root. Open such a diagram now (that is, select Cameron Peabody and click on the **View All Relatives** button ⬚ on the main application toolbar).

There is no particular set of diagram options that you need for Diagram-based Editing, but for the purposes of this tutorial, it is useful to be able to specify a well-defined set. The easiest set of options to specify is the installation settings.

Steps

1. Click on the Diagram menu, then Settings, and then Restore Installation Settings.
2. If for some reason you wish to preserve your default settings, click 'No' when asked if you want to update your default settings. Otherwise, click 'Yes'.

*Tip: It is not required, but it's usually a good idea to use Spouses in Own Box as the **Spouse Display Option**, when doing Diagram-based Editing, especially if you're planning to add children.*

Status Bar If you don't know what the *status bar* is, find it now. In the bottom left corner of the main application window (also known as the *frame window*) you should see the text 'For Help, press F1'. The area occupied by that text, and stretching beyond it the full length of the window, is the status bar. It doesn't hurt to look at it from time to time. Sometimes (as when doing Diagram-based Editing) it displays useful information.

---

[13] See *Click-and-Drag to Add Parent* below, for suggestions as to how you can add a parent for Fiona Andrews.

78

Click-and-Drag to Add Spouse

Arrange the diagram so that you can see Daniel Peabody with space to spare around his box.

Steps

1. Click on the box, and, keeping the button pressed, drag the mouse to the right, until the mouse is roughly in the area that a spouse of Daniel Peabody's would be displayed if he had one. If you did this correctly, a dotted box should appear to the right of Daniel Peabody's box. You may just be able to see 2 dotted marriage lines connecting the dotted box to his box. The status bar should display the text "Add Spouse". Release the mouse button.
2. A context menu appears with 3 options: *Add Spouse (new record)*, *Link Existing Record as Spouse*, and *Cancel*. Click on *Add Spouse (new record)*. An empty spouse box appear to the right of Daniel Peabody's box and the **Property Box** appears in its *floating* mode. Its title reads "Individual: [unnamed person]". Enter the name 'Pamela Jean Winters' for the new spouse and press **Tab**. The spouse box, next to Daniel's box in the diagram, now shows the text 'Pamela Jean Winters'. You may have to move the Property Box to see this. If you find it more convenient, you can of course *dock* the Property Box at the side of the window.

Click-and-Drag to Add 2nd Spouse

Make sure that you can see both Daniel Peabody and Pamela Winters clearly, and that you can see the area to the right of Pamela Winters' box. We are going to add a 2nd spouse for Daniel Peabody – 2nd not just in the sense that it's the 2nd one we add, but also in the sense that she was the 2nd person that Daniel Peabody married.

Steps

1. Click on Daniel Peabody's box, and, keeping the button pressed, drag the mouse to the right again. This time you must drag further than before, until the mouse is roughly to the right of Pamela Winters' spouse box. When you can see the dotted box to the right of Pamela Winter's box, and the text "Add Spouse" in the status bar, release the mouse button.
2. On the dropdown menu that appears, click on *Add Spouse (new record)* to create a new record for Daniel's 2nd wife. Enter her name as 'Isabel Thompson'.

If Isabel Thompson had been Daniel Peabody's first spouse, you could have added her as such by clicking on Daniel Peabody's box, and dragging to the left.

Click-and-Drag to Add Children

We will now add 3 children for Daniel and Pamela. You could click-and-drag on Daniel's box to add a child for him and Pamela – but only because Pamela is his first wife. It's probably better to get into the habit of clicking and dragging on spouses to add children, because this produces the results you want for all marriages, and not just the first.

Steps

1. Click-and-drag on Pamela Winters' box – dragging downwards. A dotted box should appear below and between her and Daniel's box. A dotted line should go up from it, to meet the double ('marriage') lines connecting Daniel and Pamela. The status bar should display the text "Add Child". Release the button.
2. The context menu this time should show 4 options:
   - Add Son (new record)
   - Add Daughter (new record)
   - Link Existing Record as Child
   - Cancel
3. Click on Add Son (new record).
4. Enter the new child's name as "Michael Peabody" in the **Property Box**.
5. Repeat steps 1 to 3 to add another son, Anthony. Add Anthony as the younger brother of Michael – that is, make sure you drag both downwards and slightly to

the right, so that the dotted box overlaps the right half of Michael Peabody's box. The new box should be created to the right of Michael Peabody's box (younger children always display to the right of older children).

6. Finally, repeat steps 1 to 3 again, to add another son, Robin. Although you're adding him last, let us assume that he was actually the middle child of the three. To add him as such, you should drag downwards and roughly between Michael and Anthony's boxes.

Cancel Click-and-Drag If you want to cancel a click-and-drag, while doing it, you can either press the **Esc** key, or press the right mouse button, before releasing the left mouse button. Or you could simply release the mouse button, at a time when no dotted box was displayed. Or, you could just release the mouse button. If a context menu appears, you can cancel it by clicking anywhere other than the menu, or by clicking on the **Cancel** menu command. You will only get a context menu if there had been a dotted box (indicating a relative that could be validly added) at the point where you released the mouse button.

So do not be afraid to experiment. Clicking-and-dragging on boxes will not result in new records accidentally being created. Nothing will happen until you explicitly click on a menu to indicate that you want a record to be created or linked. And even if you did create a relative and then realise it wasn't what you meant to do, you can just click **Undo** on the **Edit** menu to undo it.

The Dotted Box With that in mind, click-and-drag again on Pamela's box. Don't release the mouse button, but drag out of her box, and then move the mouse in a complete circle round her box. You should find, if you draw a wide enough circle, that there are 4 possible positions that you can drag to which will result in dotted boxes appearing – all different positions for a new child for Pamela and Daniel. When you drag *above* Pamela's box or to the *side* of it, you see a dotted line connecting her box to the mouse position, but no dotted box. If you look at the status bar at these points, you will see a message explaining why you cannot add a relative at these points.

You will have gathered by now that a dotted box indicates that Family Historian will create a relative for you if you want it to – and the position of the box indicates what kind of relative it will be, and where it will fit in relative to other relatives.

Cancel the drag round Pamela's box without creating any new relatives. Try the same with Daniel's box. There are 8 possible positions where you could create relatives for him (4 spouse positions and 4 child positions). Can you find them all?

Why couldn't you add a parent for Pamela? Why couldn't you add a parent for Daniel? (hint: keep your eye on the status bar while dragging).

Add Child for 2nd Spouse You should by now know how to add a child for Daniel and Isabel. The only significant point is to remember to click and drag on Isabel's box, and not on Daniel's box. Do it now, and create a son for the two of them called 'Charles Peabody'.

Hint: drag downwards, make sure you can see a dotted box before you release the mouse button, and look at the status bar if you want confirmation that you're doing the right thing (or an explanation if no dotted box appears). Don't worry if the box isn't aligned with other children that Daniel has.

Re-order Spouses ⬆ ⬇ Re-ordering spouses if very simple. We will now make Isabel Thompson Daniel's first spouse to illustrate this.

Steps

1. Click on Isabel Thompson's box.

2. Click on the **Move Up** button ⬆ on the main toolbar. Isabel Thompson is

now displayed as Daniel's first wife.

Re-order Siblings

The same buttons are used for re-ordering siblings. We will now make Sally Prentice Salt the older sister of Naomi Prentice Salt. Arrange the diagram so that you can see Naomi Prentice Salt, and her sister Sally. Ordinarily when you re-order a pair of siblings, you could click on either of the siblings and move that. But in this *All Relatives* diagram, Naomi only appears in an *Ancestor* box. So in this case, we must use Sally's box.

Steps

1. Click on the box for Sally Prentice Salt.

2. Click on the **Move Up** button [↑] on the main toolbar. Sally is now Naomi's older sister.

Crossed Lines

Unlike other trees, you can get lines crossing over each other within *All Relatives* trees, as you do now with this one. This only occurs with horizontal dotted line connections to ancestors. If you want crossing lines to be solid rather than dotted, you can configure this in the Lines tab of Diagram Options.

Click-and-Drag to Add Parent

Lastly, we will add a father, Thomas Andrews, for Fiona Andrews. Fiona should be visible in the current diagram. Try adding a father to her now by clicking-and-dragging upwards. You should find that the status bar says "Can't add parent – this tree does not display parents of spouses".

So how can we add her father? Of the various ways you could do it, here are three:

- You could open another diagram – one of a type in which Fiona Andrews' father *would* be displayed (such as an *All Relatives* diagram for Fiona Andrews). Then you could click-and-drag upwards from Fiona Andrews's box to add her father in that diagram.
- You could insert an *All Relatives* tree for Fiona into the current diagram, and click-and-drag on her box in that, to add a parent.
- You could use the **Property Box** to add a father for her.

All three are good options. Certainly there is no problem about using a combination of Diagram-based Editing and Property Box-based editing. The results will be the same, and the diagram will update itself to show the correct information, irrespective of where the change occurred (if you have multiple Diagram Windows open, you will find that if you edit one, they will all update themselves to show the latest information). We will use the first option.

Steps

1. Display a new *All Relatives* diagram for Fiona Andrews (e.g. click on her box within the current diagram and then click on the *All Relatives* button [⊡] on the main application toolbar). A new Diagram Window opens (you should be able to see two diagram icons for two diagram windows in the Navigation Bar).
2. Click-and-drag upwards on her box. When the dotted box appears, release the mouse button.
3. A context menu appears with four options: Add Father (new record), Add Mother (new record), Link Existing Record as Parent, and Cancel. Select Add Father (new record).
4. A new box is created and the **Property Box** appears (if it wasn't already open). Enter the name of the new parent as 'Thomas Andrews' and press the **Tab** key.

Select Multiple Boxes in a Diagram

The Diagram Window allows you to select as many boxes at a time, as you want. One technique to do this is to click in the background of the diagram and holding the mouse button down drag the mouse to form a stretchy box, to surround all the boxes you want to select. If you zoom far enough out, you can easily select all the boxes in a diagram using this technique.

Alternatively (or additionally – because these two techniques can be combined) you can add or remove individual boxes to, or from, an existing selection by pressing the **Ctrl** key, while clicking on a box. So if you press the **Ctrl** key and click on five unselected boxes in turn, all five boxes will be selected.

To select all boxes in a diagram, click on **Diagram**, then **Select & Marks**, and finally **Select All Boxes** (or just press Ctrl-A). This submenu contains yet more useful selection options, including options to invert a selection, or to select an entire branch of boxes.

Selecting multiple boxes is useful for a number of purposes. You can select records for deletion, or records that you want to set Records Flags for (see **Record Flags** on the **Edit** menu). You can mark boxes or hide them (this will be covered in later chapters). All of the **Box States** (see the Diagram menu) can be set or cleared using multiple selection. If you have a multiple selection and you click on the Media button on the main application toolbar, and you then choose **View Media for Selected Records**, the *Multimedia Window* will show all pictures of (all multimedia records linked to) all the selected records.

Deleting Relatives in a Diagram

You can delete one or more of the Individual records displayed in a diagram, by selecting them and pressing the **Del** key (or clicking on **Delete** on the **Edit** menu). A confirmation dialog will appear, asking you if you want to delete selected diagram items, or if you wish to delete actual data records. When you delete a diagram item, no change is made to the data in your records. It is just your diagram that you are changing. But if you choose to delete data records, you are not just altering the current diagram – you are deleting actual records. Consequently, if you take the latter option, a second confirmation dialog will be displayed and you will have to tick a box in that to confirm that you know what you are doing.

Make Regular Backups

Effectively then, before you can delete any records from a diagram, you have 3 levels of confirmation to get through (that is, two dialogs and a tick box) before the records are actually deleted. Consequently there should be no way that anyone could accidentally delete any records while working on a diagram. **Nevertheless, if your data is of value to you, you should take regular backups anyway. Remember that backups protect you not only from hardware and software errors, but probably most importantly of all, against your own mistakes.**

Save Changes

Finally, save the work that you have done. Click on the **Save** button ![Save] on the main application toolbar. If you have **Autosave** enabled (see Chapter 1), this may not be necessary.

9 Setting the Style, Layout & Content of Diagrams

Diagrams were introduced in Chapter 3 and we looked at some of their basic features. Chapter 8 was devoted to using diagrams interactively for diagram-based editing. In this chapter we will continue where we left off, and look at some more features of diagrams.

Open Tutorial File

We will illustrate some of the things you can do using a tutorial file: "Tutorial – Chapter 09". Start by opening this file.

Steps

1. From the **Project Window**, click on the **More Tasks** button, and then in the dropdown menu click on **Samples**, and finally **Tutorial – Chapter 09**. The file opens and Cameron Peabody is displayed as the focus person in the Focus Window. There are a few, very poor quality, monochrome pictures.
2. Select Cameron Peabody and open the *All Relatives* diagram for him (click on the **View All Relatives** button ⬚ on the main application toolbar). Make sure that the Spouse Display Option is *Spouse in Own Box*. The All Relatives diagram opens.

Restore Installation Settings

Before continuing, to ensure consistency with this book you should use default options in your diagrams, for now – i.e. the 'installation settings'.

Steps

1. Click on the Diagram menu, then Settings, and then Restore Installation Settings.
2. If for some reason you wish to preserve your default settings, click 'No' when asked if you wish to use the installation settings as default settings in the future. Otherwise, click 'Yes'.

At this point, pictures should be visible (albeit very poor quality pictures) for Cameron Peabody, Jean Clare Anderson, and Daniel Peabody.

'On-the-Fly' Changes to Diagram Options

In most genealogy programs when you generate a diagram, you specify your options and the program builds a diagram using those options. If you then decide that you want to change an option, you can't change it for that diagram. You have to create another one. This process does not fit well with the way human beings work. A better process is this:

- Build the diagram with the current default options
- Look at it and decide if you like it.
- Make changes and/or modify diagram options and see what the effect is
- Repeat this process until you are happy with the results

That is what Family Historian lets you do. In most cases, if you change a diagram option (e.g. from the **Diagram Options** dialog), Family Historian will simply update the existing diagram to reflect the change. If you have expanded branches, resized or moved boxes, or made other changes, it doesn't matter. The diagram will be kept the same (or as near the same as is consistent with the options you have chosen) and will be dynamically updated to reflect the new options.

This makes it easy for you to experiment and try things out until you are happy with the results. We will see how you can use this approach to change diagrams in this chapter.

There are, however, a small number of diagram options (marked in red in the **Diagram Options** dialog) which cannot be handled in this way, and which require the diagram to be rebuilt if they are changed (see Figure 36 below). If the diagram is rebuilt, all existing diagram elements will be discarded, and the diagram will be re-created.

Figure 36 – The General tab of the Diagram Options dialog. Items coloured red cannot be changed 'on-the-fly'. If you change them, the diagram will have to be rebuilt.

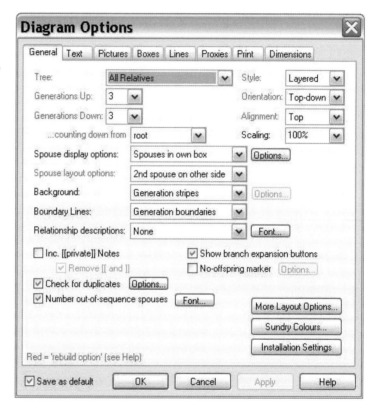

Charts vs. Working Diagrams

Family Historian diagrams are classed as either *Working Diagrams* or *Saved Diagrams*. Saved Diagrams are also sometimes called *Charts*. They are diagrams that have been saved in the Family Historian Chart format.

With charts you will always be warned and given the chance to cancel, if you make a change to diagram options that would require a rebuild. Also if you close a chart (or take some other action that would force the chart to be closed), you will always be given the chance to save any unsaved changes you have made to the chart.

With working diagrams, you can choose how much warning you wish to be given in both scenarios. The default is that you will always be warned if you have made significant changes to the diagram since it was created, before the diagram is closed or if you make changes that require a rebuild. You can configure this in the **Diagrams** tab of the **Preferences** dialog.

Text: Content, Font and Style

Family Historian gives you complete control over the content of boxes. It can display any and all text in an Individual's record. Not only that, it can display any text in any record that is even linked, in whatever way, however indirectly, to the Individual's record. The contents of boxes are specified by *Text Schemes*.

Figure 37 – The Text tab of the Diagram Options dialog. The current text scheme is "Birth, Marr, Death".

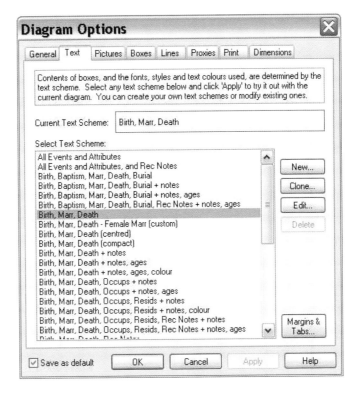

The Text Tab

Diagram Options Dialog

Text Schemes can be simple or complex. They specify not only what text appears in boxes, but also the fonts used, styles, text colours, indentation, text-alignment and more. Family Historian comes with a number of standard text schemes. We will now view the effects of some of them.

Steps

1. Arrange your diagram so that you can comfortably read the text. It doesn't matter if you can't see all boxes. Try to arrange things so that you can see Sarah Watts and Cameron Peabody at least.
2. Open the **Diagram Options Dialog** and choose the *Text* tab (see Figure 37 above).
3. The **Current Text Scheme** field shows the text scheme currently in use in the diagram. It should currently say "Birth, Marr, Death".
4. Select "All Events and Attributes" in the list of text schemes and click on the **Apply** button. Move the Diagram Options Dialog to one side if necessary so that you can see what effect this has on the contents of boxes. You should see that Cameron Peabody's box, for example, is much bigger and lists all his events and attributes.
5. Now select "All Events and Attributes, and Rec Notes" and press **Apply**. Now record notes appear in the boxes as well.
6. Now select "Birth, Marr, Death, Occups, Resids + notes, colour". Press **Apply**. This text scheme puts event notes and causes in green italics (e.g. see the cause of Cameron's death).
7. Select Name Only (compact) and press **Apply**. This text scheme is usefully compact if you don't have much space and just want names.
8. Try out any other text schemes, pressing **Apply** after each one to see what it does. Then select "Birth, Marr, Death" again, and press **Apply** to get back to the starting point.

Name, Date and Place Formats

A common requirement is to change name, date and place formats throughout a diagram. We will now see how to do this. At this point, you should still be looking at the **Text** tab of the Diagram Options dialog and the **Current Text Scheme** should be "Birth, Marr, Death".

Steps

1. Move the Diagram Options Dialog to one side so that you see Sarah Marie Watts' box, without having to close the dialog.
2. Select "Birth, Marr, Death" in the list and click on the **Edit** button. The **Edit Text Scheme Dialog** appears (see Figure 38 below). The Edit Text Scheme Dialog enables you to change every aspect of a text scheme, and add or delete any items you like.
3. Find the **Name Format** field near the top-left corner of the dialog. Its current value is "Full" (i.e. show full details for names). Move the dialog so that you can see Sarah Marie Watts box. Change the Name format to "Preferred" and press **Apply**. This displays a shortened version of a person's name. Sarah Watt's middle name, 'Marie', no longer appears.
4. Now select "Surname First" as the name format and press **Apply**. This time her name displays as "Watts, Sarah Marie".
5. Locate the **Date Format** field to the right of the **Name Format** field. Change the date format from 'Compact' to 'Abbrev(3)' and press **Apply**. Sarah's date of birth changes from "12 Dec 1907" to "12/12/1907".
6. Change the **Date Format** to 'Year' and press **Apply**. Now her birth is just given as 1907.
7. Locate the **Place Format** field to the right of the **Date Format** field. Change the place format from 'Tidy' to 'Short'. Now Sarah's place of birth has changed from 'Durban, South Africa' to just 'Durban'.
8. Click on the **Help** button. In the help that appears, scroll down to the description of the fields for **Name Format**, **Date Format** and **Place Format**. These in turn have links to pages for *Name Formats*, *Date Formats* and *Place Formats*. Follow these links for an explanation of what all the different formats are. When you've finished looking at this, close the Help again.
9. Click on the **Installation Settings** button to reset the text scheme back to its default values, and click on the **OK** button to apply the changes and close the dialog .[14]

Create Custom Text Schemes

Creating a custom text scheme of your own is straightforward. You click on the **New** button in the *Text* tab of the Diagram Options dialog. The *Edit Text Scheme* dialog appears (see Figure 38 below). You have to give the scheme a name and select the items you want from the list of *Available Items* on the left. With each selected item, you click the right chevron button [>] to add it to the Text Scheme. Depending on the items you have selected, a dialog may appear giving options relating to the item you are adding. Each item added is listed in the *Items Used in This Text Scheme* list on the right. To remove an item from the Text Scheme, select it in the *Items Used...* list and click on the left chevron button [<].

If you wish to change the order of any items, select them and use the **Move Up** [↑] and **Move Down** [↓] buttons to move them up or down the list.

When you have finished, click **OK**. The new text scheme will appear in the Text Schemes list in the **Text** tab of the Diagram Options dialog. Don't forget to select it and click **Apply** to use it with the current diagram.

At this point, you should still be viewing the **Text** tab of the Diagram Options dialog. Click now on the **Help** button. In the Help that appears, scroll down until you find the help for the **New** button. Find the link entitled "Create a Simple Text Scheme" and click on it. This help page takes you through a detailed example of how to create a simple text scheme. Work through this example now to create a custom text scheme.

---

[14] A common mistake in Windows is to think that if there is an **OK** button and an **Apply** button you have to press Apply before pressing OK to apply your changes. You don't. They both apply changes. The only difference is that OK also closes the dialog and Apply doesn't.

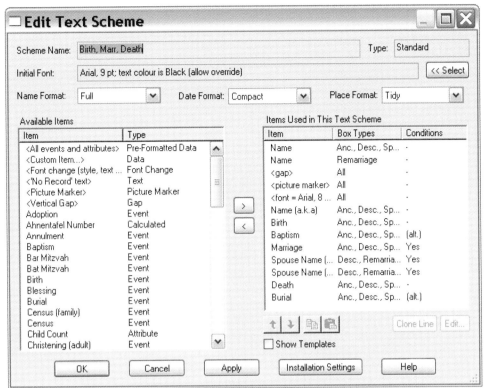

Figure 38 – the Edit Text Scheme Dialog for the "Birth, Marr, Death" text scheme.

Clone a Text Scheme A good alternative approach, if you want to create a new text scheme, is to take one that is as close as possible to what you want, and make a copy of it using the **Clone** button. Thereafter you can modify it to fit your requirements.

Modify Existing Text Scheme You can modify any text scheme – either a custom scheme or a standard scheme. We have already seen how to do the latter when we changed name, date and place formats in the "Birth, Marr, Date" text scheme. The first thing to do is to select the text scheme you wish to edit in the list of text schemes in the **Text** tab of the Diagram Options dialog, and then click on the **Edit** button to open the *Edit Text Scheme Dialog* (see Figure 38 above).

You can do extensive modifications to any text scheme just by adding, deleting, and re-ordering items as described in the previous section. A simple approach to modifying schemes is to delete items you want to change and re-insert them by selecting them in the *Available Items* list and clicking on the right chevron button

to add them. When you re-insert an item, you will be prompted for options. For example, when you insert a *Birth* item the dialog will allow you to specify a label to use (e.g. "Born:") the number of instances you require (all, first only, last only) [15], which details you want about the birth (date, place, cause, notes), how you want the item to be aligned (left, right, centred, justified), and whether you want some special text to be output if there are no birth details. Choose the options you want, or accept the defaults, and press **OK** to add.

A complication to be aware of is that when you add a single item from the *Available Items* list, you sometimes get multiple items in the *Items Used...* list. Usually these items form an *Item Group*. See the Help for more details about Item Groups and how to identify them. If you wish to modify an item which has been inserted as an Item Group, be sure to delete all lines in the Item Group before re-inserting the item.

---

[15] You can have as many instances of any event or attribute as you like; though it would be unusual for an Individual to have multiple recorded birth events.

Equally if you wish to re-order an item that has been inserted as an Item Group, be sure to keep all the lines together. You can select each line in an item group by the usual technique of selecting the first, and then pressing-and-holding the **Ctrl** key while clicking on the other lines in the group, to select them all.

Changing Fonts & Styles

The Help page "Create a Simple Text Scheme" (see Create Custom Text Scheme above) gives an example of how to modify an existing scheme to change the font and style of different items within the scheme.

Advanced Text Schemes

Most people will be able to do everything they ever need to do using the techniques already described. But there is much more that can be done if you want to drop down to the level of creating your own custom text scheme items, or modifying existing text scheme items.

To add a custom text scheme item, you must be looking at the **Edit Text Scheme Dialog** (see Figure 38 above). Select '*<Custom Item…>*' in the *Available Items* list and click on the right chevron button to add it. The **Edit Template Item Dialog** is displayed and you can configure the item there. Alternatively, select an existing item in the scheme in the *Items Used…* list on the right hand side, and click on the **Edit** button to edit it (again, in the **Edit Template Item Dialog**).

Click on the **Help** button within the **Edit Template Item Dialog** for extensive help on configuring template items, including links to advanced features which allow you to control almost every aspect of text scheme items.

Override Text

It can sometimes happen that you wish to change the standard text, and do something special for a particular individual. You can do this by carefully modifying the text scheme you are using. First, set a distinctive *Record Flag* for the Individual in question (create a new one if you do not already have a suitable one). Any item in a text scheme can be made conditional upon any given record flag being set or unset. By referring to the appropriate record flag, you can change the text scheme to output special text (or not output text) for that person only.

See Chapter 16 for more on Record Flags.

Show Pictures in Diagrams

You can insert pictures 'manually' into a diagram. We will look at that in the next chapter. You can also get Family Historian to automatically display a picture of each person in each box. We will look at this now.

Each person's pictures are ordered by *preference*. As we saw in Chapter 2, you can change a person's picture preference order in the Multimedia tab of the **Property Box** for that person.

The Picture Tab

Diagram Options Dialog

If you use the default options, pictures should already be showing for Cameron Peabody, Jean Clare Anderson, and Daniel Peabody. To control the display of these pictures open the Diagram Options dialog if it isn't already open, and click on the **Pictures** tab.

If you wish to display pictures of Individuals in boxes in your diagram, you will usually set the **Preference** field to 1 or 1st. If you don't wish to display pictures in boxes, set the **Preference** field to 0 or None. Occasionally you may wish to display 2nd or 3rd preference pictures, in which case set the **Preference** field accordingly.

Silhouettes Where some individuals have no picture, it can sometimes look better if you display a silhouette image for them, as a substitute. If you want to do this, tick the box 'Show silhouette if no picture (m/f only)'. One silhouette will be displayed for men. Another will be displayed for women. If the sex of an individual is not recorded, no silhouette will be displayed for them. Click on the Silhouettes button to view the standard silhouette images used. You can use this dialog to choose your own silhouette images to use, if you want to do that.

Later we will see how you can override these settings, and specify for individual boxes whether you want them to display silhouettes or not.

Pictures and Box Types By default, pictures are not displayed for all box types, but you can configure that. You can also control where box pictures are displayed: to the left of the text, to the right of the text, or 'within the text'. Press the **Help** button for detailed help on the various options.

Box Features We have already seen how you can control the content of a box. Other features of a box that you can control include the background (box fill) colour of the box, and the colour and thickness of the box frame if there is one (box line), the shape of the box – if you opt to have a box at all – and the box shadow colour, position and size (if you opt to have a shadow).

B&B-style Icons Box features can even include little 'icons' (tiny pictures) which display below the box – like the little icons in a Bed-and-Breakfast catalogue that tell you whether a room has a TV or an en suite shower. You could, for example, have a little men-at-work icon to show which boxes you are currently working on, or have a ship icon for sailors. How you use these features is of course entirely up to you. There is no limit to the number of icons that can be displayed below each box. You can associate icons with record flags, set on the records themselves. Family Historian comes with a number of standard icons, but you can design your own if you wish.

To learn more about how to use B&B-style icons with boxes, click the Help button on the **Boxes** tab of the Diagram Options dialog.

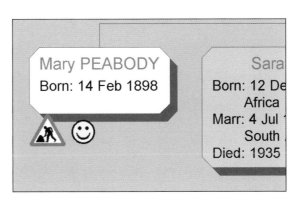

Figure 39
An example of the
use of B&B style icons.

Conditions More often than not, you will not want all boxes to look the same – you certainly wouldn't want them to all have the same icon, for example. You may want each generation to use a different box colour. Or you may want one set of relatives to be coloured green, and another set to be coloured red. You may want ancestor boxes to have a green background, a crinkly box shape, and a brown shadow; and you may want descendant boxes to have a yellow background, rounded box corners, and no shadow. You might want females to have red text, and round box edges, and males to have blue text and hard box edges. Family Historian lets you define conditions, prioritise them, and assign features to them to suit your requirements.

The Boxes Tab

Diagram Options Dialog

Open the Diagram Options dialog if it isn't already open and click on the **Boxes** tab. It is here that you define both conditions, and the box features you wish to associate with them.

The conditions are listed in the top half of the dialog, in order of priority. The features shown in the bottom half of the dialog, in a tabbed list, are the features associated with the condition selected in the top half.

The default look for Family Historian diagrams includes sex colouring (overriding the default text colouring for names, specified in the Text Scheme). Make sure that 'Sex' is selected in the Condition List. Notice that the tabbed list below has 3 tabs: 'Male', 'Female', and 'Unknown Sex'. Click on each of these tabs in turn and confirm that they specify 3 different text colours.

Now click on 'Box Type' in the Condition list. When you do this, the tabs change in the tabbed list of features. There are now 6 tabs and they are 'Root', 'Ancestor', 'Descendant', 'Spouse', 'Remarriage' and 'Proxy'. Click on the Spouse tab. The dialog should look like Figure 40 below. Click on the **Edit Features** button. The **Box Features Dialog** opens. Click on the coloured button in the **Box Fill** area and select the pink colour. Press **OK**, and then press **OK** again to close the **Box Features Dialog**. Now back in the Boxes tab of the Diagram Options dialog, press **Apply**. You should see that spouse boxes in the diagram all go pink.

Click **Edit Features** again. This time tick **Box Shape**, and select 'Two Step Corners' as the shape. Tick **Box Shadow** and select '<no shadow>' as the shadow. Press **OK** to close the **Box Features Dialog** and return to the Boxes tab of the Diagram Options Dialog. Notice that all the features you specified are now listed in the *Features* list. Click **Apply** within the **Boxes** tab of the Diagram Options dialog. Notice that spouse boxes no longer have a shadow (although other boxes still do) and they have slightly crinkly 'two step' corners.

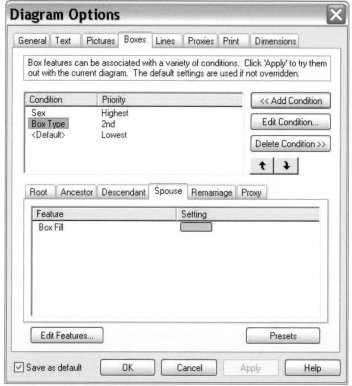

Figure 40 – the Boxes tab of the Diagram Options dialog. The picture shows the features associated with the Box Type condition. In the example, features can be specified for 6 different box types, each of which has its own tab. The Spouse tab is currently selected.

Presets

To get you started, and give you an idea of some of the things you can do, some *presets* have been defined for you. These are complete sets of conditions and

90

associated feature sets. Click on the **Preset** button now and choose 'Generations - Basic' from the list.   Press **OK** to confirm that you wish to replace existing box conditions and features and then press **Apply** to apply the preset to the current diagram. The Root box should still be coloured white, but you should now see that all other boxes are rectangular and coloured by generation. Now try the 'Generations - Ornate' preset. This is the same as the previous one except that each box has bevelled corners and a shadow. Try all the other presets. The 'No Box' preset is handy for getting rid of boxes. The default look is 'Box Types - Ornate'.

You should appreciate that the presets do not do anything that you could not do for yourself. They are just examples. Click on the **Help** button to learn how to add your own conditions and how to control the features that the conditions are associated with. A good exercise is to look at the preset and see if you can work out how they achieve the results they get.

When you have finished experimenting, select the 'Box Types - Ornate' preset once again, and apply it to the current diagram.

The Lines Tab

Diagram Options Dialog

The next tab in the Diagram Options dialog is the **Lines** tab which allows you to control the look and thickness of lines connecting boxes. If you want to control the thickness and colour of lines round boxes, you do this in the **Boxes** tab.

'Crossing Lines' are only used for the horizontal section of lines connecting Ancestors to their parents in All Relatives trees. By default, crossing lines are dotted so that when these lines cross over other lines (which they can do – hence the name) there is no confusion about which is which. However, if you prefer these lines to be solid, you can choose that option here.

Cross Out Marriage Lines for Divorced Couples

By default, Family Historian will put a little cross through the marriage lines of couples who are divorced (determined by the **Marriage Status** field). Dotted marriage lines are used for couples who never married or whose marital status is unknown. You can override these settings in this tab.

Proxy Boxes

The next tab in the Diagram Options dialog is the **Proxies** tab which deals with *Proxy Boxes*. Proxy boxes are a special kind of box that are only used in *All Relatives* trees, and even then, only direct ancestors of the tree root can have them. They are used to show where an ancestor fits in, in amongst their siblings, in the context of the ancestor's own parents' family.

Owing to the way the *All Relatives* tree works, it can happen that a given ancestor's box is located physically a long way from the part of the tree which shows their parents and their siblings. In a situation like that, someone viewing the diagram might look at the parents, wonder who their children were, and find themselves having to follow a long line across the diagram, to find out.   Rather than let this happen, Family Historian allows you to show two boxes for each ancestor. One box (box type *Ancestor*) shows the ancestor above and between the ancestor's children. The other box (box type *Proxy*) shows the ancestor among his or her siblings, below his or her parents.

It is common practice to display proxy boxes with a transparent background and with a dotted line frame as in Figure 41 below, but you don't have to display them like that. The appearance of Proxy boxes is controlled, like the appearance of any other box, in the **Boxes** tab.

 It is also common to show less information in Proxy boxes than you show in other boxes to avoid unnecessary repetition. But again, that's up to you. It is the text scheme (chosen in the **Text** tab) that determines what text goes in to a Proxy box.

It is also common not to show pictures in Proxy boxes, even if you are showing them in other boxes. That is configured in the **Pictures** tab.

The Proxies Tab

Diagram Options Dialog

The display of Proxy boxes is controlled from the **Proxies tab** of the Diagram Options Dialog. If you don't want to use Proxy boxes at all, tick *Never show proxy boxes*. Otherwise, choose the settings you want and Family Historian will build (or rebuild) your diagram accordingly. But your options don't end there. As we will see shortly, you can hide or show any box in any diagram. And that includes Proxy boxes. So if the Proxy tab options don't give you quite the results you hoped for, you can hide unwanted Proxy boxes. You can also unhide ones that were hidden, if you wish.

Press the **Help** button on the Proxy tab to learn more about Proxy boxes and your choices with regard to displaying them.

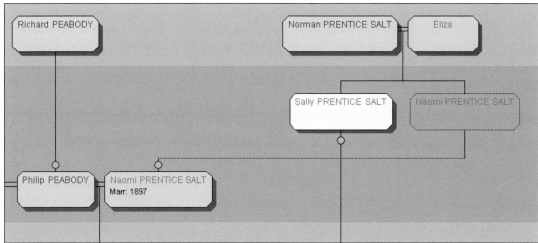

Figure 41 – Part of an All Relatives diagram for Cameron Peabody. Naomi Prentice Salt has 2 boxes. The one on the right is a Proxy box.

The Dimensions Tab

Diagram Options Dialog

The **Print** tab and print options are covered separately in Chapter 11. Beyond the Print tab, the next and last tab of the Diagram Options dialog is the **Dimensions** tab.

The size of any given box is mainly determined by the text scheme (which in turn determines font sizes) and the amount and type of data in the records of the Individuals in the diagram. Other factors include pictures and picture settings, and text margins. The corner size and the text area indent (box shape features, set in the Boxes tab) will also affect the box size and shape. None of these things are set in the Dimensions tab. But almost every other size and dimension in a diagram is set here. This means that you have precise control over how Family Historian lays out diagrams. Dimensions are set using your preferred unit of measurement (see **Preferences**).

To illustrate the effect of changing dimensions, switch briefly back to the **Text** tab, select the "All Events and Attributes, and Rec Notes" text scheme and click **Apply**. Cameron Peabody's box is now tall and thin. Switch back to the **Dimensions** tab and set the **Maximum box width** to 4" (or the equivalent in your preferred unit of measurement if you don't use inches). Click **Apply**. Now Cameron Peabody's box is much shorter, but also much wider.

Click on the **Help** button for an explanation of all the various dimensions. Take a moment to click on the **More Dimensions** button and view these too (click the **Help** button in that dialog for more help with these).

Finally, back in the **Dimensions** tab, click on the **Installation Settings** button to restore the installation (default) settings. Switch back to the Text tab and select the "Birth, Marr, Death" text scheme once again, and click **Apply**.

The Diagram Background

By default, an All Relatives diagram has a striped background, with each stripe corresponding to a generation. What if you want a different kind of background? As an exercise we will set the background now to plain white.

Steps

1. Select the **General** tab of the Diagram Options Dialog. Find the **Background** field and set it to 'One Colour'. Click **Apply** and observe that the background is now all grey. There should also be faint thin lines where the stripe edges had been. These are the boundary lines. We will get rid of them in a moment.
2. Click on the **Sundry Colours** button on the same tab. The **Colours Dialog** appears. Select 'Background if one colour' in the *Items* list. Then select the colour white in the displayed set of Basic Colours and click on the << **Select** button. You may be surprised to see that the background colour of the diagram changes to white *immediately*. This is just a convenient feature of the Sundry Colours dialog. Whatever colours you select are immediately displayed in the current diagram. However, this is only to allow you to see what the effect of your colour selection is. If you clicked **Cancel** at this point, the colours would immediately revert to what they had been. Do not click **Cancel**. Click **OK** to close the Colours Dialog. The colour selection has now been applied.
3. To get rid of the boundary lines, set the **Boundary Lines** field (still in the **General** tab of the Diagram Options Dialog) to 'No Boundaries' and click **Apply**. The boundary lines disappear and you now have a white background.

*Tip: If you wanted a plain white background for a print out of your diagram, there is no need to do any of the above. By default, the background of a diagram doesn't print anyway (this is configurable in the **Print** tab using the **Print Background** tick box).*

Background Picture

It can be effective to display a tree over a faded background picture. To do this, find the Background field again, and this time choose the 'Picture' option. A dialog appears to let you choose your preferred background picture, and how faded you want it to be. You can also specify how you want it laid out. As always, experiment with the options until you find the look you want.

Remember to tick Print Background in the Print tab of Diagram Options if you want the picture to appear when the diagram is printed.

Background Texture

Instead of a picture, you may prefer your diagram to have a textured background or pattern. You can do this too. Find an image which gives the look you want when the image is repeated. Then choose this image as your background picture, and select 'Tile' as the **Layout**.

Sundry Colours

Text colours can be set in text schemes (see the **Text** tab). They can also be overridden as a box feature (see the **Boxes** tab). All other colours relating to boxes are set in the **Boxes** tab. That still leaves several other colours that are set from the **Sundry Colours dialog**. As we have just seen, background colours are set from there. If you are using background stripes, you can set the stripes colours. If you are using a single background colour, you can set the 'one colour'. The two other colours for backgrounds – 'background if anc. colouring' and 'background if desc. colouring' – are only applicable if the Background field is 'Depends on diagram type'. In that case, they affect the appearance of the Ancestors diagram, the Descendants diagram, and the Ancestors and Descendants Diagram (i.e. all diagrams except the *All Relatives* diagram). Click on the **Help** button in the **General** tab and look at the help for the **Background** field for an explanation of this setting.

Duplicates   If you still have an All Relatives diagram open for Cameron Peabody you should be able to see that both Cameron Peabody and Jean Anderson occurred twice in that diagram. This happened because the diagram show's Cameron Peabody's relatives, and Jean Anderson is related to him in 2 ways: she was his wife, and she was his cousin.

Where an Individual has more than one box in a diagram, the boxes are called 'duplicate boxes'. Given that in practice, individuals are frequently related to one another in more than one way, it is necessary to devise a strategy for handling this in diagrams. It might seem desirable, at all costs, to arrange the diagram so that even if people are related in more than one way, you still never get more than one box per person. If you are lucky with your data, this approach can sometimes give good results. However, frequently the results of such an approach are not good. The problem is that in order to be able to arrange things so that each person gets only one box, you have to be prepared to make a great many compromises on other important features of diagrams. It may be necessary, for example, to separate spouses so that they are nowhere near each other on the diagram. Parents may end up far removed from their children. Siblings may be separated from siblings; and siblings and spouses may need to be shown in the wrong sequence. The end result is often that diagrams become a complicated mess – difficult to make sense of, and unappealing to look at. That is why this strategy was not adopted with Family Historian.

Linking   The strategy adopted for dealing with duplicates, is not to try to eliminate them all.
Ribbons   Instead, Family Historian provides features for automatically detecting duplicates wherever they occur. Duplicated branches are closed off to eliminate all unnecessary duplication. Then each occurrence of remaining duplicated individuals or families are linked together using a curved coloured ribbon which flows across the diagram. If an Individual has three boxes on a diagram, all three boxes will be linked with a single curving ribbon that flows through them.

Family Historian supports two kinds of ribbon links: ribbons linking individuals and ribbons linking families. The main difference between them is that Family links have an oval at each end, positioned between and below the spouses in a family, and connected to the two spouses. Individual links have no oval, and connect directly to the Individual boxes.

Duplicate options are configured in the Duplicate Options Dialog (see Figure 42 below). To open the Duplicate Options Dialog, tick the **Check for Duplicates** box in the **General** tab of the Diagram Options dialog (if not already ticked) and then click on the **Options** button next to it. By default, Family Historian will use Family links in preference to Individual links where possible. This is recommended to keep the number of linking ribbons to a minimum.

A number of different colours are used for ribbons, allocated more or less at random, to make it easier to follow ribbons across the diagram.

The Duplicate Options Dialog provides a number of options for controlling how duplicates are handled and how duplicate links are displayed. Click on the **Help** button for more details.

Check For   The options set in the Duplicate Options Dialog affect how duplicates are detected
Duplicates   and handled when you first create a new dialog. They will also be applied if you insert a tree into an existing diagram. However, they will not prevent you expanding branches (using the expansion buttons) to explore branches, and thereby finding, or 'creating' more duplicates. When you insert a tree, you might choose to first disable duplicate checking if you wanted, initially at least, duplicated branches to not be closed off. If you do this, you may wish to re-enable, and re-apply

94

duplicate checking, to an existing diagram. You can do this at any time by clicking on **Check For Duplicates...** on the Diagram menu.

Find Duplicates

The ribbons make it easy to locate duplicates visually, but there is another way. If you are viewing a box for an Individual and want to find other boxes for him or her, select the box and click **Find Next Box for Individual** on the Diagram menu. This will switch the selection to the next instance of that box on the diagram. A quick way of doing this is just to press the **F3** key.

Find in Diagram

What if you want to find someone in a large diagram and you don't know where there are any boxes for him or her? When you are viewing a large diagram, it is not always easy to locate a particular person just by scrolling. If you know which person you are after, the quick way to find them is to use the **Find in Diagram** command on the **Edit** menu. This command opens a **Selector** dialog. Find the Individual in the Selector dialog and then add them to the right-hand side.

The **Find in Diagram** command can be used within a diagram to find a person in that diagram, or it can be used in from any other window, to find a person in the most recently-viewed diagram. This is useful because if you can see the person you want in another window such as the Focus Window, you can click on their record to select them. Then if you click on **Find in Diagram**, when the Selector dialog opens, that person will be pre-selected, so you just need to click **OK** to find them in the Diagram Window.

If there is more than one box for the person in question, the command will find the first only. You can then press **F3**, if you wish, to see if there are any others.

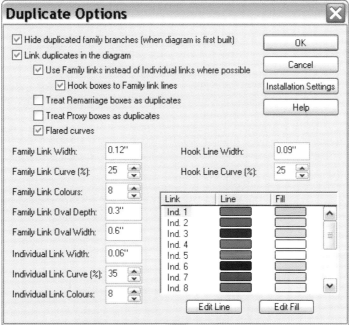

Figure 42 – the Duplicate Options Dialog

Marking Boxes

It sometimes happens that you want to mark a particular box on a diagram for some reason. Perhaps you want to scroll elsewhere and want to make sure that the box you are looking at now is easy to find again. Or if you are checking some aspect of boxes for whatever reason, you might use a mark to mark the boxes you have already checked.

By default, marked boxes are displayed with a bright yellow background, but you can configure this using *Sundry Colours* (see the **General tab** of the Diagram

95

Options dialog).

The easy way to mark one or more boxes is to select them the boxes[16] and press **Ctrl-M** (that is, press-and-hold the **Ctrl** key and then press **M**). Press **Ctrl-M** again to unmark.

The **Select & Marks** menu (off the Diagram menu) has various options relating to marking boxes (as well as selecting them). If you can't remember the **Ctrl-M** combination, you can use **Mark/Unmark Boxes** menu command to do the same thing. You can also **Clear All Marks** and **Select Marked Boxes**.

Set/Clear Marks Using Query   We have not yet looked at queries, but as we shall see when we do, they can be a useful tool for analysis. Suppose you had a diagram of ancestors and you wanted to see which of them had died of a stroke. You could include the cause-of-death in the Text Scheme easily enough, but if you had a large number of ancestors, it might not be easy to see which of them had had what. A better approach would be to use a query to automatically mark all of the ancestors in the diagram who had died of a stroke.

Diagram Orientation   By default, diagrams are oriented top-down. But they can also be oriented left-to-right, right-to-left, or bottom-up. This is set using the **Orientation** field in the **General** tab of the Diagram Options dialog – see Figure 36 above.

Standard Diagram Types   When Family Historian is installed, it comes with a set of pre-configured standard diagrams. Four of these standard diagrams (the default set) are the 'core' diagrams that have buttons on the application toolbar. To access all standard diagrams, see the **Standard Diagram Types** menu, which is on the **View** menu.

Diagrams For Couples   All Family Historian diagrams (except fan charts and the Everyone diagram) can have either an Individual or a couple as diagram root. If you use the **Standard Diagram Types** menu to open a diagram – even one of the 'core' diagrams – a dialog box will be displayed allowing you to confirm who you wish to be the diagram root. At this point, you can also specify if you want the root to be an Individual or a couple. When you choose 'couple', you have to select the couple in question by selecting the Family record in which they figure as spouses or parents.

When you use the 4 toolbar buttons for the core diagrams ⟦ icons ⟧ to open a diagram, you have to have previously selected the diagram root. Ordinarily you will select an *Individual* record; but if you want a couple to be the root, you must previously have selected their *Family* record. For convenience, if you select two boxes in a diagram, Family Historian will interpret this as a selection of their Family record, if they are a couple. For example, we will display an *All Relatives* diagram for Cameron Peabody, and his second wife, Jean Clare Anderson.

Steps

1. Display an *All Relatives* diagram for Cameron Peabody. Ensure that the **Spouses in Own Boxes** button ⟦ icon ⟧ is checked).
2. Click on Cameron Peabody's node to select him, if not already selected.
3. Hold the **Ctrl** key down and click on Jean Clare Anderson's node, to select her too. Release the **Ctrl** key. Both Cameron Peabody and Jean Clare Anderson should be selected – and no-one else. Now click on the **View All Relatives** toolbar button ⟦ icon ⟧.
4. A new diagram appears. Notice that both Cameron Peabody and Jean Clare Anderson are displayed in white – the colour of the root node. The data displayed is similar to the data displayed before, but there is an equal balance between the 2 root boxes, and thus a slightly different emphasis to the previous

---

[16] See *Select Multiple Boxes in a Diagram* in Chapter 8 if you can't remember how to do this.

diagram which focussed primarily on Cameron Peabody.

Select Family Record in Focus Window

Selecting a Family record for a couple in the **Focus Window** is easy – just click on the **Marriage Box** (see Chapter 1) for the couple in the *Spouses & Children* or *Parents & Siblings* tabs. With this selection, if you click on any of the 4 core diagram toolbar buttons, the displayed diagram will have that couple as the diagram root.

Select Family Record in Records Window

You can also selecting a Family record in the **Records Window**.

Steps

1. Switch now to the **Records Window**.
2. Locate Cameron Peabody's record. Expand his record. You should be able to see one field labelled 'Parents family' and two labelled 'Spouse family'. You can see that "... of Philip PEABODY and Naomi PRENTICE SALT" references a family record (as do the other two) because of the presence of the family record icon ▦ next to the text. Select "... of Philip PEABODY and Naomi PRENTICE SALT" and click on the **View Ancestors** button ⛓ on the main toolbar. A diagram is displayed showing the ancestors of both Philip Peabody and Naomi Prentice Salt. Leaving them both selected, click on the button for each of the other 3 diagram types in turn.
3. Repeat step 2 for Cameron's two spouse families. Finally click on **Close all Non-Essential Windows** on the **Window** menu, to close all the Diagram Windows you opened.

Box Alignment

Select Cameron Peabody now and click on **Pedigree Chart – All Gens** on the **Standard Diagram Types** menu (under the **View** menu). In the dialog box that appears, confirm that the **Tree Root Type** is 'Individual' and that the **Root Person** is Cameron Peabody, and press OK.

We will use this diagram to illustrate the role of the **Alignment** field in the **General** tab of the **Diagram Options** dialog. Open Diagram Options now and experiment changing the Alignment field value from right to left, clicking **Apply** each time. You should see that boxes which had been aligned on one side, switch to being aligned on the other side.

Ancestors & Descendants trees have additional alignment options, 'Inner' and 'Outer', so that, for example, ancestors can be left-aligned while descendants are right-aligned.

The Everyone Diagram

The *Everyone* diagram (see **Standard Diagram Types**) shows everyone in the current family tree file, and all of their relationships. It does this by creating a diagram which has multiple trees in it, all stacked up one above the other. You will almost always want to move the trees around, to get a better-looking layout (see Chapter 10 for how to do this).

Fan Charts

To open a fan chart, click on **Fan Charts** on the **View** menu. You will be able to choose the chart type (Half, Quarter or Full), the number of generations, the text contents and other aspects of the required fan chart. Fan charts are displayed in the Diagram Window. Double-click on a 'box' within the fan chart to view the Property Box for the person in question (or right-click on it and select 'Properties').

You can configure the contents of fan charts to show any information you want. Fan charts are also dynamic – that is, if you change relevant details of a person's record (e.g. a person's name), the fan chart will update immediately to show the new information. Creating or deleting relationships does not cause a fan chart to update. To force a fan chart to update in this case, right-click on it and click **Refresh** on the dropdown menu that appears (or click **Refresh** on the **Windows** menu). If you choose **Format** from the same dropdown menu, you can also

97

configure other aspects of the fan charts appearance. If you choose **Ungroup,** from the **Grouping** submenu of the same dropdown menu, you will find that you can pull a fan chart to pieces and format the pieces separately, to create particular effects, if you wish to do that.

Later we will see that you can combine fan charts and trees in one diagram.

Create Custom Diagram Types

We saw earlier how you can create custom text schemes. You can also create custom types of diagram. Suppose, for example, that you regularly want to be able to use a diagram to view census details that you have accumulated about a given person's immediate family. Lct us say that you want to able to select a given person and click on one menu command to see a diagram showing their parents and grandparents, uncles, aunts, cousins, siblings and children. And for each person, you want to see what census data you have accumulated about them.

To do this, all you need do is create a single example of the kind of diagram you want. In the imagined case you would use an *All Relatives* diagram limited to 2 generations up, and 1 generation down, from the root. You would choose an appropriate text scheme (custom or standard) and decide on the diagram orientation, the look and style of the boxes, and other details.

Having created your example, click on **Diagram** > **Save Diagram As** > **Custom Diagram Type**, and give the new diagram type a name. Thereafter, to open a diagram of the new type, select the Individual (or couple) that you wish to be the root of the new diagram, and select the new menu from the **Custom Diagram Types** submenu, which is accessible from the **View** menu.

When a new custom diagram type is created, not all details of the current diagram are saved as part of the new diagram type. Any information which you have to specify when you open the diagram (such as the new root) is not saved. Also, if you insert any additional trees into your example diagram, these will also not become part of the new custom diagram type. But any other diagram elements – such as text boxes or arrows – that you insert into the diagram, will be saved as part of the diagram type. So you could use text boxes as floating diagram titles if you wanted to, for example. You could even create a new custom type of fan chart if you wanted to.

We will look at some of the additional (non-tree) elements that you can insert into diagrams in Chapter 10.

Do not confuse creating a new type of diagram with simply saving the current diagram to a file. The latter is discussed in Chapter 10.

Modify Custom Diagram Types

Effectively, you modify a custom diagram type by re-creating it. But the easy way to do this is to open an instance of the diagram. Then open the Diagram Options dialog and make whatever changes you need to make to it. Finally, click on **Diagram** > **Save Diagram As** > **Custom Diagram Type**, as you did when you first created it. You will find that the diagram's name has been remembered in the **Custom Diagram Name** field; so you can leave that unchanged and click **OK** to save changes.

Delete Custom Diagram Types

To delete a custom diagram, choose the **Delete Custom Diagram** command at the foot of the **Custom Diagram Types** menu. Select the diagram you want to delete from the list that appears and click the **Delete** button to delete it.

Re-use the Diagram Window

When you select a record and click on any of the diagram buttons to open a new working diagram, Family Historian will normally open a new Diagram Window to display it. However, you can specify that you would prefer Family Historian to re-use an existing Diagram Window, rather than opening a new one, if you wish. This is specified in the Navigation pane of Preferences.

If you have opted to re-use Diagram Windows, and you have a working diagram that you definitely want to keep, you can ensure that Family Historian will not re-use this particular Diagram Window by locking it. To do this, either click on the

Lock Window button on the toolbar when the relevant window is active, or right-click on the icon for the relevant window in the Navigation Bar, and select **Lock Window (prevent reuse)** from the dropdown menu that appears.

The issue of locking does not apply to all diagrams. Once a diagram as been saved to a file it is no longer considered a working diagram – it is now categorised as a *chart*. Diagram Windows displaying charts are never re-used. You cannot lock a chart, and you never need to. In effect, charts are *always* locked.

There is no limit to the number of Diagram windows that you can have open at any one time. Each open window will have an icon on the Navigation Bar. It will also have a menu command (for switching to it) at the bottom of the Windows menu.

Just as you can open multiple Diagram windows, you can also open multiple Multimedia, Report and Book windows too. And these too can be locked, in the same way that you can lock a Diagram Window. But 'locking' a window has no effect if you aren't re-using windows of that type (which, again, is specified in the Navigation pane of Preferences).

Unlike these other window types, you can only have one Focus Window, one Records Window and one Query Window. These are always re-used and can never be locked.

10 Smart Trees and Wall Charts

Diagrams in Family Historian, as we have seen, are tightly integrated into the program, and are used for a number of purposes – such as browsing, editing, and navigation. But another very important role for diagrams is for making wall charts.

A 'wall chart' at its simplest, is a diagram that you print off and stick on the wall. But it could just as well be an image file that you email to a relative. If you are planning to put together a chart to print or send to others, many of the features that we have already looked at – including most of the features we looked at in the previous chapter – will be relevant. But the likelihood is that you will have additional requirements over and above the requirements we have looked at so far. You may want to add titles, text, annotations, arrows, lines, boxes and other details to your chart. You may want to add pictures (over and above any pictures in boxes). You may want to add additional trees or fan charts. You may want to hide some individuals, and branches, and enlarge the boxes of others to emphasize them. You may want to move boxes, branches and trees around to make best use of space. You may want to change aspects of the appearance of particular boxes. You may want to distinctively pick out lines connecting particular boxes, or entire branches. You will certainly want to save your chart in a file, so you can work on and improve it over time.

In this chapter we will look at how you can do all of these things, and more.

Open Tutorial File

We will illustrate some of the things you can do with charts using one of the tutorial files: "Tutorial – Chapter 10". This file contains a new group of fictitious people. From the **Project Window**, click on the **More Tasks** button, and then in the dropdown menu click on **Samples**, and finally **Tutorial – Chapter 10**. The file opens and Anthony Munro is displayed as the focus person in the Focus Window.

The *Everyone* Diagram

Now open the *Everyone* diagram. To view this diagram, click on **View > Standard Diagram Types > Everyone**. Click on the **View Whole Diagram** button ⚙ now on the main toolbar, to view the whole thing. You will see that the diagram contains three trees positioned vertically, one above the other. The topmost tree is the biggest. It is linked to the next tree down by a duplicate family link (see *Duplicates* and related sections in the previous chapter).

The *Everyone* diagram adds enough trees to a diagram to show everyone in the file, and all of their relationships. The trees are always stacked up vertically one above the other. Later we will see how you can move trees round and put them wherever you want.

Restore Installation Settings

Before continuing, to ensure consistency with this book you should use default options in your diagrams, for now – that is, the 'installation settings'.

Steps

1. Click on the Diagram menu, then Settings, and then Restore Installation Settings.
2. If for some reason you wish to preserve your default settings, click 'No' when asked if you wish to use the installation settings as default settings in the future. Otherwise, click 'Yes'.

Diagram Statistics To confirm that the *Everyone* diagram is showing all the Individuals in the file, click now on **Diagram Statistics** on the **Diagram** menu. In the Diagram Statistics dialog the first line gives the number of boxes (50) and the second gives the number of Individuals (48). The discrepancy is because 2 Individuals have duplicate boxes.

The Diagram Statistics dialog has other useful information such as the number of pages, the current scaling, the size that the diagram will be when printed, and more.

File Statistics Now click on **File Statistics** on the **File** menu and confirm that the number of Individual records in the current file is indeed 48. The File Statistics dialog shows the count of all records, and also tells you the name and location of the current GEDCOM file, which can sometimes be useful.

Open All Relatives Diagram Back in the *Everyone* Diagram, click on Michael Smith Munro's box (right at the top) and click on the **View All Relatives** button . When you do this, the new diagram opens in a new diagram window. Open **Diagram Options** and set **Generations Up** and **Generations Down** to 'All'. Press **OK** to close Diagram Options again. (Figure 43 shows a part of the resulting diagram). This diagram only shows 35 Individuals, as only 35 Individuals in the file count as relatives of Michael Munro. In Family Historian, a son-in-law counts as a relative (by marriage); but your son-in-law's parents and his other ancestors are not counted as relatives of yours. So, for example, none of Jonathan Hodge's ancestors count as relatives of Michael Munro.

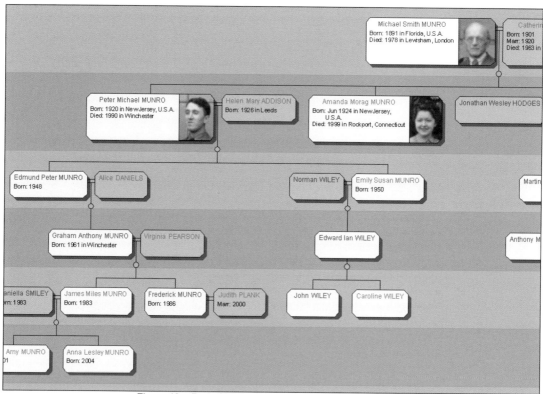

Figure 43 – Part of Michael Munro's All Relatives diagram.

Enable Moving/ Resizing Now select Amanda Morag Munro's box (she is Michael Munro's 2nd child). Let us suppose that you wish to enlarge her box. Before you can move or resize any boxes, you must enable moving/resizing. To do this click on **Enable Moving/Resizing** on the **Diagram** menu, or click on the *Enable Moving/Resizing* Button on the toolbar. Do this now. When you do this, the eight little selection boxes ('selection markers') round the edges of Amanda Munro's box change from blue to white.

Also, where the line going up from Amanda Munro's box meets the horizontal child bar connecting her to her siblings, there is now a tiny little white diamond (see Figure 44 below). Finally, a dialog appears called the Movement Control Box (see Figure 50 below).

Figure 44 – Moving/Resizing has just been enabled. Notice the white selection boxes called 'selection markers', and the tiny white diamond where the vertical line going up from Amanda Munro's box meets the horizontal line (the 'child bar') above it.

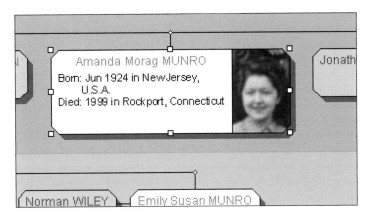

Resize Box   To resize Amanda Munro's box, click-and-drag on any of the little white selection markers. For the purposes of this example, make sure when you do this that you make her box taller as well as wider. Increase the size until it is at least twice the height it had been, comfortably overlapping the boxes below. When you release the mouse button, notice that the entire row has become deeper and all rows below her box have moved down.

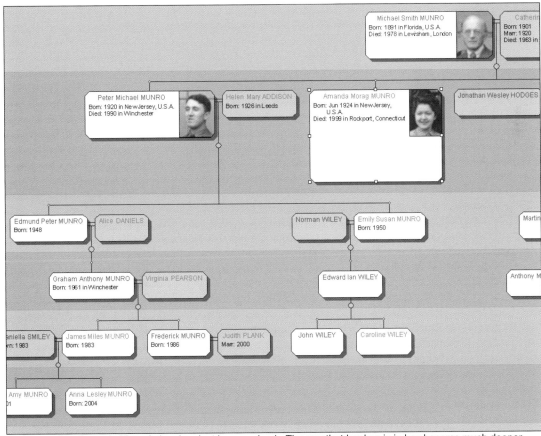

Figure 45 – Amanda Morag's box has just been resized. The row that her box is in has become much deeper. Compare the size of the background stripe with Figure 43. The boxes in rows below have all moved down.

Box Size Affects Row Size

Now right-click on Amanda's box. A dropdown menu appears with a number of options. The first five menu items are *box states*, three of which are currently ticked, including **Box Size Affects Row Size** and **Attach to Row**. The former means that the row that Amanda's box belongs to, is automatically made big enough to fit her box. It means that if her box is made so tall that it becomes the tallest box in the row, the row must be made bigger too. All boxes have **Box Size Affects Row Size** set by default. So the depth of the row is determined by the tallest box in the row – which in this case is Amanda's box.

Now click on **Box Size Affects Row Size** to untick it. When you do this **Attach to Row** is automatically unticked too. Now the size of Amanda's box no longer affects the size of the row that her box belongs to, and the row shrinks back to its previous depth. Her box now extends down below its row. And there has been a sideways adjustment so that her older brother Peter's descendants do not overlap her box. See Figure 46 below.

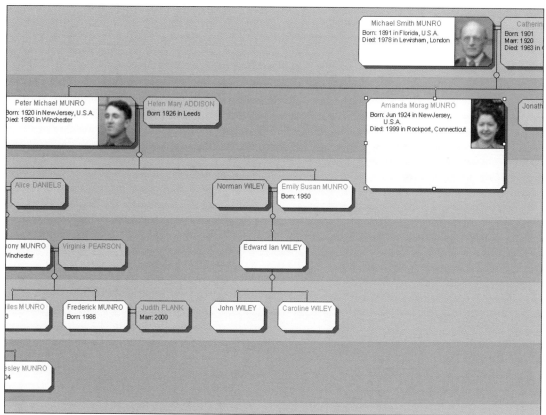

Figure 46 – **Box Size Affects Row Size** has been unticked on Amanda's box. The row that her box belongs to has shrunk back to its previous size, and her box now extends down below the row.

Autosize Box

Right-click once more on Amanda's box. This time tick **Autosize Box**. By default, every box has this box state enabled; but it is automatically disabled (unticked) when you manually resize a box as we did just now. When you enable **Autosize Box** on Amanda's box, you should see that it snaps back to its previous size so that once again it fits within its row. It is no longer competing for space with Peter Munro's descendants, so they move back to where they had been, and the diagram once again looks like Figure 43.

Five Types of Drag-and-Move Actions

Clicking on the **Enable Moving/Resizing** button ⊕ enables (as the name suggests) both resizing *and* moving. Family Historian supports five different ways of moving all or parts of trees by a click-and-drag action. The five types are:

- Box Move
- Bar Move

- Fixed Point Move
- Tree Move
- Everything Move

We will look at each in turn.

Box Move   Click now on Amanda's box itself and holding the button down, drag downwards. If you hadn't enabled moving/resizing, this would be an *add-relative* action (see Chapter 8); but now it is a *move-box* action.

As you drag down, notice that other boxes jump sideways to get out of the way. If you drag slowly you will see that they move apart to let Amanda's box get past, but will move back the moment there is space for them to do so. They always leave a minimum gap between boxes (you can adjust these gaps in the **Dimensions** tab of the **Diagram Options Dialog**), so no box ever comes close enough to actually touch Amanda's box.

Drag Amanda's box downwards until it is roughly in line with Edward Wiley's box, and then release the mouse button. Now the diagram should look roughly like Figure 47 below.

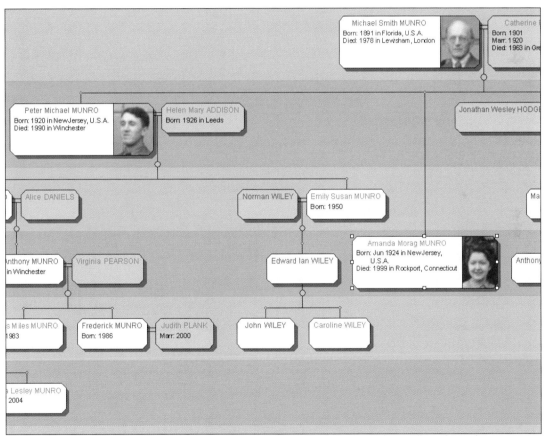

Figure 47 – Amanda's box has been dragged downwards. The other boxes have adjusted to make room.

Include Box in Row   Now right-click again on Amanda's box. Notice that both **Box Size Affects Row Size** and **Attach to Row** are unticked (in fact all box states for this box are unticked at present, except **AutoSize Box**). What do you think would happen if you ticked either of these states now?

The answer is that nothing happens if you tick **Box Size Affects Row Size** because Amanda's box – even allowing for gaps above and below – is not taller than the row

105

that it came from. But if you tick **Attach to Row** you will see a big change. Do this now: tick them both in turn[17]. Now the row that Amanda's box belongs to suddenly becomes much deeper until it extends below where her box is now. And all rows and boxes in generations below hers have to move down. This is shown in Figure 48 below. Notice that once again, the boxes don't just move down. They also close in to make the most of the available space.

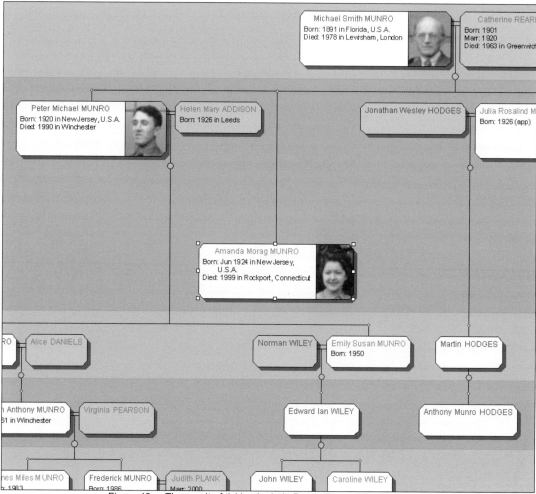

Figure 48 – The result of ticking Include Box in Row on Amanda' box.

Box Move is a Branch Move

Right-click on Amanda's box and untick **Attach to Row** so that the diagram once again looks as it did in Figure 47.

When you clicked-and-dragged on Amanda's box to move it down, this is called a *Box Move* in Family Historian. You can click-and-drag on any box to do a box move. When you do this, you will not move just that one box but its whole branch. If the box is a *descendant* box type, you will move all of its descendant boxes too, and any spouse boxes attached to that box. Moving a spouse box is like moving a descendant box – it works the same way. Move an *ancestor* box is the same again, only this time you move all ancestors of the box, as well as any spouses.

To illustrate the above, click now on Norman Wiley's box and drag downwards, passing Amanda Munro's box, till his box is roughly in line with Anna Lesley Munro's box. When you did this you moved not just Norman Wiley's box (a spouse box), but also Emily Susan Munro's box (his wife) and all of their

---

[17] 'Ticking X' in this context is a convenient short-hand for "right-click on the box and click on the X menu command, so that it becomes ticked".

descendants. Once again, other boxes moved out of the way as needed to make the best use of available space.

Align With Others in Same Row
Right-click on Norman Wiley's box and tick **Align with Others in Same Row**. This state is set by default on all boxes, but becomes automatically cleared when you manually move a box. When you re-enable it, you should find that Norman Wiley, his spouse and all his descendants spring back to where they had been and once again the diagram looks like Figure 47.

Box Moves Are Outwards Only
When you dragged Amanda Munro's box downwards, you had to drag it downwards (or back up). You couldn't drag it sideways. Box moves are *outwards* only (or more accurately – *outwards or back*). If your diagram has top-down orientation, you can only drag a descendant box downwards (or back); and you can drag an ancestor box upwards (or back). If you were using left-right orientation, you could only drag a descendant box rightwards (or back); and you could only drag an ancestor box leftwards (or back).

Bar Moves
We saw earlier that when we enabled moving and resizing by clicking on the **Enable Moving/Resizing** button ⊕ tiny little white diamonds appeared on the horizontal child bar above Amanda Munro. In fact, *all* horizontal child bars have them. You can click-and-drag on any of these little white diamonds, and when you do so, you are doing a *Bar Move*. Actually you don't have to click-and-drag on the diamonds themselves. You can click-and-drag anywhere on any of the horizontal bars. However, suppose a parent had only one child, as Jonathan Hodges

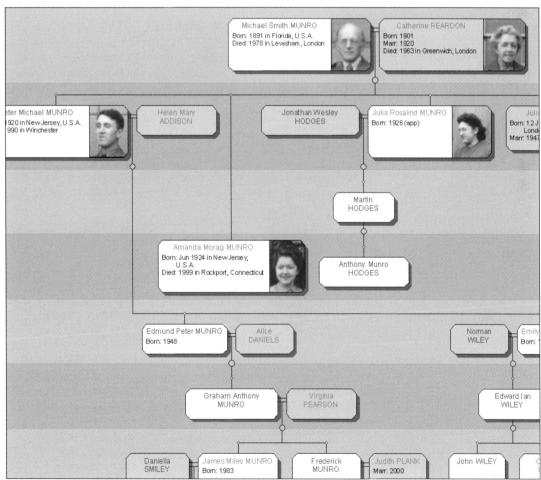

Figure 49 – The results of a Bar Move.

and Julia Munro do, for example. In that case, there is no horizontal bar to click on. But there is still a tiny white diamond and you can still click-and-drag on that.

107

You can do bar moves not just with descendant branches, but also with ancestor branches too. The little white diamonds appear on the horizontal line linking an ancestor to his or her parents (the *parent bar*) and you click-and-drag on that to do a bar move.

To illustrate how bar moves work, click now anywhere on the horizontal child bar, just below Peter Munro's box linking all of his children. Keeping the button pressed, drag downwards until you are comfortably below Amanda Munro's box. Then continue dragging, but to the *right* this time, until Alice Daniels' box is more or less below Amanda Munro's box. The results should look roughly like Figure 49 above.

Sideways Bar Moves
When you move a bar, you move all branches attached to that bar. And like a box move, you move it outwards and back. But unlike a box move, you can also move it sideways as well. And as with all moves (and all box resizes), other boxes and branches within the same tree will automatically move out of the way and make the best use of available space.

Box Moves Work with Multiple Selection
You can only move one bar at a time, but you can move any number of boxes at the same time. Simply select them all using any of the usual techniques for selecting multiple boxes, then click on any one of them to drag them all. The only restriction on this is that they must either all be ancestor type boxes, or none of them can be ancestor type boxes. They cannot be a mixture of ancestors and non-ancestors.

The Movement Control Box
When you clicked on the **Enable Moving/Resizing** button ⊕ the **Movement Control Box** appeared (see Figure 50 below). This dialog box is always open when moving and resizing is enabled. The **Movement Control Box** is another of those dialog boxes, like the Property Box, that doesn't prevent you doing things in other parts of the program, when it is open.

Figure 50 – The Movement Control Box

Fixed Point Moves
When you first enable moving and resizing, the default mode is *Box and Bar* (see Figure 50). In this mode, any click-and-drag on a box is a *Box Move*. And *Bar Moves* are also enabled.

To enable *Fixed Point Moves* click on **Fixed point** in the Movement Control Box. Do this now. When you do this, the little selection markers continue to be white, and you can still click-and-drag on a selection marker to resize a box. But the tiny white diamonds have gone. You cannot do either Box Moves or Bar Moves in this mode.

Click on Anthony Edward Munro's box and click on the **Set** button in the Movement Control Box. When you do this, a thick orange frame surrounds Anthony Munro's box (see Figure 51 below). It has been marked as a *fixed point*. Now when you click and drag on other boxes, they will move relative to that fixed point.

Separating Spouses

Try this now: click-and-drag Julia Fish's box to the left. And click-and-drag Susan Dowling's box to the right. Notice that, as always, the rest of the diagram automatically adjusts itself to accommodate the change you are making. Notice that as well as separating them you can also drag them back together again. Do that now with Anthony's spouses – drag them back next to him.

Separating Siblings

Now find Julia Munro's box (Anthony Munro's older sister). Zoom back and scroll if you need to. You will remember from Chapter 3 that pressing-and-holding the space bar switches you momentarily into Grabber mode ([image]) so that you can then click-and-drag anywhere on the diagram to move the whole diagram. It's a very useful technique so worth remembering, and it works even if you are moving-and-resizing. Try it now to reposition the diagram so that you easily see Julia Munro's box. Try to arrange things so that you can still see Anthony Munro's box too.

Now click-and-drag Julia Munro's box to the left. If Julia had had younger siblings, they would have been pushed left too. Now drag her box back.

Now try it again but this time try clicking-and-dragging on her spouse or child or grandchild. Notice that it doesn't make any difference which you click-and-drag on. The whole of Julia's branch moves together.

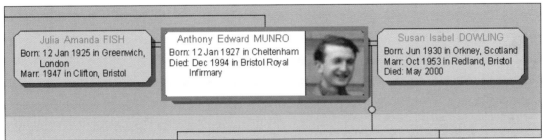

Figure 51 – The thick red frame round Anthony Munro's box shows that it has been set as a fixed point. Clicking-and-dragging on either of his spouses will move them away from him (or back)

Separating Entire Branches

We've already seen that you can use fixed point moves to drag spouses away from each other, or back towards each other. And you can do the same thing with siblings. But it works just as well with cousins too. In fact you can set a fixed point in any box in any branch, and drag entire neighbouring branches away from, or back towards, the first branch. Try this now.

Find Caroline Wiley's box (2nd bottom row) and make it a fixed point – that is, select her box, and then click on the **Set** button in the Movement Control Box. You can only ever have one fixed point at a time, so setting a new one cancels the previous one. Now click on any box in the branch to the left (e.g. Daniella Smiley, Carolyn Munro, Frederick Munro, etc). Notice that it doesn't make any difference which you pick, you can drag the whole branch leftwards, or back towards the fixed point.

We have illustrated fixed point dragging with descendant branches; but it works just as well with ancestor branches too.

*Tip: A quick way to set a fixed point is to press-and-hold the **Alt** key on your keyboard while clicking on a box. As long as moving/resizing is enabled this will make the box a fixed point.*

Cancelling Fixed Points

You can cancel a fixed point by clicking on the background of the diagram when the Alt key is held down. This will switch you back to *Box and Bar* mode. Alternatively, if you switch to any other Drag-and-Move mode in the Movement Control Box (see Figure 50 above), or if you disable moving/resizing by closing the

Movement Control Box, or by unticking **Enable Moving/Resizing** in the Diagram menu, this will also automatically cancel the current fixed point if there is one.

Tree Move So we have looked at 3 kinds of drag-move action: box, bar and fixed point. The 4th kind is tree move. Click on **Tree** in the Movement Control Box, and then click-and-drag on any box in the diagram. When you do this, the entire tree moves. As the current diagram only contains one tree, you are (in this case at least) effectively moving the entire diagram. If you have a diagram that contains multiple trees, you can move each one of them separately, using a tree move.

Move Everything & Scaling The last kind of drag-move action is the **Everything** move. When you move *everything* in a diagram, what you are really doing is moving the whole diagram in relation to the printed page. This topic will be covered in Chapter 11.

You can also use the Movement Control Box to adjust the *scale* of a diagram. This too will be discussed in Chapter 11.

Tip: If you click on **Everything** as a drag-and-move action in the Movement Control Box, you will find that Family Historian insists on switching to show page boundaries. We will look at this in Chapter 11, but for now, if you want to revert to not showing page boundaries, untick the **Show Page Boundaries** button on the Diagram toolbar.

Shift Spouses The current spouse layout option puts a man between both of this spouses if he has two, as Anthony Munro has. You can choose a different spouse layout option for the whole diagram in the *General* tab of the Diagram Options dialog. Or you could simply shift the spouses around on the diagram.

Select Anthony Munro and click on the left of the topmost pair of **Shift Box** buttons labelled 'Spouse': [«] (the 'left shift spouse button'). That moves Anthony to the left of both of his spouses. Now click twice on the right shift spouse button [»] to move him to the right of both of them.

Now click on Julia Fish and click again on the right shift spouse button. Notice that she now has a little '1' to the right of her box, and Susan Dowling has a little '2' next to hers. By default, spouses are numbered if they are shown out-of-sequence. But you can prevent this if you wish by unticking **Number out-of-sequence spouses** in the **General** tab of the Diagram Options dialog.

Using the shift spouse buttons you can arrange spouses in any order you like.

Shift Siblings Now select Anthony Munro's box again. The bottom pair of **Shift Box** buttons are labelled 'Sibling'. Click on the left shift sibling button. Anthony swaps places with his elder sibling Julia. Click on the right shift sibling button to swap them back.

Shift vs. Move Up/Down You may remember from Chapter 8 that you can re-order spouses and siblings using the **Move Up** [↑] and **Move Down** [↓] buttons on the application toolbar (or the equivalent commands on the **Edit** menu). You may be wondering what the difference is between using the **Shift** buttons and the **Move Up/Down** buttons?

The answer is that the **Shift** buttons simply shift boxes around in the diagram. They do not change your records in any way. When you use the **Move Up/Down** buttons to re-order spouses and siblings, however, you are changing the data in your records. It is true that when you use the **Move Up/Down** buttons, the boxes change order too; but they do this because they are reflecting the underlying order of the spouses and siblings in your records.

In summary then, use the **Move Up/Down** buttons for *Diagram-based Editing*. But use the **Shift** buttons when you just want to change the appearance of a diagram, for the purposes of putting together an attractive chart.

Hide Boxes   You can hide boxes whenever you want, whether moving/resizing is enabled or not. Right-click on Ian Stephen Munro's box and click on **Hide** in the dropdown menu that appears (or you could have used the **Hide Selected Boxes** command on the **Hide/Show Boxes** submenu of the **Diagram** menu). Notice when you do this, not only does Ian Munro's box disappear, but his entire branch does too – which includes his wife's box, and all of his descendant boxes.

You can hide any box, except a tree root. You cannot hide the root of a tree. But you can get rid of the tree altogether by deleting it as we will see shortly. When you hide a box the whole of that person's branch will be hidden too. You can hide a spouse box without hiding any descendant boxes that the spouse is attached to; but not vice versa. So, for example, if you had hidden Charlotte Carrington's box, Ian Munro's box would not have been hidden. But when you hid his box, hers was hidden too.

The **Hide Selected Boxes** command works with multiple selection. But often that's not needed, because as we've seen, you can hide an entire branch by just hiding one box.

Show Hidden Boxes   As well as being able to hide boxes, you can also unhide them again. To do this, you first have to make the hidden boxes visible by clicking on **Show Hidden Boxes** on the **Hide/Show Boxes** submenu of the **Diagram** menu. Do this now. When you do this, all hidden boxes become visible again – in this case, Ian Munro and his branch.

Unhide Boxes   When you select a box and click **Hide** you are setting the *Hidden* box state on that box (see the **Box States** menu on the **Diagram** menu). When you show hidden boxes, any box that has the *Hidden* box state set displays with a purple background. In this case, there's only one – Ian Munro's box. Although Charlotte Carrington's box disappeared when you hid Ian Munro's box, the *Hidden* box state is not set on her box, so it has no purple background. Her box was not hidden because her box state was *Hidden* (it wasn't and isn't), but because she belonged to Ian Munro's branch, and *his* box had the *Hidden* box state.

Right-click on Ian Munro's box. Notice that the *Hidden* state is ticked. Click on that command to untick it. His box reverts to its normal colour.

Now untick **Show Hidden Boxes** on the **Diagram** menu so that hidden boxes are no longer made visible. Note that no boxes disappear when you do this. If you hadn't unchanged the *Hidden* state of Ian Munro's box, he and his branch would have disappeared again.

Smart Trees   As we have seen, in Family Historian, trees automatically adjust themselves to accommodate any change you may make – such as moving a box, moving a branch, resizing a box, expanding a branch, or hiding or showing boxes. This ability to automatically adjust their layout to accommodate changes, is what is meant when trees in Family Historian are called *Smart Trees*.[18]

Insert into Diagram Submenu   We will now look at how you can insert additional trees and other items, into an existing tree. Click on **Insert into Diagram** on the **Diagram** menu. This submenu has a long list of items you can insert into any diagram. A more convenient way of accessing this submenu is to right-click on the background of the diagram. The

---

[18] Trees are also *dynamic* (which means that they automatically reflect changes in the underlying data) and *interactive* (which means that you can use them interactively – e.g. to change your underlying data using diagram-based editing).

Insert into Diagram submenu is accessible on the dropdown menu that appears. It is usually even more convenient still, however, to insert items from a toolbar. There is a toolbar with buttons for all the items you can insert into a diagram. This is the Shape toolbar.

The Shape Toolbar

To open the Shape toolbar, click on the **Display Shape Toolbar** button  on the main Diagram toolbar. The Shape Toolbar appears immediately below the normal toolbar – see Figure 52 below.

Figure 52 – The Shape Toolbar

Multi-Tree Diagrams

In the ordinary way when you create a new diagram it only has one tree in it. But any diagram can have any number of trees in it. There are four kinds of tree:

- Ancestor
- Descendant
- Ancestor and Descendant
- All Relatives

Every tree is one of those. For each tree type there is a corresponding diagram, but the reverse is not true. The 'Everyone' diagram is made up of multiple Ancestor and Descendant trees. There is no 'Everyone' tree.

Figure 53 – The Choose Tree Dialog

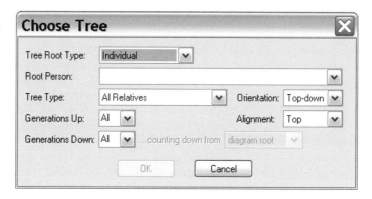

Insert Tree

When you insert a new tree into an existing diagram it is inserted into the centre of the window as you are now looking at it. So it is a good idea, before inserting a tree, to first arrange the window to leave a suitable empty space in the centre of the window. There is no need to do this very carefully. You will be able to reposition the new tree once you have inserted it. But there is no point in creating unnecessary confusion by inserting one tree straight on top of another.

We will now insert a tree into the current diagram.

Steps

1. Click on **View Whole Diagram** to zoom back out. Then press the spacebar to switch temporarily to **Grabber** mode and click-and-drag downwards on the diagram (anywhere on the diagram) to move the whole diagram downwards, until the topmost box is near the bottom of the window.

2. Click on the **Add All Relatives Tree** button on the Shape toolbar (or use the **Insert into Diagram** submenu). The **Choose Tree Dialog** appears (see Figure 53 above). Set **Root Person** to Jonathan Wesley Hodges (you will

probably need to use the 'Browse...' option in the dropdown list). Leave other settings unchanged and click **OK**. The new tree is inserted into the diagram, with a duplicate family link linking the family of Jonathan Hodges and Julia Munro, which has boxes in both trees. Anthony Munro Hodges gets a separate individual duplicate link of his own. Click on **View Whole Diagram** ⊕ to zoom back so that you can see the whole diagram again.

Move Tree After Insert

Family Historian assumes that the first thing you are likely to want to do, after inserting a tree into a diagram, is to move it to a good position. So whenever you insert a tree into a diagram, moving/resizing is automatically enabled, and the mode is automatically set to *Tree Move*.

Click-and-drag now on any box in the new tree that you have just inserted, and move it from side to side to confirm that you are in *Tree Move* mode. Notice also that the **Enable Moving/Resizing** button ⊕ is checked, that the **Movement Control Box** has appeared (see Figure 50 above), and that the **Drag-and-Move Action** is now set to *Tree*.

Trees are Smart, Diagrams Aren't

Now move the new tree so that some of its boxes overlap the original tree. Notice that the trees *will* overlap. The original tree does not move to get out of the way of the new tree. You may be wondering why not. Aren't trees supposed to be smart?

The answer is that trees *are* smart. It is diagrams that are not smart. Or, if you prefer, another way of saying the same thing is that trees are only smart *internally*. A tree will automatically adjust itself to accommodate changes to boxes *that are part of that tree*. But trees do not move to get out of the way of other trees. Nor will they adjust themselves to avoid other diagram elements that we will be looking at shortly – namely pictures, text boxes, rectangles and lines. So there is nothing to stop trees from overlapping if you want them to. If you don't want them to, it's up to you to position them so they don't.

Front-to-Back Ordering

You will have noticed that the boxes from the new tree appear in front of the boxes of the original tree. Suppose you wanted the new tree to be behind the original tree? Do this now. Right-click on any box in the new tree. In the dropdown menu that appears, click on **Order** and then **Send to Back**. Notice that where the new tree overlaps with the old tree, it is now the new tree boxes that are behind the old tree boxes.

Check For Duplicates

We looked at duplicates in chapter 9. In general, you will usually want to keep the number of duplicate boxes to a minimum. We could have reduced duplication by stipulating that we only wanted one generation of descendants when we inserted the new tree. Or we could simply click on the expansion box beneath one of the sets of boxes for Jonathan Hodges and Julia Munro to hide their descendants who are unnecessarily duplicated. But you can also get Family Historian to do it for you. Click now on the **Check for Duplicates** command on the **Diagram** menu, and press **OK** to confirm the warning dialog that appears.

When you do this, you should see that the descendant branch of Jonathan and Julia in the new tree is closed. Jonathan and Julia still have duplicate boxes, so there is still one duplicate family link; but their descendants are no longer duplicated.

The reason that the branch was closed in the *new* tree and not the *old* tree was that we had moved the new tree to the back. **Check for Duplicates** works from front to back. Duplicate branches are closed in the trees at the back, rather than in the trees at the front.

All trees (and for that matter, all diagram elements) are ordered relative to one another, front-to-back. If the trees don't overlap, you won't be able to simply see in what way they are ordered, but they are nevertheless. When you first insert a tree, it will be ordered so that it will appear in front of all other existing diagram elements. But as have seen, you can change that. Think about front-to-back ordering before using **Check For Duplicates** to make sure you get the results you want.

Cancel Moving/ Resizing

Find a suitable place to put the new tree and then cancel moving/resizing. You do this by unchecking the **Enable Moving/Resizing** button ✛ or by closing the Movement Control Box.

Tree Type in Status Bar

When you only have one tree it's easy enough to remember what kind of tree it is. Often you can see at a glance just by looking at it, that it is an *Ancestor, Descendant, Ancestor & Descendant* or *All Relatives* tree. Sometimes, however, you can't easily tell just by looking at it. And if you have multiple trees in one diagram, it is easy to forget. And yet it does make a difference. You can do things with one type of tree that you can't do with others. You can add ancestors by clicking-and-dragging on all trees except *Descendant* trees for example.

You can easily find out what kind of tree you are looking at. Just click on any box in the tree, and the tree type will be displayed in the status bar.

Delete Tree

If you want to get rid of a tree, it's easy to delete it. Just click on any box in the tree and press the **Delete** key on your keyboard. You can do this whether or not moving/resizing is enabled. When you do this the **Confirm Delete** dialog appears. The purpose of this dialog is to establish whether you are simply trying to make a change to your diagram, or whether you wish to delete data records.

Remember that diagrams in Family Historian are used for diagram-based editing, as well as for putting together wall charts. You *can* use a diagram, if you wish, to identify records you wish to delete, and delete them. So Family Historian needs to know what your intentions are.

In this case, however, we don't want to delete any data records. We just want to change the diagram (and get rid of a tree), so leave the default dialog setting which is to *Delete selected diagram items only*, and press **OK**.

When you do this, another warning message is displayed. This time, Family Historian is warning that if you proceed one entire tree will be deleted.

Each Tree Counts As Just One Diagram Element

For the purposes of deletion, and for other purposes too – such as front-to-back ordering – each tree counts as just *one* diagram element. You can't delete individual boxes within a tree. If you want to get rid of them, you have to *hide* them. So the message that appears now is to make sure that you realise that you are about to delete an entire tree. Click **OK** to confirm. The new tree has now disappeared. No changes have been made to any of data records.

Do not worry, incidentally, that you might forget what you are doing and accidentally delete data records when you didn't mean to. If, when the first warning dialog had appeared, you had chosen the non-default option labelled "Delete data records for selected boxes (you will be required to confirm)", another confirmation dialog would have appeared entitled "Confirm Delete Records" with "CAUTION! Please read carefully…" at the top. The dialog would have explained carefully what you were about to do and suggested alternative actions if it wasn't what you meant to do. Before you could delete anything you would have had to tick a box saying "I understand that X records will be deleted" (where X is the number that you were about to delete). Only when you had done that would the **Delete Records** button have become enabled; and you would then have had to click on that to actually do the deletion. So it's not something that anyone is likely to do inadvertently. And if they did, they could click **Undo** on the **Edit** menu to undo it anyway.[19]

Insert Picture Into Diagram

We have seen how Family Historian will automatically display pictures of Individuals in boxes for you, if you ask it to (see the **Pictures** tab of the Diagram Options dialog). You can also manually insert pictures into diagrams as separate diagram elements, by clicking the **Add Picture** button on the Shape toolbar (or the **Picture** command on the **Insert into Diagram** submenu). If you have a suitable picture you can try this now. The formats supported are bitmap, jpeg, gif, pcx, tif (or tiff), png, targa, or wmf.

Just as there is no limit to the number of trees you can have in a diagram, there is also no limit to the number of pictures or other diagram elements that you can have in a diagram.

Moving & Resizing Pictures

Moving and resizing pictures (and indeed all diagram elements other than trees) is very easy. There is no need to enable moving/resizing (that is for trees only). Simply click on the picture. The selection markers for pictures are always white. Click-and-drag on any of them to resize the picture. By default, when you resize a picture its aspect ratio (the ratio of height to width) is always maintained.

Rotating Pictures

When you select a picture, as well as the eight white selection markers at each corner and side, there is also a small round green circle attached to the picture at the top (see right). Click-and-drag on this green circle to rotate the picture.

Format Picture

Right-click on a picture and choose Format from the dropdown menu that appears, to bring up a **Format** dialog for it (or just double-click on the picture). This dialog has three tabs: **Image**, **Line and Fill** and **Shape**. The **Fade Image** field on the **Image** tab is used to fade the image to white. If you set the value to 75%, the picture will look very faint, and close to white.

Use the fields on the **Line and Fill** tab to specify whether you want a border round the outside of the picture, and if so, how thick and what colour.

Finally, in the **Shape** tab, you can unlock aspect ratio if you want to be able to resize a picture without maintaining its aspect ratio. You can also set the rotation here. So if you wish to cancel a previous rotation, set the value to 0. Click on the **Help** button for more help on the options available to you.

Insert Text Box

To insert a text box into a diagram, click on the **Add Text Box** button on the Shape toolbar (or on **Text Box** in the **Insert into Diagram** submenu). When you do this, the cursor will change to look like a cross-hair: . Click-and-drag on the diagram to draw a stretchy box where you want the text box to go. When first inserted, a text box just has the word 'Text' in it. To change the text, open its Format dialog (double-click on it, or right-click on it and select 'Format' from the context menu that appears). The *Format* dialog looks like Figure 54 below.

Format Text Boxes

Enter what text you want in the **Text** tab. You can use text boxes for titles or annotations, or anything else you can think of. Each text box can have its own font, alignment (left, right, centred or justified), and inner margins.

Using the **Insert Data Reference** button you can insert a data reference into the text. When the diagram is displayed, the data reference will be replaced by the name or other details of the diagram root. If you were using the text box as a title, for example, and you were creating a custom diagram type (see chapter 9) you

---

[19] But that doesn't mean you don't need to take backups! It is always a good idea to take regular backups to protect you against all the things that can go wrong – and especially to protect you against your own mistakes.

might use text like this: "Relatives of %INDI%". The data reference is the '%INDI%' bit. If a custom diagram type had that title, it would show the correct title, no matter which Individual had been selected as the root.

The **Line and Fill** tab (see Figure 54) allows you to specify whether you want a frame round the text, and if so how thick and what colour. You can also specify whether you want the areas behind the text to be 'filled' or transparent, and (if filled) what colour.

When you have entered details, press **OK** to close the **Format** dialog.

Text boxes can be moved, resized or rotated exactly as pictures can (except that unlike pictures, their aspect ratio is not locked by default).

Figure 54 – The Text box Format Dialog

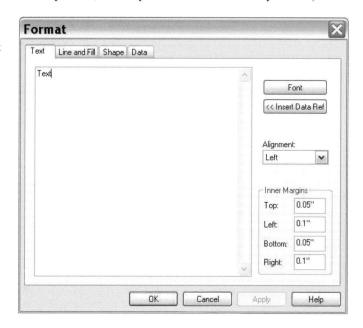

Insert Rectangle

Inserting rectangles is similar to inserting pictures. Click on the **Add Rectangle** button ▭ on the **Shape** toolbar (or click on **Rectangle** on the **Insert into Diagram** submenu). Then click-and-drag on the diagram to draw a stretchy box in the shape of the rectangle you want. When you release the mouse button the rectangle will be inserted. Double-click on it (or right-click and choose Format) to open the Format dialog, if you want to change fill, line or other details.

If a rectangle has no 'fill', you have to click on the frame to select the rectangle, or click-and-drag on the frame to move it. However, if it has a fill, you can click anywhere inside the rectangle to select it, and can click-and-drag anywhere on it to move it. It can be resized and rotated like a picture or text box.

Insert Rounded Rectangle

Inserting rounded rectangles (that is, rectangles with rounded corners) is almost exactly the same as inserting ordinary rectangles. Click on the **Add Rounded Rectangle** button ▢ on the **Shape** toolbar (or click on **Rounded Rectangle** on the **Insert into Diagram** submenu). Then click-and-drag on the diagram to draw a stretchy box in the shape of the rectangle you want. When you release the mouse button the rectangle will be inserted.

The formatting options for rectangles and rounded rectangles are exactly the same. The only difference in fact is that when you select a rounded rectangle, a little yellow diamond appears near the white selection marker in the top-left corner (see right). Click-and-drag sideways on this yellow diamond to alter how rounded you want the corners to be.

116

Insert Ellipse

To add an ellipse, click on the **Add Circle or Ellipse** button ⊙ on the **Shape** toolbar. Then click-and-drag on the diagram to draw a stretchy box in the shape of the ellipse you want. When you release the mouse button the circle or ellipse will be inserted.

Insert Circle or Square

Adding a circle is exactly the same as adding an ellipse, except that you press-and-hold the **Shift** key while you click-and-drag on the diagram. If you press-and-hold the **Shift** key while adding either a rectangle or a rounded rectangle you will get a square or a rounded square.

Insert Polygon

A polygon is a multi-sided object. Adding a polygon is much like adding other shapes. Click on the **Add Polygon** button △ on the **Shape** toolbar. Instead of click-and-dragging however, click once on the diagram for each *vertex* (corner-point) that you wish to add. Double-click on the diagram to add the last vertex. A polygon cannot have fewer than 3 vertices.

Add, Delete or Move Polygon Vertices

You can resize, rotate and format a polygon just as you can other shapes. You can also add, delete or move its vertices. To do that, you must first **Ungroup** the polygon. Right click on the polygon and choose **Ungroup** from the **Grouping** submenu. When you do this, each vertex will display with a little white selection marker. Click-and-drag on a vertex to move it. Press and hold the **Alt** key while clicking on a vertex to delete it. Press and hold the **Alt** key while clicking on the edge of the polygon to add a vertex. If you want to be able to resize the overall shape, or rotate it, you must return it to its 'Grouped' state. To do that, right click on the polygon and choose **Group** from the **Grouping** submenu. Now when you select the polygon, the usual eight selection markers will be displayed around the polygon, and you can click-and-drag on any of these to resize the shape as a whole. You can also click-and-drag on the green circle to rotate it.

Insert Line

Click on the **Add Line** button ＼ on the **Shape** toolbar to add a line. Click-and-drag to add the line. Adding a multi-segment line is similar to adding a polygon.

Click on the **Add Multi-Segment Line** button ⤵ on the **Shape** toolbar, then click once on the diagram for each vertex of the line that you wish to add. Double-click to add the end-point.

Press the **Shift** key when inserting a line to force each line segment to 'snap' to the horizontal, or to the vertical.

Add, Delete or Move Line Vertices

The **Add Line** button is there for convenience only. It isn't really needed, because an ordinary line isn't a different type of shape to a multi-segment line. An ordinary line is just a multi-segment line which only has two vertices. With all lines you can add, delete or move vertices. Click-and-drag on a vertex to move it. Press and hold the **Alt** key while clicking on a vertex to delete it. Press and hold the **Alt** key while clicking on the edge of the polygon to add a vertex.

Rotating and Resizing Lines

If you want to rotate a line (multi-segment or single segment), or resize the overall shape of the line, one way would be to carefully move each vertex. But an easier way is to right click on the line and choose **Group** from the **Grouping** submenu. When you do this, eight selection markers will appear around the line as a whole, and the little green circle will appear at the top. Click-and-drag on the green circle to rotate the overall shape. Click-and-drag on any of the selection markers to resize the overall line shape.

Insert Arrow

Click on the **Add Arrow** button ⇨ on the **Shape** toolbar to add an arrow. Then click-and-drag on the diagram to specify where you want the arrow to go. Arrows can be formatted, resized and rotated like any other shape. When you select an arrow, a little yellow diamond is shown where the 'stem' of the arrow meets the head (see right). Click-

and-drag on the yellow diamond to alter the shape of the arrow.

Insert Pie Shape

There are two kinds of pie shape: with or without text. They are inserted in the usual way, by clicking-and-dragging on the diagram, to mark the area where you want them to go. You can enter text into a pie-shape-with-text, in the same way that you can with a text box.

Press-and-hold the **Shift** key when inserting a pie shape, to force it to be a segment of a circle, rather than a segment of an ellipse.

Pie shapes have two little yellow diamonds (see right). Click-and-drag on either of these yellow diamonds to alter the shape of the pie.

Insert Freehand

Click on the **Add Freehand** button on the **Shape** toolbar, and then click-and-drag on the diagram to draw a freehand line (see example right). You can format freehand lines like any other shape. You can specify the thickness, colour and solidity of any freehand lines. If you add more freehand lines they will by default have the characteristics of the last freehand line you added.

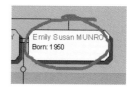

Freehand lines can be resized and rotated. If you **Ungroup** them (by right-clicking on the freehand shape and choosing **Ungroup** from the **Grouping** submenu) you can even fine-tune the shape of a freehand line by adding, deleting or moving vertices.

Shift Key

We have already seen that if you press the **Shift** key while adding a rectangle, ellipse or pie shape, you will get a square, circle, or segment from a circle, respectively. If you press it when inserting a line, each line segment will 'snap' to the horizontal or to the vertical. If you press the **Shift** key while moving a vertex for a line or polygon, the vertex will snap to be aligned horizontally or vertically with its two nearest neighbouring vertices.

If you press the **Shift** key while *resizing* a shape, its aspect ratio (the ratio of width to height) will be maintained as you resize.

Ctrl Key

If you press the **Ctrl** key when inserting or resizing most shapes, the shape will be resized relative to its centre point.

If you press both the Ctrl key and the Shift key, the effect of each will be combined.

Resizing/ Rotating Multiple Shapes

If you want to make exactly the same change to multiple shapes, you can select them all and when you resize or rotate any one of them, all the selected shapes will be resized or rotated. Press-and-hold the **Ctrl** key while clicking on a shape, to select it without unselecting other shapes. Multiple shapes can also be 'lasso'd', just as boxes in trees can.

Copy and Paste Shapes

You can copy and paste a single shape, or a selection of multiple shapes (including pictures and freehand lines – anything, that is, that can be inserted from the Shapes toolbar) within a diagram or between diagrams.

Delete Shapes

To delete shapes, just select the shapes you want to delete and then press the **Delete** key. You will be asked to confirm the deletion.

Front-to- Back Ordering

Shapes can be ordered front-to-back, relative to one another, and relative to any trees in the diagram. Right-click on a shape and select a command from the **Order** submenu.

Grouping Shapes

You can combine multiple shapes of any type by grouping them together. To do this, select all the shapes you want to group together, right-click on any one of them and select **Group** from the **Grouping** menu. When you do this, you effectively create a new grouped shape, that can be resized, rotated and formatted, as a single object. Grouped shapes can also be grouped with other shapes, and this process can be repeated indefinitely to make grouped shape objects that can be as complex as you like. You can also ungroup a shape (**Ungroup** on the **Grouping** menu) to return it to its constituent parts. When you ungroup a shape, any rotations or resizing that you had previously applied to the grouped shape, are removed. This is by design.

Any shapes (including pictures and freehand lines) can be grouped together. Trees and tree boxes, however, cannot be grouped.

Insert Fan Chart

To insert a fan chart into a diagram, click on the **Add Fan Chart** button on the Shape toolbar. When you do this, the Fan Chart dialog appears prompting you to specify details of the required fan chart. Fan charts in Family Historian are actually grouped shapes. More specifically, they consist of multiple pie-charts-with-text, grouped together to form a single object. If you right-click on a fan chart and click on **Ungroup** on the **Grouping** menu, you will be able to pull the fan chart apart, to see how it is constructed.

Fan Chart Base Person

To change the *Base Person* for a fan chart – that is, the person whose ancestors are displayed in the fan chart – right click on the fan chart and click **Format** to open the Format dialog. You can change the base person in the **Data** tab.

Creating Custom Diagram

You can create custom diagram types, based on shapes (in effect, this is what a fan chart is). To do this, you will need to understand how to use text boxes and pie-shapes-with-text shapes, to display information about whoever happens to be the diagram root. To learn more about this, click the **Help** button on the **Data** tab of the **Format** dialog.

Moving Tree Branches Anywhere

We saw earlier how to move branches within a diagram using *Box Move*, *Bar Move* or *Fixed Point Move*. In each case though there were constraints on where the branch could be moved to. But suppose you want to move a branch with no constraints? Suppose, for example, you wanted to Peter Munro's branch of the family to put it at the top of the diagram, above both of his parents?

There is no branch move that will let you do that. But using the techniques we have already learned in this chapter, you can get the desired result anyway. All you need do is hide the branch that you wish to 'move'. Then add a tree corresponding to the branch and position it in the desired location. Finally, insert lines into the diagram and using as many lines as you need, link the 'moved' branch back to where it came from.

To do this with Peter Munro, you would first hide the box for Peter Munro. When you do this, his spouse and all of his descendants will disappear. Then insert a *Descendant* tree for Peter Munro and position it where you want it to go. Finally add all the lines you need to link Peter Munro back to his parents.

Format Multiple Shapes

We have seen that you can right-click on any shape (including complex grouped shapes and pictures, etc.) and choose **Format** from the context menu that appears, to change aspects of the shape in question. You can change formatting options not just for one shape at a time, but for any number. Select all the shapes you wish to format, right-click on any one of them, and choose **Format** from the context menu that appears. The changes you make will be applied to all the selected shapes.

Format Tree Boxes

As well as shapes, you can also format tree boxes. In Chapter 9 we saw how you can specify box features of all kinds in the **Boxes** tab of **Diagram Options**. When you do this, you are associating box features with particular conditions – so, for example, a box feature, such as its shape or shadow, might be associated with the sex of the person, or the type of the box.

When you use the **Format** command to change box features, you are overriding whatever rules you had previously set up in the **Boxes** tab of **Diagram Options**, for the boxes you have selected. To format one or more tree boxes, select them all, and then right-click on one of the selected boxes and choose **Format** from the context menu that appears. When you do so the **Override Box Features** dialog appears (see Figure 55 below).

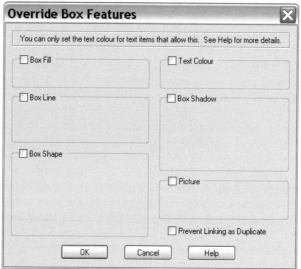

Figure 55 – The Override Box Features Dialog with no features overridden

Override Box Features   The **Override Box Features** dialog, when first displayed, shows seven check boxes, all unchecked. Each of these check boxes corresponds to a box feature. To override that particular feature, tick the check box in question. When you do so, more fields will appear in the relevant part of the dialog and you will be able to change the features in question.

Override Silhouettes   Figure 56 below shows what the **Override Box Features** dialog looks like when all features have been overridden. Boxes formatted with these options would have a yellow background and a rounded box, among other things. None of them would show a picture. Instead they would all display a silhouette image (at least they would as long as the sex of the Individuals in question had been recorded).

Prevent Linking as Duplicate   The features in the **Override Box Features** dialog are similar to those that you can specify in the **Boxes** tab of **Diagram Options**. But there are differences. One difference is the **Prevent Linking as Duplicate** option. Tick this checkbox if you do not want the linking ribbons that connect duplicates to attach to the selected boxes. See Chapter 9 above for more on duplicate boxes, and linking ribbons.

Layout & Scaling   The *Layout & Scaling* submenu on the **Diagram** menu provides a number of menu commands with powerful features for controlling various aspects of the overall layout and appearance, and scale, of a diagram. Scaling issues will be discussed in Chapter 11, but here are some of other tasks you can perform using the commands on the *Layout & Scaling* submenu:

- Make all boxes in the diagram have the same height (or width if it's oriented sideways)
- Make all boxes in each row of the diagram have the same height (or width if it's oriented sideways)
- Select a number of boxes and resize them to match the height of the tallest

- Select a number of boxes and resize them to match the height of the smallest
- Select a number of boxes and resize them to match the width of the widest
- Select a number of boxes and resize them to match the width of the narrowest
- Resize pictures in selected boxes so that the pictures fit their respective box heights (if pictures are located at the side of the text, only)
- Make all rows of a diagram the same height (or make all columns the same width if the diagram is orientated sideways)
- Reset box/row/column sizes to the default

Although you can only resize pictures to match their box heights, if the pictures are located at the side of the text, if you want to resize pictures located *within* the text, you can do this. You need to temporarily change diagram options to move pictures to the side of the text. Then manually adjust the box size to the required size. Then resize the picture, and finally change Diagram Options back to showing pictures within the text.

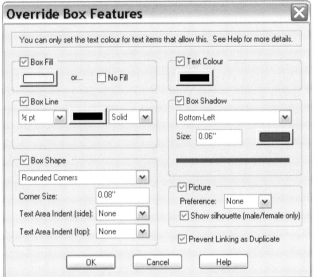

Figure 56 – The Override Box Features Dialog with all features overridden

Matching Box Sizes When selected boxes are resized, they are resized to match the size of the smallest or largest box in the group (height or width) depending on which option you chose. If you want to resize boxes to match the size of a box that is neither the largest nor the smallest of a selected group, you can do this. You just need to resize all the boxes other than the correctly-sized box, to be smaller than it. Now that it is the largest box in the group, you just add it to the selection and resize all the other boxes up to its size.

If you make all boxes the same size (height, width or both), do not assume that all boxes will continue to have the same size if you change the diagram, by expanding branches to add more boxes to it, or manually change box sizes. If you still want all boxes to have the same size in these cases, you will need to re-apply the menu command for achieving this.

Routes and the Family Connection Mapper The **Override Box Features** dialog allows you to override most aspects of the appearance of *boxes* in trees in diagrams. But what about the *lines* connecting the boxes? For this you need the **Family Connection Mapper**, which is a powerful tool for working with tree lines. You can use it to mark the lines connecting boxes – which are called *routes* in Family Historian – in powerful and flexible ways.

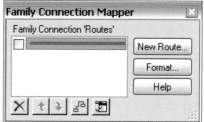

Figure 57 – The Family Connection Mapper, with only one 'route'

Connect Two Boxes

As an illustration of what you can do with the Family Connection Mapper, we will, as an exercise, connect various boxes.

Steps

1. Open a new descendant diagram for Michael Smith Munro. Make sure you are showing all of his descendants. You should know how to do this by now, but if not, go back and review Chapter 3.

2. Click on the **View Whole Diagram** button so you can see all boxes.

3. Click on the **Family Connection Mapper** button . The **Family Connection Mapper** opens (see Figure 57 above). The red line represents a *route* – a marked line connecting boxes. A diagram can have as many routes as you like. By default, a red line route is created for you automatically when you open the Family Connection Mapper, if otherwise there wouldn't be any routes listed.

4. Now click on Carolyn Amy Munro (bottom-left) to select her box. Press-and-hold the **Ctrl** key and click on Patrick Christopher Munro. If you have done this correctly these two boxes should be selected and no other boxes should be selected. Confirm that this is the case.

5. You should see that the background behind the red line in the **Family Connection Mapper** is coloured to indicate that the red line route is selected (even though the check box to the left of the red line is unticked). Click on the **Connect Two Boxes** button on the toolbar in the Family Connection Mapper. If you have done this correctly, you should see a red line connecting Carolyn Munro to Patrick Munro, looking something like Figure 58 below.

6. When you do this, you may notice that the check box for the red line route in the Family Connection Mapper is now ticked. This check box is ticked if the currently selected boxes are part of the red line route. It is unticked if they aren't. Confirm that this is the case by alternately selecting boxes that are, or are not, on the route. If you select multiple boxes, the check box will be ticked if they're all on the route, and unticked if they are all not on the route. If some are, and some aren't, it will show an intermediary state. To add any box to a route, simply select the box you wish to add and tick the check box for the route in question. Let's add Catherine Reardon, Michael Munro's wife, to the route. Select her box and tick the check box for the red line route. You should see that her box is now included on the route. If you select both her and her husband and untick the red line check box, you should see that both are now removed from the route.

Multiple Routes

There is no limit to the number of routes you can have in one diagram. We will add a second route to show this.

Steps

1. Select the boxes for Daniella Smiley and Caroline Wiley. Then click the **New Route** button on the **Family Connection Mapper**. Accept the defaults in the **Family Connection 'Route'** dialog and click **Create**. You should see that there is now a blue line as well as a red line in the Family Connection Mapper. Click

on the blue line, and then click on the **Connect Two Boxes** button ![icon] in the **Family Connection Mapper** toobar. If you have done everything correctly, you should find that there is now a blue line connecting Daniella Smiley and Caroline Wiley. Where the two routes overlap, the blue line covers the red line.

2. Click on the **Send Route Backward** button ![icon] on the **Family Connection Mapper** to move the blue line down the list, below the red line. Now you should see that the red line covers the blue line. If you want to be able to see both routes at the same time, the way to do this is to make the blue route thicker, so that it appears behind the red line route. Making sure that the blue line is selected (that is, has the selection background – whether its check box is ticked or not is irrelevant) click on the **Format** button. The **Family Connection 'Route'** dialog appears. Take note that you can use this dialog to change the colour and other details of the selected route. For now, however, just set the line size to 6 pt and press **OK**. You should now be able to see the blue route behind the red route where they overlap. The overlapping area should look something like below Figure 59 below .

This example illustrates that any box can be on more than one route. If you click on Graham Anthony Munro's box, for example, you should be able to see that the check boxes for both the red line and blue line routes are ticked in the Family Connection Mapper.

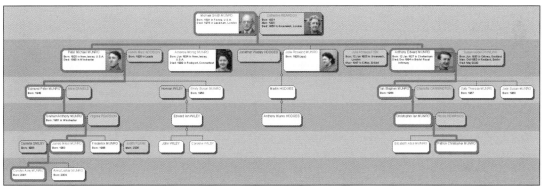

Figure 58 – Connecting Two Boxes

Non-Linking Route Boxes   You can add any box to any route. For example, to add Judith Plan to the blue line route, simply click on her box to select it and then tick the blue line check box in the Family Connection Mapper.   When you do this, her box will be framed in blue – but it will not link up with other boxes on the blue line route. This is because two route boxes only display as connected if they are directly connected to one another by diagram lines. Now add Frederick Munro to the blue line route – that is, select his box and tick the check box for the blue line route. What you should see this time is that not only does his box get frame in blue, but the lines connecting him to Judith Plank and the lines connecting to him to James Mile Munro, are also marked in blue. This is because Frederick Munro's box is directly connected to those of Judith Plank and James Munro.

Multi-Way And 'Broken' Paths   The word 'route' implies a single path from one place to another. Although you can use routes in this way, as the example shows, Family Historian routes can be much more complex than that. They can represent branching paths which feed off in multiple directions. And they can be 'broken' paths, which don't even necessarily all join up.

Colouring Branches   You can of course combine all the techniques we have learned in this chapter. For example, look at Figure 60 below. The four children of Michael Smith and Catherine Reardon have had their whole descendant branches coloured distinctively, just using the techniques we have covered in this chapter. As an exercise, see if you create the same effect.

Tip: Selecting a whole branch of boxes is easy. Right-click on a box and click on **Select Branch Boxes** to select its entire branch. For example, right-click on Peter Munro and choose **Select Branch Boxes** to select the entire branch of boxes leading out from his box. Right-click on any of the selected boxes, and choose the **Format** command to open the **Override Box Features** dialog and change the fill colour for all the selected boxes. Use the **Family Connection Mapper** to add all selected boxes to a route (you will need four routes – one for each branch). In the example, the branches have been moved apart from one another. Use **Fixed Point** moves to do this. A useful tip is that you can at any time easily select all boxes on any give route. To do that, select the route and then choose **Select Route Boxes** from the dropdown menu that appears when you click on the **Menu** button 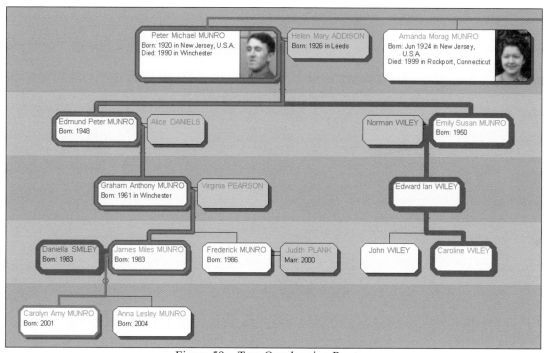 on the **Family Connection Mapper** toolbar. You may not need to do that in this particular case, but it can be useful if you want to format the appearance of the boxes on the route and need a quick way of selecting them all.

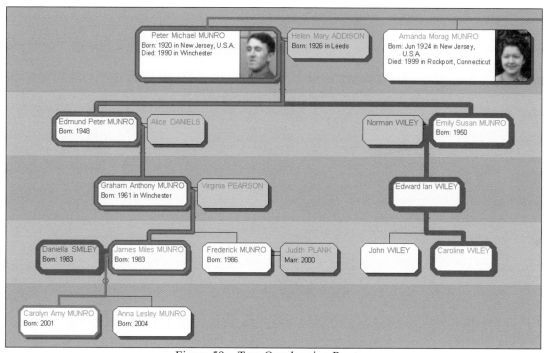

Figure 59 – Two Overlapping Routes

Saving a Diagram as a Chart File

When you are opening a diagram for browsing, navigating or editing, you don't usually need it again when you've finished whatever you were doing. You can always open another diagram as needed. But when you are creating a wall chart, or a chart that is to be kept and sent to others, your diagram is of value in itself and you will want to be able to save it.

You can save any diagram in a number of different picture formats; but if you want to be able to save it exactly as it is now – so you can open it in a Diagram Window and carry on working on it another time – you must save it as a file in *Family Historian Chart* format. To do this, click **Save Diagram** on the **Diagram** menu. This saves the diagram in Family Historian chart format. Clicking **Diagram** then **Save Diagram As** then **Family Historian Chart,** is another way saving a diagram as a file in Family Historian Chart format.

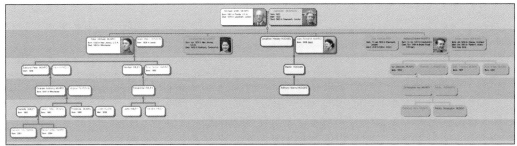

Figure 60 – Colouring Branches

Charts Can Only be Saved Within Projects

You can only save charts in the context of a Family Historian project. If you are simply using Family Historian to browse or edit a GEDCOM file, you cannot save charts. If you try to save a chart now, you will find that you are not allowed to do it. This is because we are using Family Historian to edit a tutorial file, but there is no project as such. Projects are created in the Project Window (see Chapter 1).

How to Open a Chart

When you are using Family Historian to work on a project, you can view and open any chart files you have created by clicking on the **View** menu, and then on **Saved Charts**. This will show you a list of charts that have been saved in the project and you can open any of them.

Charts are Integrated, Interactive & Dynamic

When you open a previously-saved chart you should find that – with a caveat that we will come to in a moment – it looks exactly as it looked when you saved it. Not only that, but *you can continue doing everything with it that you could do before you saved it*. The diagram is still tightly integrated. It is still dynamic. That is, if you make a change to the data in your records, the diagram will update immediately to reflect the change. It is still completely interactive. You can click on expansion boxes to hide or show branches. You can click-and-drag to add records using diagram-based editing. The trees are still smart trees. Everything is as it was before you saved the diagram. Or at least – and this is the caveat – the chart will be the same if you haven't changed any of the data that it is displaying.

Charts Reflect the Current Reality

Suppose you saved a chart of Michael Munro's relatives, but after you saved the chart, you deleted one of his children and added some new grandchildren. What would you see when you re-opened the chart?

The answer is that you will see the new grandchildren (or at least, if expansion buttons are enabled, you will see an expansion button at the appropriate place to show where the grandchildren go) and you *won't* see the deleted relatives. Charts reflect the current reality. If the data in the family tree data file has changed since the chart was saved, the chart will show the changed data. A chart does this by synchronising itself with the current data file when it is opened.

How to Ensure that a Chart Doesn't Change

If you have a chart that is just the way you want it, how can you keep a copy of it exactly as it is now, that is guaranteed to look exactly as it does now when you open it again? The answer is: you should make a copy of the entire project. Then when you want to re-open the chart, you do so by opening the copy of your original project (and, of course, you must be sure that you never change your record data in the copy of the project).

Even if you do this, there could still be changes, if you change the text scheme that the chart used, or if your chart uses pictures which are not stored as part of the project.

Saving Charts As Pictures

You can save any diagram in a choice of eleven different picture formats. The best format for most purposes (especially with large diagrams) is PDF format.

Saving Charts in PDF Format

PDF format is a very useful format. If you want to print a large chart, a good option is to save the chart in PDF format. If you take the PDF file to a print shop, they should be able to print it out exactly as you saved it.

PDF is also a good format if you want to send a chart image to someone else. To view a PDF file, everyone needs a PDF reader program such as Adobe Reader. But this is a free program and widely used already. If anyone does not already have a copy of Adobe Reader, they can download a copy from the Adobe website.

There are two ways of saving a chart in PDF file format. One way is to click on **Diagram** then **Save Diagram As**, then **PDF File (.pdf)**. When you do this, you will be presented with an options dialog, in which you can choose to fit the whole diagram on a single page, and specify a margin size. Occasionally, however, you may prefer to use the alternative method which is to create your PDF file by using the **Print** command on the **File**. If you choose this approach you should select "Family Historian PDF" as your printer (you should find that this is in your list of printers). When you 'print' to this 'printer', no actual printing occurs. Instead, a PDF file is created.

Copy Diagram

You can also copy a diagram, or part of a diagram, to the clipboard using the **Copy Diagram** command. This is available on the **Diagram** menu. When you click on **Copy Diagram**, the **Copy Options Dialog** opens (see Figure 61 below).

Choosing **All Pages** as the area to copy will result in a larger area being copied than **Whole Diagram**. The former sizes the entire grid of occupied pages. Depending on how page boundaries are positioned, this may result in a lot of unused extra space being copied. **Whole Diagram** by contrast pays no attention to page boundaries and just copies the diagram itself.

Diagrams can be copied in either enhanced metafile format or bitmap format, using either the currently displayed size (i.e. the current zoom level) or the 'actual size' (i.e. 100% zoom). Having copied a diagram in either of these formats, you should then find that you can paste it into another application – such as word-processor document. Be aware, when you do this, that many applications will automatically resize images when you paste or otherwise insert them into the document, if they are too large to fit.

Figure 61
Copy Options dialog

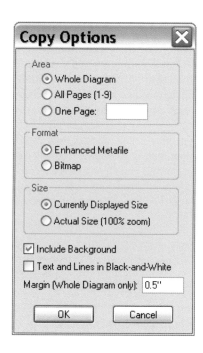

11 Scaling & Printing Diagrams

All diagrams in Family Historian can be scaled to any size and can be printed at any position you want on a sheet of paper, or over a grid of sheets of paper. You can if you wish automatically prevent boxes from overlapping with page boundaries.

In this chapter, we will look at these issues and everything to do with printing diagrams. You will need to have a printer installed and available to be used from your computer.

Open Tutorial File

We will illustrate the discussion by using the tutorial file: "Tutorial – Chapter 11". From the **Project Window**, click on the **More Tasks** button, and then in the dropdown menu click on **Samples**, and finally **Tutorial – Chapter 11**. The file opens and Cameron Peabody is once again displayed as the focus person in the Focus Window.

Locate Thomas Peabody in this file (look in the Records Window), and open an *Ancestors* diagram for him.

Saving Diagrams in PDF Format

There are two ways of saving diagrams in PDF format, one of which is to 'print' the diagram to a 'printer' called "Family Historian PDF". The reason for the quotes is that "Family Historian PDF" is not a real printer. But you create PDF files using this technique. These issues were discussed in the previous chapter, and are not covered in this one.

Print Diagram

To print a diagram, at any time, simply click on **Print** on the **File** menu. You don't have to print the whole diagram. You can print individual pages (or a range of pages) if you want to.

As we saw earlier, zooming in and out has no effect on how a diagram will look when printed. So how can you tell what a diagram will look like when printed?

Diagrams in Family Historian do not have to print on a single sheet of paper. If you want, you can – and many people do – print diagrams big enough to cover an entire wall. Assuming that your printer doesn't print wall-size sheets of paper, the only way you can do this is either to get a print shop or professional genealogy printer to print your diagrams for you, or print the diagram yourself on a large number of sheets of paper and fix them together somehow. Most printers do not print right up to the edge of the paper. If yours doesn't you will either have to accept that there will be gaps at the edges of each page, or you will have to cut off the unused edges of the paper.

Tip: If you're printing a large diagram on many pages, it's a good idea to write the page number in pencil on the back of each page to make it easier to remember how they fit together.

Show Page Boundaries

To determine how a diagram will look when printed, the first step is to find out how many pages it will print on, and which bits of it will print on which page. The ***Show Page Boundaries*** button achieves both of these for you.

Steps

1. Click on the **Show Page Boundaries** button now. The button stays depressed, and a grid of dotted lines appears behind the diagram. To ensure that

you can see the grid clearly, zoom out now (e.g. press **Num–**) until you can easily see the whole diagram and at least one extra unused grid square on each side of it. Unused grid squares (that is, grid squares which will not print) have a white background. You will probably find that the diagram occupies only a single grid square – but this will depend on your paper size and the print orientation.

2. Click the **Show Page Boundaries** button a few times to make the grid disappear and re-appear. You should notice that at the top left-hand corner of each occupied grid square is a page number. The grid squares correspond to printed pages. If you printed the diagram now, only the grid squares that have page numbers would print. The other empty grid squares with a white background would not print.

3. Click on the **View Whole Diagram** button now. The behaviour of this command is slightly different when you are viewing page boundaries. Instead of arranging the diagram so that it fits nicely inside the current window, it arranges it so that all *occupied pages* fit inside the current window. This should make it easy to see at a glance exactly how many pages will print, and where different bits of diagram will print on each of them. Now click on **Diagram Statistics** on the **Diagram** menu and confirm that the number of pages you can see is the same number displayed for 'Pages' (the third value shown).

Position Diagram on Printed Page (1)

How do you position the diagram relative to the grid of pages so that you can control its exact position on the page, when printed? There are two ways of doing this. The first is to use the **Movement Control Box**. Click on the **Enable Moving/Resizing** button on the toolbar to open the **Movement Control Box**, and then choose **Everything (position on page)** as the Drag-and-Move action. If you aren't already viewing page boundaries, when you choose this option page boundaries will automatically be enabled. Now move the mouse over the diagram.

When you do this, the mouse should look like this: Click-and-drag anywhere on the diagram to move the whole thing relative to the page boundaries. If you move the diagram so that it crosses page boundaries, into other grid squares, you should notice that all grid squares immediately display as 'occupied' the moment even part of the diagram is within their area. Untick **Enable Moving/Resizing** when you have finished moving the diagram. When you do this, the **Movement Control Box** closes.

Position Diagram on Printed Page (2)

The second way of positioning a diagram on the printed page is simply to move the grid that shows page boundaries. First ensure that the grid is visible and that you have clicked **View Whole Diagram** so that you can see all occupied pages.

Steps

1. *Grid intersections* are the points where grid lines meet. Pick any grid intersection, and move the cursor carefully so that the tip of the cursor is over the intersection. You should see that the cursor changes to this shape: .

2. Click the *left* mouse button and, keeping the mouse button pressed, move the cursor. You should find that you move the entire grid when you do this (if not, repeat steps 1 and 2 taking care to ensure that the cursor has the required shape at the moment when you click the mouse button). Move the mouse so that the intersection you are dragging is roughly between the boxes for Ian Peabody and Fiona Peabody.

3. Release the mouse button. Now click on the **View Whole Diagram** button. You should find that the diagram now occupies 4 grid squares (conceivably more if you have every small paper, but it's not likely). If you printed the diagram now, 4 sheets of paper would print.

In some ways this way of doing things may appear to be a back-to-front way of doing things. It may seem more natural to move the diagram relative to the grid, rather than move the grid relative to the diagram. But it amounts to the same thing. The effect is that you have adjusted whereabouts on the printed page the diagram will appear.

Align Page & Row Boundaries

If you press the **Ctrl** key while moving the grid it will 'snap' to the nearest row boundary (if the diagram is oriented sideways rather than vertically, you can do the same thing with the diagram columns). This is most useful if you previously used the **Layout & Scaling** submenu (off the **Diagram** menu) to set scale the diagram to fit an exact number of rows per page, and to force all rows to have the same height. See the section *Fit an Exact Number of Rows Per Page* below for more on this.

Print Preview

Now click on **Print Preview** on the **File** menu. You can use the **Next Page** button on the toolbar to step through each page in turn. If there were four occupied pages in the grid, there should be four now. Confirm that the results were what you expected. Remember that each previewed page should correspond to what you see in each page of the grid.

Printing the Background

If you used default settings for your Ancestor diagram, it should have had a striped background, and expansion buttons should be visible in the Diagram Window. But in the Preview window, the background is white, and the diagram has no expansion buttons. This is because, by default, the diagram background doesn't print, and neither do expansion buttons. Close the Preview dialog now by clicking on the **Close** button on the toolbar.

The Print Tab

Diagram Options Dialog

Open the Diagram Options dialog, and click on the **Print** tab. Tick **Print Background**, and untick **Never print expansion buttons**. Press OK to close the Diagram Options dialog and click on **Print Preview** on the **File** menu to view the preview for the diagram again. This time you should see the striped background. You should also be able to see expansion buttons.

Close the Preview window, and go back to the **Print** tab in the Diagram Options dialog now. Click the **Installation Settings** button to revert to default settings, and press **OK**.

Black-and-white and Colour printing

By default, Family Historian will print diagrams in colour. If you just want to print a draft version of a diagram, you can, if you wish, specify that text, lines and boxes should print in black-and-white only. To do this, check **Print text, lines and boxes in Black and White only** in the **Print** tab of the **Diagram Options Dialog**. You can check the effect of this by looking at the diagram in Print Preview.

Landscape vs. Portrait

When you look at the grid, are the squares wider than tall or taller than wide? If the former, your printer is currently set for *Landscape* mode. If the latter, it is currently set for *Portrait* mode. To change this, click on **Page Setup** on the **File** menu now. Does the dialog that appears look familiar? It should do. It is the Print tab of the Diagram Options Dialog, but without the other tabs. Choose the **Orientation** that want, and press **OK**.

If you have changed orientation, you should see that the grid squares have changed shape too.

Now switch back to Landscape mode if you aren't already in Landscape mode, and click-and-drag on the grid intersection to position the diagram right in the middle of a grid square (any grid square). Assuming your paper is not very small, you should find that you can the whole diagram onto one page. Press **View Whole Diagram** to view the whole thing.

Scaling

Suppose your diagram had been too large to fit onto a single page? How could you make it smaller?

The size of a diagram is affected by a great many things. For a start, there is the amount of text displayed in each box, the font sizes used for the text, the number of generations in the displayed tree(s), whether spouses are displayed in their own boxes or not, whether pictures are displayed or not, and if so at what size – not to mention the dimension settings (see the **Dimensions** tab of the Diagram Options Dialog). Even the orientation of the diagram has an effect. Top-down diagrams tend to be wide. Left-right diagrams are often more compact.

If you want to change the size of your diagram, one option is to change any or all of the above. But what if you don't want to? What if you want your diagram to print exactly as it is now, only smaller?

For this you need to adjust the **Scaling** setting. To change *scaling* open the **General** tab of the Diagram Options dialog. Set the **Scaling** field to 50% and press **OK**. Normal scaling is 100%. If you set Scaling to 50%, each box in the diagram will be half the height that it had been before, and half the width. The combined effect of this is that the diagram as a whole will take up only one quarter of the space that it had previously taken up when printed.

When you adjust diagram scaling, the diagram may appear to have moved on the printed page. Use the techniques described in the section *Position Diagram on Printed Page* above to move the diagram back into the middle of a grid square.

Set Scaling on the Movement Control Box

Scaling can also be adjusted on the **Movement Control Box** (click on the **Enable Moving/Resizing** button ⊕ to open it). You can adjust scaling either by changing the value in the **Scale** box, or by moving the slider. If you want to set the scale to a value greater than 100%, you cannot use the slider for that. Instead, enter the value you need into the Scaling box.[20] Again, you may need to adjust the diagram's position on the printed back after adjusting scaling.

Fit an Exact Number of Rows Per Page

Where a diagram displays over multiple pages, you may find it desirable and convenient to scale the diagram so that an exact number of rows will fit on each page (or columns if it's a sideways oriented diagram). This is what the command **Scale Diagram To Fit an Exact Number of Rows Per Page** does (on the **Layout & Scaling** submenu of the **Diagram** menu – the text will be suitably adjusted if the diagram is sideways oriented). If rows are not already the same size, it will adjust them to make them the same size.

As we saw earlier in this chapter, you can also get page boundaries to align with row boundaries (or with column boundaries if it's a sideways oriented diagram). See *Align Page & Row Boundaries* above for more details.

Zoom To Actual Size

Don't assume that because you've set scaling to 50% that the diagram will look small on the screen. The size of a diagram on your screen is affected by scaling; but it's also affected by the current zoom. To see a diagram at its 'actual size' (that is, at 100% zoom), click on **Reset Zoom Level to 100%** on the **Zoom** submenu of the **Diagram** menu.

The current zoom level of a diagram is always shown in the status bar as a percentage figure (except when moving/resizing is enabled). If scaling is not 100%, it too is displayed in the status bar. As scaling is also expressed as a percentage, the scaling factor always has the label 'Scale:' in front of it, to ensure that it is not confused with the zoom factor.

---

[20] You can also set scaling by clicking on **Diagram Scaling** on the **Layout & Scaling** submenu of the **Diagram** menu.

Scaling a Diagram to Fit a Page Size

You don't have to scale a diagram down to make it smaller. You can also scale it up to make it bigger. For example, a scale of 200% would double the width and height of each box.

Let us now assume that we want to adjust scaling so that whatever paper size you are using, the diagram will fit neatly onto a single page. If it is bigger than the printed page we will make it smaller. But if it is smaller than the printed page we will make it bigger.

One way to do this would be to keep adjusting the **Scaling** setting in the Diagram Options dialog until we've found the right setting to give us what we want. This would be a fiddly way of doing it though as we would probably keep having to reposition the diagram on the printed page, each time we changed the scaling setting.

There is another way of doing it. Just as you can position the diagram relative to the printed page by moving the grid, you can also effectively scale the diagram (adjust the size it will have when printed) by resizing the grid.

First, ensure that the grid is visible (click on **Show Page Boundaries**) and that you have clicked **View Whole Diagram** so that you can see all occupied pages.

Steps

1. Start by moving the grid so that the top-left corner of the occupied area is close to the diagram. Click **View Whole Diagram** again, if necessary, to ensure you can see the whole diagram.
2. Now move the cursor over the grid intersection at the *bottom right-hand corner* of the occupied area. You should see that the cursor changes to this shape again. This time, however, click the *right* mouse button and, keeping the button pressed, move the mouse slowly in the direction of the intersection in the *top-left corner* of the window. You should find that the entire grid changes size and each grid square becomes smaller when you do this. Find the position where the whole diagram fits neatly into a single grid and release the mouse button.
3. Take note of the 'Scale:' value in the status bar (or in the Movement Control Box, if moving/resizing is enabled). That is your current scaling setting. If it is larger than 100% you have enlarged the diagram to fit the page.
4. You may want to reposition the grid slightly at this point to centre the diagram nicely in its grid square.

Note: When you make the grid squares larger, you are effectively making the printed size of the diagram smaller. When you make the grid squares smaller, you are effectively making the printed size of the diagram larger. If this seems confusing, remember that each (occupied) grid square corresponds in the real world, to a printed sheet of paper , and that nothing you are doing is actually changing the size of real world bits of paper. In resizing the grid, you are actually just changing the relative size of the printed diagram, and the paper upon which it will be printed.

Tip: You don't have to use the bottom-right intersection to resize the grid. You can click-and-drag on any intersection. But in practice it is usually easiest if you use the bottom-right one.

Avoid Page Boundaries

As we have seen, diagrams can print on multiple pages, either horizontally, vertically or both. You may want to arrange your diagram so that boxes do not print over the edges of diagrams.

To ensure that boxes do not overlap the edges of pages (either at the side or at the top and bottom) click on the **Avoid Page Boundaries** button: .

If page boundaries are not visible, you should make them visible now by clicking on **Show Page Boundaries**. This just makes it easier to see what effect the **Avoid Page Boundaries** button has.

Now use the technique described in *Position Diagram on Printed Page (2)*, above, to move the grid relative to the diagram. Notice that you cannot position a grid line on top of a node. Or rather, if you do so, the diagram adjusts itself so that boxes are moved away from the page edge.

You can configure exactly how close a box is allowed to come to a page edge, when you are avoiding page boundaries. There are two settings that determine this. They are labelled **Avoid boundaries gap** ('Horz.' and 'Vert.'). These can be set in the **More Dimensions Dialog** which you can reach by clicking the **More Dimensions** button in the **Dimensions** tab of the Diagram Options Dialog.

12 Recording Your Sources

When accumulating genealogical data, it is a very good idea to document not just the information you accumulate, but also where the information came from – your *sources*. A 'source' can be whatever you choose to consider the source of your information to be. The most common kind of source would be a document of some kind – e.g. a birth or marriage certificate, or a census record. But a source could also be a person (their recollections) or, more narrowly, a particular *interview* with a person. A book could be a source, or a part of a document, a gravestone, or even another GEDCOM file (which might or might not have been created by Family Historian).

In this example, we will use a tutorial file and add a little more detail – this time about Michael Peabody. We will treat Michael Peabody himself as a source and create a source record for him. We will automatically add source citations to him as we enter the data.

We will also create another source record for a book written by Jonathan Peabody. We will retrospectively indicate that various items of information came from this source.

Open Tutorial File
From the **Project Window**, click on the **More Tasks** button, and then in the dropdown menu click on **Samples**, and finally **Tutorial – Chapter 12**. The file opens and Cameron Peabody is displayed as the focus person in the Focus Window.

Set Automatic Source Citation
We will shortly enter some data supplied by Michael Peabody. This time, however, we want all the data we enter to have source *citations*. A *citation* is a link between an item of data and a source record. A typical 'item of data' would be a field in a record. The citation indicates where the data came from.

You can, as we will see, painstakingly type in source citations for every item of data as you enter it. However, if you are entering a large number of items of data, and what you want to say about each one is that this is what Michael Peabody told you in an interview in 1998, you might find yourself feeling that there has to be a better way. In fact, there is: *automatic source citations*.

Steps

1. Click on Set Automatic Source Citation in the Tools menu. The Set Automatic Source Citation Dialog appears.
2. At the top is the **Source Record** field. Click on the << **Select** button to the right of it.
3. A dialog comes up with the title "Select Source Records" – but the list is empty. There are no source records. Click on the **New...** button to create a new one.
4. A **New Source Record Dialog** appears. In the **Title** field type "Michael Peabody". In a real-world situation, you might choose to put Michael Peabody's address in the **Note** field. Notice that all the fields appear to be chosen on the assumption that a source is a published document of some kind – perhaps a book. That's because sources frequently *are* published documents. However, as stated in the *Preamble*, sources can be whatever you consider your source of information to be. Where a source is not a document, you must use the various fields in the source record in the way that seems most appropriate. Obviously you can put whatever you like in a **Note** field. In the **Type** field enter "Person". If the others do not seem at all appropriate in a given case, you

should simply leave them blank.

5. Press the **Create** button. This takes you back to the **Set Automatic Source Citation Dialog**, with the **Source Record** field now set to Michael Peabody.
6. Set the **Entry Date** to "12 June 1998". This field is typically used to store the date that a particular entry in a document was made (e.g. in a marriage register perhaps), which is why it is labelled in this way. However, in this case, we are using it to store the date that an interview took place. Press **Tab**.
7. Set **Assessment** to *Primary Evidence* and press **Tab**.
8. In the **Note** field type "Interview at M.P.'s home, in Maidstone, Kent".
9. Leave other values as they are, and press **Set Automatic**.

Status Bar 'Flag'

In the bottom right corner of the status bar, you should see the text 'Auto-Citation Enabled'. Take good note of this. As long as auto-citation is enabled, all the *new data* that you enter, irrespective of which tools and techniques you use to enter it with, will all be automatically cited to Michael Peabody as source. And that reminder in the status bar will be there until you cancel the automatic citation. However, *existing* data, which was already there when you set the automatic source citation, is never affected by automatic source citations.

Show Sources in the Property Box

Find Michael Peabody in the Records Window, and view his record in the **Property Box**. If the Source Pane isn't already showing, click on the **Show Sources** button on the Property Box toolbar to show it. If you can't remember what the Source Pane looks like, it's marked in Figure 11 in Chapter 2 above. As you can see there, the Source Pane has (by default) a yellow background. Ordinarily it is displayed at the bottom of the Property Box when the Property Box is docked, and to the right of the Property Box when the Property Box is floating. But this is configurable.

If the Source pane is too small to be able to see easily, click-and-drag on the gripper bar that lies between it and the main Property Box data pane to resize it (gripper bars are also marked in Figure 11). You may also want to resize the Property Box itself and/or switch from docked to floating or vice versa – whatever is most convenient for you.

Steps

1. Click in the **Name** field of the *Main* tab. The **Sources For** field in the **Source Pane** now shows the word "*Name*". But the Source list below it is empty. There are no source citations for that item of data.
2. Now click in the **Born** field. The **Sources For** field switches to the word "Birth".
3. Enter the date as "22 april 1958" and press **Tab**. The Property Box now looks something like Figure 62 below (bearing in mind that the Property Box is shown floating here, and in your case it may docked, with the Source Pane at the bottom). The **Sources For** field shows the text "Birth*". In the *Source List*, there is one entry: "Michael Peabody". All other details match the automatic source citation that you set up.

To hide the Source Pane, click on the **Show Sources** button again. The button ceases to be depressed, and the Source Pane is hidden.

The Source Pane

Although the **Source Pane** was open when we added Michael Peabody's birth date, it didn't have to be. If you added Michael Peabody's details directly into the **Records Window**, without the **Property Box** even being open at the time (which can be done, using *low-level editing*, if you know how to do it), the source citations would still be set up automatically. However, if you are entering details into the **Property Box**, the **Source Pane** automatically updates itself to show the sources for whatever item of data you last clicked on (or tabbed to) in the main part of the **Property Box** – the *Data Pane*.

A potentially annoying consequence of this is that, if you are not careful, you may miss the source citation you have just created. The reason is that Family Historian only actually creates or updates field information when you tab or click away from a field. The source citation is created at the same time. But because you have just clicked away from the field, you don't now see the source citation you just created for it.

One solution is to enter the data in the field, press **Tab** to 'register' the data. Then click back (or press **Shift+Tab** to get back) into the field you just vacated. We didn't have to do this with the **Born** field because when we tabbed we moved from the birth *date* field to the birth *place* field, and these share the same citation (the citation applies to the recorded birth event details). But it could arise with other fields.

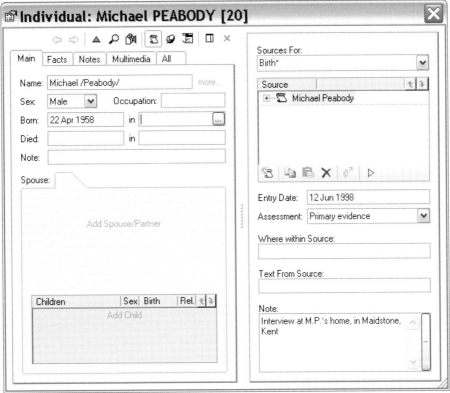

Figure 62 – the Property Box, with the Source Pane open

F5 An alternative is to press the **F5** key when you enter data in a field, instead of pressing the **Tab** key. This has the effect of forcing Family Historian to register the data you have entered or updated, but without the cursor leaving the field. The advantage is that you can immediately see not only the effects of your update in the field itself, but you can also immediately see the automatic source citation created for it. Try it now.

Steps

1. Click on the **Show Sources** button 🗒 to open the Source pane again.
2. Click in the **Occupation** field. The **Source Pane** is empty.
3. Type "Journalist". Press *F5*.
4. The **Source Pane** updates to display the Source Citation for this item of data.

It should be stressed that in terms of the underlying data created or updated, there is absolutely no difference between pressing **F5** and pressing **Tab**, or clicking elsewhere. If you are prepared to take on trust that your source citations are being created, you don't need to bother with it – indeed, you don't need to have the Source

Pane open at all.

Source Record Icon

All record types have their own distinctive record icon. The icon for Source records, you may have realised by now, looks like this: . Your file now contains one record for Michael Peabody qua *Individual*, and another record for Michael Peabody qua *Source*. Keeping clear about the kind of record you are looking at, at any given time, should help to avoid the possible confusions that might arise. The record icons give a visual clue, which should help.

Cancel Automatic Source Citation

As soon as you have finished entering all the data provided by a given source, it is a good idea to cancel the automatic source citation, so that you don't accidentally create citations you didn't want to create. To do this, click on **Cancel Automatic Source Citation** on the **Tools** menu. You should see that the status bar no longer has the "Auto-Citation Enabled" text displayed.

Add Citation

We will now retrospectively add source information to information that had been added previously. We will also create another source record – this time for a book written by Jonathan Peabody.

Steps

1. Locate Cameron Peabody, and display his record in the **Property Box**. Make sure the *Source Pane* is open.
2. Click in the **Occupation** field (containing the value 'Printer'). The **Sources For** field in the *Source Pane* shows the value *Occupation*. No source citations are listed below it.
3. Click on the **Add Citation** button in the *Source Pane* toolbar. A dialog titled "Select Record" appears, displaying the Source record for Michael Peabody. Do not select it. Instead click on the **New...** button.
4. A dialog titled "New Source Record" appears. In the **Title** field, type the title for Jonathan Peabody's book: "Printing in the 20th Century".
5. In the **Typ**e field, type "Book".
6. In the **Author** field, type "Jonathan Peabody".
7. In the **Publication Information** field type: "Bookles & Bookles Publishing".
8. Press **Create**. The new source record is created and a source citation to it is displayed for the **Occupation** field, for Cameron Peabody.
9. Set the **Assessment** field to *Primary Evidence*.
10. Set the **Where within Source** field to "Chapter 11".

Copy and Paste Citation

You would not want to have to do that much work for each item of data, if you had many items of data which required the same citation. You don't have to.

Steps

1. Ensure the citation you just created is selected. Click on the **Copy Citation** button on the Source pane toolbar.
2. Click in the **Born** field (in the Property Box *Data Pane[21]*). Press the **Paste Citation** button in the Source Pane toolbar. The **Born** field now has the same source citation as the **Occupation** field (select the citation you just pasted and note that the **Assessment** and **Where within Source** fields for this citation are the same as the ones you specified for the printer field).
3. Click in the **Died** field and press the **Paste Citation** button again. The **Died** field now has the same source citation as the **Occupation** field.

Citation Fields

You should by now have gathered that the **Entry Date, Assessment, Where within Source, Text From Source** and **Note** fields in the Source Pane, are all aspects of the citation selected in the source citation list, just above the Source Pane toolbar.

---

[21] See Chapter 2 if you aren't sure what the Data Pane is.

Although the values are frequently the same for many citations (which is why automatic source citations, and copying-and-pasting, are useful) these values can be different for each source citation.

The Sources For List

Look now at items in the **Sources For** list in the Source Pane. Each item is a field, or sometimes an entire 'sub-branch' of fields, for which data has been provided, and for which a source citation *can* be provided. The ones with an asterisk next to them are the ones for which one or more source citations have been provided.

Delete Citation

To delete a source citation, select it in the Source Pane, and click on the Delete Citation button ✕.

Go To Source Record
▷

To navigate to the source record, for a selected source citation, click on the **Go To Source Record** button ▷ in the Source Pane toolbar. You can, of course, later return to the previous record you were viewing by clicking on the **Go Back** button ⇦ in the **Property Box** toolbar.

Source Records in the Records Window

Like all records, there is a tab for Source records in the **Records Window** (some record types may have their tab hidden, but you can always unhide it from the **Record Window** tab of **Preferences** on the **Tools** menu).

Click on the Source tab in the **Records Window** now. You should see 2 records – one for Michael Peabody, and one for Jonathan Peabody's book.

Repository Records
🏠

You may have noticed, when we created the source records, that you can specify a *Repository* for a source. This is optional. You don't need to specify repositories. Each source record can have at most one – but many source records can be linked to the same repository. The repository record stores details of an address at which potentially many sources may be located. The record icon for a Repository record looks like this: 🏠.

Specifying a Source When Merging

Later we will look at how you can merge another project or GEDCOM file into the current project or GEDCOM file. As we will see, when you do this, as part of the process, you will be able to create a source record to represent the source project or file, and create source citations to link all the merged data to this source record.

13 Introduction to Queries

In this chapter we will be looking at Family Historian's support for queries. We will start by looking at what a query is. We will introduce a new Family Historian subwindow – the Query Window – and look at some of the many things that you can do with queries.

Open Tutorial File

This chapter uses the tutorial file "Tutorial – Chapter 13". From the **Project Window**, click on the **More Tasks** button, and then in the dropdown menu click on **Samples**, and finally **Tutorial – Chapter 13**. The file opens and Cameron Peabody is displayed as the focus person in the Focus Window.

What is a Query?

Queries are stored sets of instructions which allow you to specify criteria for identifying a set of records (or events or attributes) of a given type. For example, a very simple example might be: "Find me all the Individual records where the person's date of birth is later than the year 2000". A slightly more complex one might be "Find me all the Family records where the father has 'Paterson' somewhere in his name, and the word 'Australia' is mentioned in the place field for the father's birth".

When a query is 'run', Family Historian looks through the current file to find all the records of the required type which match the criteria contained in the query. The resulting set of records is called the *Result Set*.

There is much more to queries than this, however; but this definition will at least serve as an introduction.

Standard Queries

Family Historian comes with a pre-defined set of queries, called *Standard Queries*. We will look at a selection of these now.

Relations and Nearest Relationship

Standard Query

We will start by looking at the *Relations and Nearest Relationship* query. This query finds everyone in the current file who is related to a given person (whoever you choose) and shows exactly how they are related to that person. Actually, any 2 people can be related in more than one way (Cameron's 2nd wife is also his first cousin, for example). This particular query only shows the nearest relationship. Later we will look at another query that shows the nearest 5 relationships.

Steps

1. Select Cameron Peabody. You should know by now that you can select his record wherever you can see a reference to it – in the **Focus Window**, in the **Records Window**, in the **Diagram Window**, or other windows.
2. Click on the **View** menu, then **Standard Queries**, then **Relations and Nearest Relationship**. The **Query Parameters Dialog** appears with title "Enter Query Parameters". The dialog box has one field, labelled "Starting Person". The value in this field already shows "Cameron Peabody".
3. Leave the Starting Person field unchanged and click **OK**. The *Query Window* appears looking roughly like Figure 63 below.

Tip: You don't actually need to select a record before running a query. However, it can sometimes save you a little time if you do. For example, the reason that the Query Parameters Dialog showed Cameron Peabody pre-selected as the Starting Person, was that his record was the current selection when you ran the query.

The Query Window

The **Query Window** is another *subwindow*[22]. Like all Family Historian subwindows it has its own Navigation Bar Icon – the first of the two icons shown on the left. The second icon is the Query Window's toolbar icon.

Like the Records Window, the Query Window has multiple tabs. These tabs never alter. They are: *General*, *Columns*, *Rows* and *Result Set*. At the moment the *Result Set* tab is selected. Take note that the other tabs are there, but otherwise ignore them for now. We will be looking at them presently.

Above the tabs, there is a field labelled 'Query'. This field is a dropdown list, containing all the standard queries, plus any custom queries that you have created yourself. It shows the *current query* in the **Query Window**. At present, the current query is *Relations and Nearest Relationship* – the query we have just run. To the right of this field is the **Query Toolbar** *(see* Figure 63 *below)*. We will be looking at this shortly. Beyond the **Query Toolbar**, to its right, is the text 'Standard Query – read only' in blue. This simply indicates that you are looking at a standard query, and that, like all standard queries, it is read only – you can't modify it. However, as we will see presently, you can copy it, and modify the copy.

*Tip: You can open the **Query Window** at any time, without having to previously run a query from the View menu, by simply clicking on the **Query Window** button on the main application toolbar. If the Query Window is already open, you can switch to it at any time – as you can with any subwindow – by simply clicking on its Navigation Bar icon.*

The Result Set Tab

Query Window

If you use spreadsheets, the *Result Set Tab* of the **Query Window** should look familiar to you.

The columns in the *Result Set* Tab are determined by the query whose result set it is displaying. At present, you should see four columns, with headings: *Relation*, *Record Id*, *Relationship*, *Relationship from relation's point-of-view*, and finally *Relative's Generation*. You may have to scroll sideways to see all of them. Alternatively, move your cursor over the gap between any 2 column headings, until the cursor looks like this   ; and click-and-drag to resize a column.

You should see that the *Relation* column contains a list of individuals, as you might expect. The *Relationship* column shows how each person is related to Cameron Peabody, and the *Relationship from relation's point-of-view* shows what you would expect. Cameron Peabody is there too – treated as a limiting case of his own relation. His relationship to himself is given as 'root.

The *Relative's Generation* column effectively assigns a generation number to each person, giving 0 to anyone who belongs to the same generation as Cameron Peabody, -1 to anyone from the previous generation, -2 to anyone from the generation before that, +1 to Cameron's children's generation, and so on.

Sorting the Result Set

You will notice that the query is sorted in generation order, starting with the most recent generation. This sort order was specified in the query. We will see later how this is done. For now, however, note that you can re-sort the result set by clicking on any column heading.

Click now on the *Relative's Generation* column heading. This sorts the list in ascending order of generation instead of, as it was, in descending order of generation.

If you press-and-hold the **Alt** key and then click on the column heading, the list will be sorted in reverse order.

---

[22] If you can't remember what a 'subwindow' is, see the section on them in Chapter 1.

How can we now revert back to the original sort order?

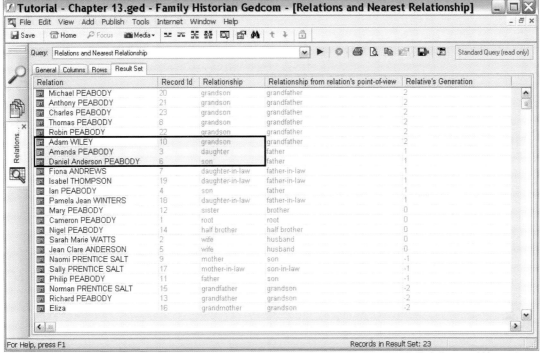

Figure 63 –The Query Window with the Result Set tab selected. The current query is Relations and Nearest Relationship. 9 cells have been selected.

Run Query

Query Toolbar

To get the *result set* to revert to its original sort, in this case, we have to run the query again. We have already seen that a query can be run from the **Standard Queries** menu, within the **View** menu. However, any query can also be run from within the **Query Window** itself.

Steps

1. Select the query you wish to run from the dropdown list labelled 'Queries:' at the top of the **Query Window**. In this case, we just want to re-run the current query, "Relations and Nearest Relationship", which is already selected.

2. Click on the **Run Query** button ▶ on the **Query Toolbar**. The **Query Parameters Dialog** appears again. The **Starting Person** field in the dialog should still contain Cameron Peabody.

3. Click **OK** in the **Query Parameters Dialog**. The query is run again, and reverts to its original sort order.

Run and Invert Result Set

Query Menu

If you look at the status bar, at the bottom of the application window, you should see that it says "Records in Result Set: 23". That may seem surprising. There are 24 Individual records in this file. Isn't everyone in the file related to Cameron Peabody? Who is missing?

It is very easy to find out which record has been excluded by this query.

Steps

1. Click on the **Query Menu** button 🗏 at the right-hand end of the **Query Toolbar**. A dropdown menu appears.

2. Click on the menu command: **Run and Invert Result Set**. This command runs a query in exactly the same way as it is ordinarily run, except that instead of

displaying all the records which match the query, it displays all the records which don't. You should see the **Query Parameters Dialog** appear again, with the **Starting Person** field still showing Cameron Peabody.

3. Click **OK**. The query is run again, but this time the 'inverted' result set is displayed.

The inverted result set contains one record only – that of Thomas Andrews. The other columns are all blank. The fact that these columns are blank is of course quite reasonable if Thomas Andrews is not related to Cameron Peabody. But why isn't he?

Select Record in Result Set

Just to the left of the text 'Thomas Andrews' in the first cell of the result set, you should see that there is a little Individual record icon – the identity card icon ▉. You may remember from earlier chapters on the **Records Window**, that it is a general principle that text which has a record icon next to it represents the record itself. And so it is here. Records can be selected in the *Result Set* tab, by clicking on any cell which contains a record icon.

To select a single cell in the Result Set tab you just click in it. This gives it a thick border. If the first cell is not already selected, click in it to select it now, and then click on the **Property Box** button ▉ in the application toolbar (or just double-click on the cell). The **Property Box** appears and shows record details for Thomas Andrews. Now click on the **View Descendants** button ▉. If spouses are not already being displayed, click on the **Spouses in Own Box** button ▉ too. You can see from the diagram in the **Diagram Window** that Thomas Andrews is the father of Fiona Andrews, who is the 'spouse' (they never married, although they had a child together) of Ian Peabody. Ian Peabody, you may remember, is Cameron Peabody's son.

This explains why Thomas Andrews doesn't count as a relative of Cameron Peabody. For most purposes (such as this query), Family Historian treats as a relative of a given person, X, anyone who is a descendant of X, an ancestor of X, a descendant of an ancestor of X, or a spouse of any of these people. It will also count as a relative of X anyone who is a relative (by the above definition) of X's spouse. And Thomas Andrews, uniquely in the current file, does not match any of those criteria, for Cameron Peabody. He is Cameron Peabody's son's father-in-law; but not, by our definition, a relative of Cameron Peabody as such.

More Standard Queries

Close the **Diagram Window** and the **Property Box** but leave the **Query Window** open. If you accidentally closed it, click on the **Query Window** button ▉ on the main application toolbar to re-open it.

We will now look at a selection of other standard queries.

Relations and 5 Nearest Relationships

Standard Query

The *Relations and 5 Nearest Relationships* query is similar to the *Relations and Nearest Relationship* query, but instead of showing just one way that a person is related, it shows up to five ways that they are related. Like all queries, you can run this query either from within the **Query Window**, or from a menu command (**View** then **Standard Queries**, then **Relations and 5 Nearest Relationships**). We will run it from within the **Query Window**. For a change, we will look this time at the relatives of Jean Clare Anderson.

Steps

1. Click on the **Query** field at the top of the **Query Window**, and select *Relations and 5 Nearest Relationships* from the dropdown list.

2. Click on the **Run Query** button ▶ on the **Query Toolbar**.

3. The **Query Parameters Dialog** appears. Select Jean Clare Anderson[23] and click **OK**.

The result set for this query has 7 columns and 23 rows (that is, 23 records match the query – which in this case means that Jean Clare Anderson has 23 relatives in the current file). The first column is labelled 'Relation'. The second is 'Record Id'. The remaining 5 are all labelled 'Relationship'. The first relationship column shows how the given person is most closely related to Jean Clare Anderson. The second relationship column shows the second-closest relationship, and so on. For example, Cameron Peabody's closest relationship to Jean Clare Anderson is that he is her husband. His second closest relationship to her is that of *cousin*.

Contains Text

Standard Query

Now run the *Contains Text* query. Type 'Maidstone' into the **Enter Text** field when prompted. The result set contains Michael Peabody only.

This is a useful query. It finds all the Individuals that have any fields which contain the entered text – in this case, it found the only record with any connection with Maidstone.

Fact Date Warnings

Standard Query

Now run the *Fact Date Warnings* query. Notice that this time the **Query Parameters Dialog** does not appear. Some queries, such as this one, do not take any parameters. Some take several parameters.

When you run this query, the result set appears but with no cells showing. In the status bar it should say "Records in Result Set: 0". That is not an error. This query finds all events and attributes which have dates that, for one reason or another, look improbable. The current file doesn't contain any. To show how it works we will have to create an improbable date.

Steps

1. Click now on the Focus Window tab in the Navigation Bar to switch back to the Focus Window. Open the Property Box for Cameron Peabody and change his date of birth from 3 Jan 1901 to 3 Jan 1701. Press the tab key. When you do this a little balloon appears which says "Possible Error. Date is earlier than the Individual's earliest expected birth date, given their death date". Click on this balloon, or press the Esc key, to close it.

2. Click on the Query Window in the Navigation Bar to switch back to the Query Window and press the **Run Query** button ▶ to run the query again. This time the result window should show three rows. Why three rows for one improbable date? The answer is that Family Historian doesn't know that the problem is with the Birth date. It merely knows that the dates for Cameron Peabody's birth, marriage and date look as if they can't all be right. This query lists up to three possible warnings for each date. In the present case there are two warning strings for two of the dates, and one for the third. Scroll sideways now and check all five warnings. You will see that the same warning occurs twice for the Death date. This is because the Death date is a range, and Family Historian checks both 'ends' of the range. In this case, both are improbable for the same reason.

Data-Linked Cells

We have already seen that some cells in a query result set provide links back to records. If you select any cell which displays a record icon to the left of the text (such as the Individual record icon 🖻 which displays next to Cameron Peabody in the 4th column) and click on the Property Box button 📑 on the toolbar, you can view the record in question in the Property Box. Double-clicking on the cell

---

[23] If Jean Clare Anderson is not shown in the dropdown list, select 'Browse...' to open the Select Records dialog. Click on Jean Clare Anderson in the list on the left side, and click on 🔳 to add her to the selection on the right side. Press OK.

achieves the same thing, as does right-clicking on the cell and choosing **Properties** from the dropdown menu that appears. This is because these cells are *data-linked* – they are linked back to records.

Locating Fields in the Property Box

Not all data-linked cells are linked to records. Some are linked to fields. The cells in the first column of the current result set are all data-linked. If you double-click on any of them, that actual field will be displayed in the Property Box. Try it now. Double-click on the cell which contains "4 Jul 1926". When you do this, the Property Box is opened (if it had been closed) at the Facts tab, showing events in the life of Cameron Peabody, and his marriage to Sarah Watts, on 4th July 1926, is selected.

When you double-click on a data-linked cell, Family Historian will show that field in the Property Box, in what it judges to be the most suitable tab. If you right-click on a data-linked cell a dropdown menu appears. Choosing **Locate In Property Box** does the same thing as double-clicking. Choosing **Locate in All Tab** however will ensure that the field is displayed in the **All** tab of the **Property Box**.

Cells are not data-linked if they contain calculated values or messages – data in other words that isn't a straightforward representation of a particular record or field value. In that case, there is no field or record which is associated with the value in the cell. Double-clicking on these cells does nothing.

If a cell is data-linked, its text is coloured black by default. Non-data-linked cells have text which is coloured grey by default. Look now at Figure 63 above. The cells in the first column have black text, and hence are data-linked. All the others have grey text and are not data-linked. These colours can be changed in the **Query Window** tab of **Preferences** if you wish.

Birthdays (all)

Standard Query

Now run the *Birthdays (all)* query. This is another query that does not require any parameters, so the **Query Parameters Dialog** does not appear.

Why are there only 5 records in the result set? Because this query ignores all records where the month of birth is not recorded. Only 5 records satisfy that, in this file.

Although the sample is not big enough to show this properly, this query sorts the result set by month, and within month, by day, and within that, by name of the Individual. However, as always, you can re-sort the list by clicking on any column heading.

Birthdays (for given day and month)

Standard Query

Run the *Birthdays (for given day and month)* query. This is an example of a query that takes more than one parameter. When the **Query Parameters Dialog** appears, enter 2 in the **Month** field, and 14 in the **Day** field, to find out who was born on Valentine's Day. You should see that only Mary Peabody was. All the cells are data-linked. Double-click on either the month, day or year to view the details of Mary Peabody's birth in the **Facts** tab of the Property Box.

Search For Orphans

Standard Query

The standard query *Search For Orphans* is a useful one if you want to locate any records for individuals who are not related to anyone else. In fact, not only can you use it for this, but you can also use it to identify small groups of individuals who, although related to one another, are not related to other individuals in the file.

Run the query now. It doesn't take any parameters. There should be one row in the result set for each individual in the file – i.e. 24. The way it works is that each individual is assigned a 'pool' number. The value of the pool number is arbitrary. The significance of it is that all individuals sharing the same pool number are directly or indirectly related to one another. Cameron Peabody, as we saw, is not directly related to Thomas Andrews, but they are indirectly related (they are each related to Ian Peabody, for example).

In this example, all individuals in the file have a pool number of 1. This shows that they are all directly or indirectly related to one another. However, if you added a new unrelated individual and ran the query again, the new person would have a pool number of 2, which would show that they were not directly or indirectly related to anyone in pool 1.

The query is sorted by descending order of pool number. By looking for pool numbers which are only held by a small number of individuals, or just by one, you can easily identify small isolated groups, and orphans.

Boys' Names

Standard Query

The standard query *Boy's Names* is another that takes no parameters. Run it now. It lists all the given names of the males in the current file. There is an exactly similar one for girls' names. It includes the year of birth, where known, so that you can see not only which names have been popular, but when they were popular.

Named List Members

Standard Query

We haven't looked at *Named Lists* yet. They will be discussed in Chapter 16. However it is worth mentioning the *Named List Members* query. It is a very simple query that prompts you to specify a named list, and then returns the Individuals who are members of that list. This can be useful if you want to use a Named List where a query is expected (e.g. in *Split Tree Helper*, or using a query to mark boxes in a diagram). It effectively allows you to use your Named List as if it were a query.

All Individuals

Standard Query

If you want to print off the Records Window, this is the query to use. Its columns correspond to the Records Window columns (when first installed). If you want the columns sorted by Record Id, click on the Record Id column heading.

All Events

Standard Query

The *All Events* query lists all events recorded in the current file, in order of date, with the most recent events first. Events (and attributes) can have up to two 'owners' in Family Historian. For an Individual event like birth or death, the 'owner' is just the Individual. However, Family events – like Marriage or Divorce – are said to be 'owned' by both of the spouses in the Family record. This is why there are two columns labelled 'Individual 1' and 'Individual 2' for the two possible owners.

All Facts

Standard Query

The *All Facts* query is similar to the All Events query, but it includes *attributes* as well as *events*. The difference between events and attributes, you may remember, is that the latter have values where the former do not. Occupation, for example, is an attribute – and its values might be 'Printer', 'Journalist', 'Farmer' etc. For this reason, the *All Facts* query has a 'Values' column. The Values column will always be blank for events.

Print Query as Report

All queries, including queries you create yourself (custom queries) can be printed as a report. To see what a query will look like when printed, click on **Print Preview** on the **File** menu. Do this now, to see what the *Boys' Names* query looks like when printed as a report.

Print Preview

Query Toolbar

As **Print Preview** is a command you are frequently likely to want to use with queries, there is a button for it – the **Print Preview** button – on the **Query Toolbar**. This button is there for convenience only. There is no difference in effect between clicking on this button, or the **Print Preview** command on the **File** menu.

Print Preview is only available if you have a printer installed.

Configure Query Reports

Although standard queries are read only, for most purposes, you can still control some aspects of how they will print as reports. In particular, the width of the columns of a report when printed correspond approximately to the relative width of the columns in the Result Set tab. By clicking and dragging on the intersection between column headers (when the cursor looks like this:) you can resize columns in the Result Set tab, which in turn will determine the width of the same columns when printed.

Click now on the *General* tab of the **Query Window**. Most of the fields in this tab are grey, but you will notice that the **Orientation** and **Multi-page handling** fields at the foot of the window, are not grey. The **Orientation** field determines whether this report prints in *Landscape* or *Portrait*.

The **Multi-page handling** field determines what Family Historian does about reports which are too *wide* to fit onto a single page (reports which are too *long* to fit onto a single page are not considered a problem – you just get multiple pages in the report). The best solution, if at all possible, is to arrange your report in such a way that it can fit within the width of a single page (by adjusting column sizes if necessary). However, if this is not possible, you effectively have to choose between simply discarding any data which is too wide to fit onto one page (this is the *Max. one page across* option), or you have to accept that you will get a *grid* of report pages when the query is printed. In the latter case, you can choose between numbering these pages *Across then down*, or *Down then across*.

To see how many pages you will get when a report is printed, use **Print Preview**.

Standard Query Descriptions

While we are looking at the *General Tab* of the **Query Window**, notice that it contains a **Description** field. Each standard query is described in this field.

Select the first query in the **Query** field: *Age At Death (all)*. Notice that the **Description** field describes what this query does. Now click the *Down Arrow* key on your keyboard once. If the keyboard focus was still on the **Query** field (that is, you haven't clicked anywhere since you clicked on it) the query will change to *Age at Marriage (all)*, and you can read its Description. Click the **Down Arrow** key again, to step through each query in turn and see what it does. This is an easy technique for browsing the list of queries.

Later when we look at custom queries, you will see that you can write your own descriptions for them in this field.

The Query Toolbar

We have already looked at the **Run Query** button ▶ and the **Print Preview** button 🔍. We will now look at the remaining buttons on the **Query Toolbar** (see Figure 64 below).

Tip: As with all Family Historian toolbars, if you simply move the cursor over a button and pause briefly, a small floating message will appear next to it as a brief reminder of the function of the button. These messages are sometimes called 'Tool Tips' or 'Bubble Help'.

Figure 64 – the Query Window toolbar

Cancel Query

⊗

Query Toolbar

Do not be concerned if you do not recognise this button. The **Cancel Query** button ⊗ spends most of the time in its greyed state, in which it looks like this: ⊗. It is only enabled when a query is actually running. You click on it if you want to cancel the currently running query. However, if you have a moderately powerful computer, you may find that queries run so quickly that there is no time to cancel them before they have completed. This does not mean that the **Cancel Query** button does not work on your computer. It just means that the queries take very little time to run.

Print

Query Toolbar

Like the **Print Preview** button the Print button is on the **Query Toolbar** for convenience only. There is no difference in effect between clicking on the **Print** button on the **Query Toolbar**, and clicking on the **Print** command on the **File** menu.

Queries and Spread-sheets

We have already noted that you can print any query as a report. Almost equally useful is the fact that you can also easily copy all or part of a query's result set into a spreadsheet. Modern spreadsheet applications are usually powerful programs that can be used for sophisticated data analysis, and can produce all kinds of charts and graphics for you.

Select Multiple Cells

Before you can copy cells, you must first select the cells you wish to copy. We have already seen how you can select a single cell in the *Result Set* tab of the **Query Window** by simply clicking in the cell. Users of spreadsheet applications will know that you can also select a range of cells by clicking in the top-left cell and, keeping the mouse button depressed, drag down to the bottom right cell that you wish to select (i.e. this is a single action click-and-drag). The 'bottom right' cell can, of course, be in the same column as the 'top left' cell, if you just want to select a column, or in the same row, if you just want to select a row.

An easy alternative to click-and-drag, which is particularly useful for a large range, is to click in the top-left cell of the range you want, then scroll until the bottom-right cell is visible, press-and-hold the **Shift** key, and click again in the bottom-right cell. Figure 63 above shows an example of a result set in which a grid of nine cells (in three rows of three columns each) have been selected.

Copy Selected Cells

Query Toolbar

Having selected the cells you want, you can then click on the **Copy Selected Cells** button on the **Query Toolbar** to copy the cells to the clipboard[24]. Pressing **Ctrl-C** does the same thing.

If you have a spreadsheet application, try copying a range of cells to it now.

Steps

Select the range of cells you want in the Result Set tab (the whole result set if you like), then click **Copy Selected Cells** to copy the range to the clipboard (don't be concerned that nothing obvious apparently happens when you click on the button).
Now open your spreadsheet application and start a new, empty worksheet. Click in a cell in your worksheet, and paste the contents of the clipboard into the worksheet. Typically you can do this by clicking on **Paste** on the **Edit** menu in the spreadsheet. Alternatively, pressing **Ctrl-V** will usually achieve the same thing. The contents of the selected range of cells are copied into the spreadsheet.

Locate in Property Box

Query Toolbar

We saw earlier how you can locate a field or record in the Property Box by simply double-clicking on it, if it is a data-linked cell (see earlier sections in this chapter). This button does the same thing with the currently selected cell. If the currently selected cell is not data-linked, the button will be greyed.

Save Results to File

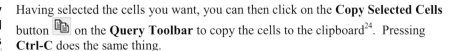

Query Toolbar

As well as copying the contents of a result set to the clipboard, you can also save the entire contents of a result set as a file. When you click on the **Save Results to File** button a dropdown menu appears giving you the choice of formats: PDF, CSV, and Text.

If you are planning to open your file in another application such as a spreadsheet,

---

[24] The 'clipboard' is the name for a hidden holding area within Windows that items are copied to, prior to being pasted.

word-processor or database application, you should use CSV format.

Saving a result set to a file can be useful in various ways. For example, if you have a Word-processor which has a Mail-Merge facility (which any decent one should do) you could use a result set to generate standard letters to other genealogists, or create custom reports using your word-processor. See your word-processor documentation for instructions on how to do this. Again – for this kind of purpose, CSV format is ideal.

PDF format is most useful when you want to send a Query result set to someone as a *report*. The PDF format is designed so that PDF files look the same, whichever computer you view them on.

Query Menu

Query Toolbar

When you click on the **Query Menu** button ![icon], the last button on the **Query Toolbar**, a small dropdown menu appears with a few extra menu commands. We have already looked at the **Run and Invert Result Set** command.

Five of the commands will be discussed in Chapter 16. These are

Add Row Records to Named List
Remove Row Records From Named List
Set Flag on Row Records
Clear Flag on Row Records
Add Selected Cell Records to Named List

The **Save Result Set As** submenu effectively does the same as the Save Results to File button (see previous discussion).

The **Locate in Property Box** and **Locate in All Tab** menu commands are the same menu commands that you get in the context menu that appears when you right-click on a data-linked cell (see the section "Locate Fields in the Property Box" above).

The **Options** command lets you set print margins, and change various fonts and colours. One of the fonts, *Query Window Results*, is the font used in the Result Set tab. The others are fonts used when a query is printed.

The other commands on the **Query Menu** all concern custom queries. We will look at custom queries in the next chapter.

Delete Multiple Records

We have already seen in Chapter 8 that you can select multiple records in diagrams. Another way to select multiple records is to run a query which returns those records. Then select all the cells that represent those records. Remember that a cell which represents a record has a record icon to the left of the text.

One reason you might want to select multiple records is if you wanted to delete them all. To do this, click **Delete** on the **Edit** menu (or press the **Delete** key). When you do this, a message will warn you that you are about to delete records, and give you the opportunity to cancel.

Using a query to select multiple records that you wish to delete is especially useful when you want to split a Family Historian file. There is a dialog designed to help with precisely this scenario, called the **Split Tree Helper** dialog. It is discussed in Chapter 15.

Tip: Another way to delete multiple records is to put them into a Named List, and then use the command **Delete All Records in Named List**. See Chapter 16 for more on Named Lists.

Delete Multiple

It sometimes happens that you don't want to delete multiple records, but you do want to delete multiple fields within a record. Suppose, for example, that you want

Fields to delete all birth and death details from a file. Simply run a query that shows the fields you want, select them all (i.e. select all the cells that represent the fields) and press the **Delete** key. As always, you will be given a warning and an opportunity to cancel, before any data is actually deleted.

It may, of course, be that there is no query which conveniently includes the fields or records that you want to delete. In that case, you will have to create one yourself. Custom queries are the topic of the next chapter.

14 Writing Custom Queries

This chapter continues exactly where the last chapter left off, so if you haven't already done so, you should read the previous chapter first.

In this chapter, you will learn how to create, change and delete custom queries.

Open Tutorial File
Like the previous chapter, this chapter uses a tutorial file to illustrate the issues discussed. From the **Project Window**, click on the **More Tasks** button, and then in the dropdown menu click on **Samples**, and finally **Tutorial – Chapter 14**. The file opens and Cameron Peabody is displayed as the focus person in the Focus Window.

Custom Queries
Custom queries are queries that you create yourself. Queries are not stored in GEDCOM files. They are kept completely separate and maintained by Family Historian. This means that both standard and custom queries can be used with any GEDCOM file.

Once you have created a custom query, you never have to explicitly save changes to it, as you do with family tree files – changes are automatically saved as soon as you make them.

New Custom Query
To create a new custom query, open the Query Window (by, for example, clicking on the Query Window button ▦ on the main toolbar), then click on the **Query**

Query Menu
Menu button ▣ on the Query Window toolbar, and finally click on **New Custom Query** in the dropdown menu that appears. A dialog box will appear in which you have to specify the name of the new query, and its type. The name must be unique among custom queries. A custom query can, however, have the same name as a standard query.

There are nine types of query – one for each record type ('Individual', 'Family', 'Source', etc) and one labelled 'Fact (event or attribute)'. An Individual query produces a result set that consists of Individual records. If you like, they 'return' an ordered list of records. A Source query produces a result set consisting of Source records (returns an ordered list of sources); and so on. A *Fact* query produces a result set consisting of *fields within records* – the fields which store event or attribute data. So Fact queries are a little different from all other queries in that they alone do not return records.

If you run a new custom query, without making any changes to it, you will find that if it is a record type query, the result set will consist of every record of the required type, in unsorted order. If it is a Fact query, the result will consist of every fact (every field that stores a fact) in the whole file.

What is a Record?
In case you're not sure what a *record* is, it is essentially an imaginary box that Family Historian uses to store data in. One such box is kept for each Individual, Family and Source (and other things) in your project. An Individual record is a different *type* of record to a Family record, which in turn is a different type of record to a Source record. The difference consists partly in what you do with them, and partly in what kinds of data you store in them.

What is a Field?
A field is an item of data within a record. *Birth date* is a field within an Individual record, for example.

What is a Fact? We looked at this in Chapter 6. In Family Historian, the word 'Fact' is often used as shorthand for 'Event or Attribute'. Everyone should know what an *event* is: **Birth**, **Death**, **Christening** ... are examples of events. An *attribute* is anything that is associated with a value. For example, **Occupation** is an attribute, the value for which would be 'printer' in Cameron Peabody's case. Another example is **Marriage Count**. In Cameron's case, the value for this attribute would be '2'.

In a sense, **Name** and **Sex** are both attributes too; but in Family Historian (and GEDCOM), you will not see name and sex information listed under 'Attributes'. If you like you can think of them as attributes which are too important to be listed with the other attributes.

In the context of a Fact query, a 'Fact' is a particular type of field within a record – that is, one used for storing event or attribute data. Facts can be Individual facts or Family facts – that is, they can be found in (and can only be found in) Individual and Family records.[25]

Save As Custom Query Returning now to the Query Menu: As stated earlier, you cannot modify a standard query (apart from configuring it for printing), but you can copy it, and modify the copy.

Query Menu

Steps

1. Ensure that the query you wish to copy is the current query in the **Query Window** (select it in the **Query** field at the top of the **Query Window** if it isn't already selected).
2. Click on the **Query Menu** button 🖅 and select **Save as Custom Query** from the dropdown menu that appears.
3. By default, the name field will show the name of the current query. If you are copying a standard query, you don't actually have to change this, although you may wish to. Set the query name to whatever you wish it to be. The custom query is created. You will not be allowed to use the name of another custom query.

Copy or Rename a Custom Query There are no menu commands for copying or renaming custom queries. But you don't need any. **Save as Custom Query** can be used to make a copy of any query. If you want to rename a custom query, use **Save as Custom Query** to copy it, then delete the original. This amounts to the same thing as renaming it.

Delete Custom Query To delete a custom query, first make sure it is selected as the current query in the **Query Window** (using the **Query** field in the top left corner of the **Query Window**). Then click on the **Query Menu** button 🖅 on the **Query Toolbar,** and choose **Delete Custom Query** in the menu that appears. You cannot delete standard queries.

Query Menu

You can also delete custom queries from the **Custom Queries** submenu of the **View** menu.

The *Parent Names* Sample Query As a first example, we will create a custom query that finds all the individuals in the current file whose father was called 'Philip' and whose mother was called 'Naomi'.

We will create a simple version of this initially, and will gradually look at ways to enhance it.

---

[25] It should be recognised that the way the words 'fact', 'event' and 'attribute' are used here is close to ordinary English, but not quite the same. A dictionary might tell us that the information we record in notes, say, are also facts. But they don't count as facts in the slightly-specialised way that we are using the term here.

Steps

1. Open the **Query Window** if it is not already open (e.g. by clicking on the **Query Window** button on the main application toolbar).
2. Click on the **Query Menu** button on the **Query Toolbar**, and select **New Custom Query** from the dropdown menu.
3. Set the name of the query as 'Parent Names'. The type should be *Individual*. Click on **Create**. The new query is created.

The General Tab

Query Window

Click on the *General* Tab of the **Query Window** (see Figure 65 below). The **Query Type** field should contain 'Individual'. The **Read Only** field is unchecked. You can check this field if you have finished making changes to a custom query, and want to ensure you don't absent-mindedly make further changes to it, or delete it. For now, though, leave this unchecked.

Enter the following description, as a reminder to yourself, in the **Description** field: "Finds all the individuals in the current file whose father was called 'Philip' and whose mother was called 'Naomi'."

Title and Subtitle

The **Title** and **Subtitle** fields are used when a query is printed as a report. The **Subtitle** field usually contains the date (there is a choice of formats). If you want to specify your own subtitle, select 'Custom'. When you do this, a box appears to the right of the subtitle field, and you can enter your custom subtitle there.

Leave the **Subtitle** field as it is for now, but change the **Title** field to 'Parent Names'.

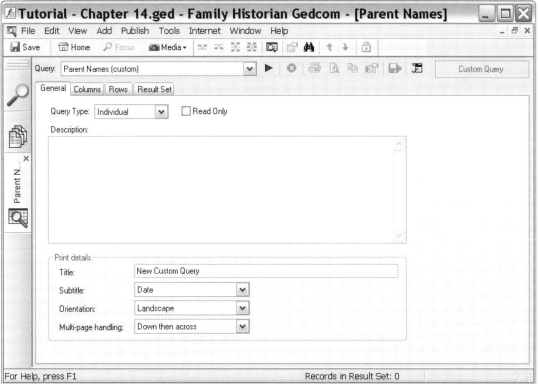

Figure 65 – the General tab of the Query Window

The Columns Tab

Query Window

We are looking for all individuals whose father is called 'Philip' and whose mother is called 'Naomi'. What information do we want to see about the individuals that we find who match this? Obviously we want to see the name of individuals found. But perhaps we would also like to see their parents' full names, and perhaps some

153

other details. For now, we will opt to see the following information:

- Individual's full name
- Father's full name
- Mother's full name
- Individual's date of birth
- Individual's place of birth

We can modify this later if we want to, but this will do for a start. Click on the *Columns* tab (see Figure 66 below).

The Column List

Columns Tab

On the right of the window is a box labelled 'Columns'. This is the ***Columns List***. The **Columns List** has four columns: *Heading*, *Expression*, *Sort* and *Hidden*. Each *row* in the list corresponds to a *column* in the result set. At present, there is only one row. This row has 'Individual' in the *Heading* column and '%INDI%' in the *Expression* column. When you create a new custom query, Family Historian automatically creates one column for you, by default; so that if you run the query without doing anything else, you will see one column in the result set.

The Fields List

Columns Tab

On the left of the window is a box labelled 'Fields'. This is the ***Fields List***. This lists all of the possible fields you can have in queries of this type. If the query is a record-type query, it shows all fields in records of the query type (*Individual* in the current case). As we have seen before, GEDCOM fields are hierarchical. Fields can have sub-fields, which in turn can have more sub-fields, and so on.

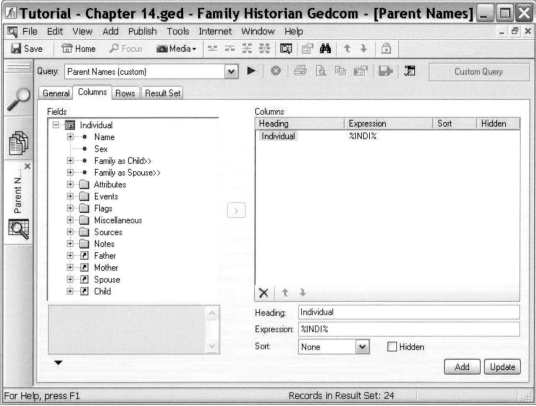

Figure 66 – the Columns tab of the Query Window. 'Family as Child>>' has been expanded in the Fields List.

Add Field as Column

`[ > ]`

Columns Tab

To see the value of any field, listed as a column in the result set, you simply need to select the field in the **Fields List**, and click on the **Add Field as Column** button `[ > ]` to the right of the list, to add the field in question to the **Columns List**. Then, when you run the query, the new column will appear in the result set. We will do this now. The current query should still be *Parent Names* at this point. If it isn't, select *Parent Names* in the **Query** field at the top of the window.

The default column that was provided when the query was created, will do very well as our first column. This means we only need to add four more.

You will notice that there are four items at the end of the 'Individual' branch, labelled *Father*, *Mother*, *Spouse* and *Child*. These do not represent fields as such. They are *shortcuts* from one record to another – which is why each of them has the shortcut icon 🔲 next to them. In practice, shortcuts are very convenient, and ordinarily you would use them in this query. We will look at shortcuts in a moment, but for this example, we will show you how to construct this query without using shortcuts. So ignore these items for now.

Steps

1. Click on the expansion button ⊞ next to *Family as Child>>* to expand that branch. Do not double-click on the text, as that will cause the field *Family as Child>>* to be inserted as a column in the **Columns List** (if you did it anyway, don't worry – we will see shortly how to delete columns). Now select *Father>>* and click on the **Add Field as Column** button `[ > ]`.
2. Now select *Mother>>* and click on the **Add Field as Column** button again.
3. Now close the expanded branch for *Family as Child>>*, and expand the branch for *Events*. Find *Birth* in the expanded branch, and expand that too. Finally, under *Birth*, select *Date* and click on **Add Field as Column**.
4. Still looking under *Birth*, select *Place*, and click on **Add Field as Column**.

*Tip: An alternative to clicking on the **Add Field as Column** button is just to double-click on a field name.*

There should now be five items – each corresponding to a result set column – listed in the **Columns List**. The values in the *Expression* column of the **Columns List** will no doubt seem quite strange. The values in the *Heading* column should be a little more intuitive, but even one or two of these may seem odd. Nevertheless, ignore them for now, and click on the **Run Query** button ▶ now to run the query. This action should switch you to the *Result Set* tab, and there should be 24 rows – one row for each Individual record in the current file (we haven't yet got round to being selective), arranged in 5 columns. The heading for each column should correspond to the headings in the Column List, and you should be able to see that for each individual found, the first column gives their name (with an Individual record icon 🔳 next to it). The 2nd column gives their father's name (if known) with the same icon. The 3rd column gives their mother's name (if known) with the same icon. The 4th column gives their date-of-birth (if known), and the 5th column gives their place of birth.

Now switch back to the Columns tab.

Making Sense of the Field List

Columns Tab

As we know, GEDCOM fields are hierarchical; so it should not be too surprising that birth date is stored in a field called *Date* which is a sub-field of a field called *Birth*, and that birth place is stored in a field called *Place* which is another sub-field of *Birth*. Remember that sub-fields *qualify* (that is, provide more details about) their 'parent' field.

In case you're wondering, there is no field called *Events*. Fields of different types are sometimes grouped together into categories in the **Fields List**, just to make it easier to find the ones you want. Categories always have the folder icon ▢ next to them. *Birth* is an event, which is why it is listed under *Events*. You cannot add *Events* itself as a column. Conversely, any row which does not have the folder icon can be added.

Whereas a person's birth date and birth place are stored in their own record, the names of their parents are not stored in their own records. Instead, they will have a field, called *Family as Child*, which stores a link to a *Family* record. The Family record in turn contains more fields, including fields which hold links to all the *Individual* records for the members of the family.

What this shows is that although a result set is, essentially, an ordered collection of records, the data displayed for each record does not actually have to come from the record itself. It can also come from other records linked to it. And that is what has happened here. By inserting the field we did, we effectively have got Family Historian to traverse a link from the original individual, to that person's family record (as child); and then traverse again from that family record to the individual record for the father.

Tip: Any field in the field list which stores a link to another record always ends in '>>'.

Shortcuts

▢

Columns Tab

It is useful to understand how records are linked together, because for some purposes you may need to know this. However, in practice, most of the time you will find it much easier and more convenient to use *shortcuts*, when you want to create an expression which refers to a person's parents, spouses or children. Shortcuts are not fields. They are just there to make it easier for you to reference one record from another.

Shortcuts are easy to identify because they have the shortcut icon ▢ next to them. If you want to add a column for maternal grandfather, for example, you could do this somewhat laboriously by expanding the branch for *Family as Child>>*, then within that expand *Mother>>*, then within that expand *Family as Child>>*, then within that select Father>>, and then click on the **Add Field as Column** button. Alternatively, you could expand the ▢ *Mother* shortcut, select the ▢ *Father* shortcut within that and then click on **Add Field as Column**. The two approaches achieve the same result, but the latter technique is simpler.

Change Column Headings

Columns Tab

Look now at the columns you created a few sections back. The first column is labelled 'Individual', which is fine. The second column is labelled 'Family as Child Father', which is not. You should think of the column headings that Family Historian generates for you as useful reminders of what the field contains. But you should always be prepared to have to adjust them to make them more presentable.

Steps

1. Click on *Family as Child Father* in the **Columns List** now. Notice that all the values for the selected column are now displayed in the fields below the **Columns List**. Find the field labelled ***Heading*** and change the value of this field from 'Family as Child Father' to 'Father'.
2. Click on the **Update** button (bottom right corner).
3. Now click on *Family as Child Mother* in the Columns List, and use the same technique to change the heading to *Mother.*

Now run the query again, and confirm that the column headings are what they should be.

Expressions

You may be wondering what the significance of the values in the *Expression* column are. *Expressions* determine what data is displayed in the column (as we will see later, you can also use expressions in filters – and even in report titles and subtitles).

There are 2 different kinds of expression: *functions* and *data references*. All the expressions we have looked at so far have been *data references*. [26] We will look at an example of a *function* expression shortly.

Handling Multiple Instances

You do not have to construct data references as Family Historian will always generate them for you. You just have to select the fields you want from the **Field List** and click on the **Add Field as Column** button ⬚. The only qualification to this, however, concerns *instances*. The data references that Family Historian generates always retrieve the *first* instance of each of the fields referenced. But what if it is not the first instance that you want? In that case, you should get Family Historian to generate the field as normal, but modify the instance value in the expression. For example, the expression for a person's father generated earlier was

INDI.FAMC>HUSB>

If you select the column by clicking on the heading, the expression is shown in the **Expression** field below the **Column List** as

INDI.FAMC[1]>HUSB[1]>

These 2 forms are equivalent. The latter shows the field instance information explicitly, the former does not. The default instance is always 1, if not specified.

If you want the *second* Family as Child (for people who have more than one set of parents), you only have to change the first [1] to a [2] (and remember to press the **Update** button to register the change)[27].

The Rows Tab

We have chosen the columns we want, but we haven't yet selected the records we want. This is what we will do now.

Query Window

Select the *Rows* tab (see Figure 67 below). The top part of the Rows tab contains a box with 3 column headings. These are *Filter, Param.,* and *Parameter Label.* This box is called the **Filter List**.

Add *General* Filter

We need to filter the result set. We want to only include records for individuals whose father is called 'Philip' and whose mother is called 'Naomi'.

Rows Tab

At the bottom of the Rows tab is an area with three tabs: *General, Relations and List.*

Steps

1. The *General* tab should already be selected, but if not, click on it now to select it.
2. The **Condition** field should be set to *Add If...*

---

[26] We have come across data references before when looking at text schemes in Chapter 9 above. The technically-minded may be interested to know that data references are usually just sequences of GEDCOM *tags* (GEDCOM field names) separated by either a '.' or a '>' (the latter indicates a link from one record to another record). For example, in the expression 'INDI.FAMC>HUSB>', *INDI* is the GEDCOM tag for an **INDI**vidual record. *FAMC* is the '**FAM**ily as Child' field within that, which stores a link to a Family record. The **HUSB**and field in the Family record stores a link to the Individual record for the father/husband figure in the family. A proper discussion of data references is beyond the scope of this book, but there is more information about them in the Help. Look up 'Data References' in the Help index.

[27] You may be wondering why HUSB also has an instance indicator. You can't have more than two spouses/parents in a family record, but they can both be the same sex. If you have two male partners in a family record, they will both be recorded using the HUSB tag. So there can be more than one.

3. The **Expression** field must refer to the father's name. To the right of the **Expression** field is a button with 3 little dots ⬚. Click on this now. The **Data Reference Assistant** dialog appears. Expand the branch next to *Family as Child* and then expand *Father*. Then select *Name* and press **OK**[28]. The text 'INDI.FAMC[1]>HUSB[1]>NAME[1]' appears in the Expression field.
4. Set the **Operator** field to *Contains.*
5. Type *Philip* into the **Value** field.
6. Press the **Add** button (bottom right). A row is added to the **Filter List**.
7. Now set the **Condition** field to *Exclude Unless...*
8. This time **Expression** field must refer to the mother's name. Click on the little button ⬚ to the right of the **Expression** field. In the **Data Reference Assistant** dialog, expand the branch next to *Family as Child* and then expand *Mother*. Select *Name* and press **OK**. The text 'INDI.FAMC[1]>WIFE[1]>NAME[1]' appears in the Expression field.
9. Set the **Operator** field to *Contains.*
10. Type *Naomi* into the **Value** field.
11. Press the **Add** button (bottom right). A second row is added to the **Filter List**. At this point the Rows Tab should look like Figure 67 below.

Now click on the **Run Query** button ▶. This time there should be only two rows in the result set: one for Mary Peabody and one for Cameron Peabody. They are of course brother and sister. Their parents are shown as Philip Peabody and Naomi Prentice Salt.

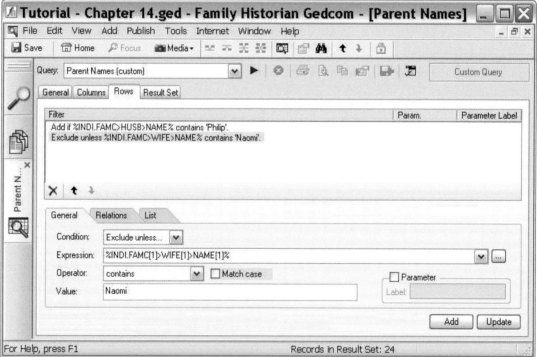

Figure 67 – the Rows tab of the Query Window. Two filters have been added.

How Filters Work   Each row in the *Filters List* represents a *Filter*. Filters created using the General tab are called *General Filters*, filters created using the Relations tab are *Relation Filters*, and filters created using the List tab are *List Filters*.

When a query is run, Family Historian applies each filter in turn. It is important to appreciate that *filters are applied in sequence*, starting with the first filter in the list,

---

[28] Alternatively, you could use the *Father* shortcut.

then working down through each in turn to the end of the list.

The Result Set and the Input Set When Family Historian runs a query and applies its filters, it starts by creating two lists, called the *Input Set* and the *Result Set*. You will never see any references to the Input Set in the program. It is only used by Family Historian internally while the query is being run, and is discarded when the query has completed. Nevertheless, it is helpful to know about it, to make sense of how filters work.

The *Result Set* is not just an internal list. We have heard many references to 'result sets' before. Result sets are the lists of items (records or facts) which are displayed in the Result Set tab of the **Query Window**, when a query has finished running.

When Family Historian runs the *Parent Names* query, it starts by putting all items of the query type (all Individual records if it's an Individual query, or all *facts*, if it's a fact query) into the Input Set. The Result Set list is empty at this point.

As stated earlier, Family Historian then applies each filter in turn.

For each filter, if the filter has an *Add* condition (*Add if...* or *Add Unless...*), Family Historian will look through the Input Set to find items that match (if it is an *Add If...*) or don't match (if it is an *Add Unless...*) the condition specified in the filter. Any items found will be moved from the Input Set to the Result Set.

If the filter has an *Exclude* condition (*Exclude if...* or *Exclude Unless...*), Family Historian will look through the *Result Set* to find items that match (if it is an *Exclude If...*) or don't match (if it is an *Exclude Unless...*) the condition specified in the filter. Any items found will be moved back from the Result Set to the Input Set.

In our example, when the *Parent Names* query is run, Family Historian will initially move all Individual records into the Input Set and leave the Result Set empty. When it applies the first filter, it will look through the Input Set and find all the records where the father's name contains 'Philip'. It will move all of these records into the Result Set. When it has finished doing that, it will move on to the second filter and apply that. Because this is an *Exclude* condition, it will look through the Result Set and find all the records there where the mother's name is *not* Naomi ('*not*' because it is an *Exclude Unless...*). It will move all such records back into the Input Set.

The combined effect of these 2 filters is to leave in the Result Set all and only records where the father's name is 'Philip' and the mother's name is 'Naomi'.

First Filter has *Exclude* Condition If the Input Set always initially contained all of the items, an empty filter list would mean an empty Result Set. Equally if the first filter had an *Exclude* condition, it would never have any effect. For this reason, Family Historian uses the following rule when initialising the Input Set and the Result Set, *before* applying filters:

If the filter list is empty, or if the first filter has an *Exclude* condition, it puts all items (of the relevant query type) into the Result Set and leaves the Input Set empty. Otherwise – that is , if there is at least one filter and the first one has an *Add* condition – it puts all the items into the Input Set and leaves the Result Set empty.

More on Filters As we have seen, filters are applied sequentially. When applying filters, Family Historian simply moves items forwards and backwards between the two lists (the Input Set and the Result Set). At any given time, while the filters are being applied, each item is always in one, and only one of these lists. It is never in both lists at the same time. It can never have more than one occurrence in a list. That is why you will never see the same items occur more than once in the Result Set tab of the **Query Window**.

There is no limit to the number of filters you can have in a query. Nor is it the case that there are any special rules to say that you can't move an item from one list to another if you had previously moved it the other way. In fact a series of filters might easily result in the same item shuttling forwards and backwards any number of times between the two lists, as the filters are applied. Do not make the mistake of attributing undue complexity to filters. In fact their role is quite straightforward, once you have understood it.[29]

Benefits of Sequential Filtering

The main benefit of sequential filtering is that you can have steps which make reference to the results of the previous step. This is never done with *General* or *List* filters, but as we shall see shortly, it is done with *Relation* filters. For example, you can have one filter which adds all of the ancestors of a given person. The next filter can then stipulate that you should also add all descendants of *those* people (the people in the Result Set at this point). A further filter could then go on to add the ancestors of everyone who is *now* in the Result Set, and so on. This way of working is very useful when you are dealing with family tree relationships.

Using Parameters

Rows Tab

Instead of looking for records where the name contains 'Philip' and 'Naomi', we might want to make our query more generally useful, so that it can be used to search for records, using a pair of parent names that you supply when the query is run. For this you need *parameters*.

Make sure that you are now looking at the Rows tab.

Steps

1. Select the first filter in the list, by clicking on the text in the first column. The filter details are displayed below the **Filter List** in the General filter tab.
2. Click on the **Parameter** check box. The **Label** field becomes ungreyed.
3. Enter "Father's Name" into the **Label** field. Click on the **Update** button to update the filter.
4. Select the second filter in the list. This filter's details are now displayed in the General filter tab.
5. Click on the **Parameter** check box. The **Label** field becomes ungreyed.
6. Enter "Mother's Name" into the **Label** field. Click on the **Update** button to update the filter.

Now run the query again, by clicking on the **Run Query** button [▶]. The **Query Parameters Dialog** appears. Change the father's name to 'Peabody' and the mother's name to 'Jean'. Press **OK**. This should produce a result set with 4 records – one child of Cameron Peabody and Jean Clare Anderson, and three children of Daniel Anderson Peabody and Pamela Jean Winters.

Tip: If you want the same parameter value to be inserted into different filters, just make sure that you use exactly the same label each time.

Using Qualifiers

Rows Tab

Suppose that what we wanted was a query that only checked the *first* name of a person's mother? For the convenience of this tutorial, we will arbitrarily assume that this requirement only applies to the mother's name and not to the father's name.

Steps

1. Select the second filter in the list (the 'Exclude Unless...' filter that refers to the mother's name).
2. Click on the button with 3 dots [...] to the right of the **Expression** field. Expand *Family as Child>>*, then *Mother>>* (or use the *Mother* shortcut if you prefer),

---

[29] Some peoples' reaction is to see this way of applying filters as inefficient, and to anticipate that Family Historian queries will run slowly. In fact, however, this is not the case. Family Historian queries are efficient and run very fast.

then *Name*. The *Name* field has various sub-fields, but listed before them are a number of possible *qualifiers* for the *Name* field. *Qualifiers* always begin with a ':' and they have no field icon next to them. Unlike subfields, qualifiers do not represent distinct items of data. Rather they are used for qualifying the way the value in a field is presented. For example, the :FIRST qualifier for the name field effectively pulls out the first name from the *Name* field. Select *:FIRST* now and press **OK**. The **Expression** field in the *General* filter tab now reads: INDI.FAMC[1]>WIFE[1]>NAME[1]:FIRST (unless you used the shortcut, in which case it will read: INDI.~MOTH[1]>NAME[1]:FIRST).

3. Ensure that the value for **Operator** is *Matches* (we're looking for an exact match on first name). Press the **Update** button.

Run the query again, and again specify 'Peabody' as the father's name and 'Jean' as the Mother's name. This time there should only be one match - for Daniel Peabody, the son of Cameron and Jean Clare Anderson. Pamela Jean Winters is now excluded as a mother's name, by the 2nd filter.

Some fields have qualifiers, some don't. Qualifiers are especially useful with all date fields and, as we have seen, with name fields.

Tip: If you want to look more closely at the effect of qualifiers, run the standard queries Qualifiers for Dates and Qualifiers for Names. These queries have no filters. They are designed to illustrate the effect of different qualifier types.

Add Record Id

Now suppose that you want to modify your query again, to add the record id for each record found, and also the record ids of that person's father and mother (if any).

Record Ids are not stored as fields in Family Historian. They are held internally in the record itself. So to retrieve a record id, you cannot use a data reference as we have done up to now. Instead, you must use a *function*. If you have used Microsoft Office products, such as MS Excel, you may have encountered functions before. Support for functions is a powerful feature that allows you to make use of derived or calculated data.[30]

In Family Historian, as in MS Excel, function names begin with an '=' sign. In this example we will be using the function '=RecordId()' which returns the record id of the current record.

Steps

1. Confirm that the current query is "Parent Names" (select it if it isn't).
2. Select the *Columns* tab.
3. Click on an unused part of the **Columns List** so that no existing column is selected. The **Update** button becomes greyed (you don't actually *need* to do this, but it clears the fields we are about to enter data into, and ensures that you won't accidentally update an existing column by mistake).
4. Insert "Record Id" into the **Heading** field below the Columns List.
5. Insert "=RecordId()" into the **Expression** field below that, taking care to ensure that you have entered it exactly like that.
6. Click on the **Add** button. If you entered the Expression field value incorrectly, a message will warn you that the expression is not recognised, in which case, correct the error, and press **Add** again.

---

[30] A proper discussion of functions is beyond the scope of this book. There is a complete list of all Family Historian functions, as well as detailed information about how to use them, in the Help. To find this, look up 'Functions' in the Help index.

Re-order Columns

Columns Tab

Let us suppose that we want *Record Id* to be the second column.

Steps

1. Select *Record Id* in the *Heading* column and click repeatedly on the **Move Up** button ⬆ on the bottom toolbar, until *Record Id* is the second column in the list.
2. Now run the query again, and confirm that the Record Id column does display the record id, and is the 2nd column in the result set.

Specify Column Sort

Columns Tab

You specify how you want the result set to be sorted as part of the column data, in the Columns tab. Each column has a **Sort** field value – which can be *Ascending*, *Descending* or *None*. For sorting purposes, columns on the left take precedence over columns on the right. For example, if the first column was *Surname*, and it was to be sorted in descending order, and the second column was *Given Name*, and it was set to be sorted in ascending order, the result set would appear to be sorted in descending order of surname. However, where two or more records shared the same surname, those records would be sorted additionally in ascending order of given name.

If you wanted the result set to be sorted by given name first and then by surname, you could do this by simply moving the given name column up, so that it came before surname.

If you didn't want to re-order the columns in the result set, but still wanted the given name sort to take precedence over the surname sort, you can still do this. You should set the **Sort** field value to *None* for both columns, and then create copies of each column, using the original **Sort** values, and with the **Hidden** field checked. These hidden columns will not appear in the result set. They are used for sorting purposes only. You can put them anywhere in the **Column List**, but it is usual to add them to the end of the list. To get the sort precedence you want, you would only need to make sure that the hidden *Given Name* column came before the hidden *Surname* column.

Delete Column

Columns Tab

To delete a column, you need only select it in the **Column List** and click on the **Delete** button ✖ on the bottom toolbar.

The *Born After 1900* Sample Query

In the *Parent Names* sample, we created a custom query that used only general filters. We will now create a custom query that also uses a *relation* filter.

For this example, we will create a query that attempts to find all people who were born after 1900. We will do this first by creating a general query to find everyone whose birth date falls after 1900. However, some people will not have a birth date specified, and will consequently be excluded. So to find at least some of these people, we will also include anyone who is *descended* from anyone whose birth date falls after 1900.

Add Relation Filter

Rows Tab

We must start by creating the new custom query.

Steps

1. Open the **Query Window** if it is not already open, by clicking on the **Query Window** button 🖼 on the main application toolbar.
2. Click on the **Query Menu** button 📃 on the **Query Toolbar**, and select **New Custom Query** from the dropdown menu.
3. Set the name of the query as "Born After 1900". The type should be 'Individuals'. Click on **Create**. The new query is created.
4. Click on the Rows tab and select the general filter tab if not already selected.

5. The **Condition** should be *Add If...*
6. Click on the button with 3 little dots ⬚ to the right of the **Expression** field. The **Data Reference Assistant** dialog appears. Expand the *Events* branch, and within that expand *Birth*, and then select *Date* within that. Press **OK**. The text 'INDI.BIRT[1].DATE' appears in the **Expression** field.
7. Set the **Operator** field to *was later than.*
8. Type *1900* into the **Value** field.
9. Press the **Add** button (bottom right toolbar). A row is added to the **Filter List**.
10. Click on the **Run Query** button ▶ to run the query. Notice that there are only four records in the result set.
11. Now return to the Rows tab, and click on the *Relations* filter tab.
12. Leave the **Condition** field as *Add If...*
13. Set **Relationship** to *Descendants.*
14. Leave **Max Generations** blank (i.e. no maximum).
15. Set **Of** to Anyone in the current result set.
16. Leave **Inc spouses of relatives** unchecked, and press the **Add** button to add the filter to the filter list.
17. Now, run the query again. This time there should be 12 people in the result set (in the status bar in a pane on the right, it should say "Records in Result Set: 12").

Delete Filter

Rows Tab

To delete a filter from the current query, you need only select it in the **Filter List** and click on the **Delete** button ✖ on the bottom toolbar.

Re-Order Filters

Rows Tab

To re-order a filter, select the filter that you want to move, and click either the **Move Up** ⬆ or **Move Down** ⬇ buttons, until the filter is in the position you want.

Relation Filters that Reference a Single Individual

Rows Tab

Look now at the *Relations* filter tab within the *Rows* tab. You will notice that as well as specifying *Anyone in the current result set*, as the *Of* value, you can also specify *This Individual*. When you do this, you have the option, if you want to, of specifying a value at this point for *This Individual* (you do this by clicking on the box and selecting 'Browse...' to open a Select Records dialog). However, there is no need to specify a value at this point. Family Historian requires that any relation filter which uses *This Individual*, must take a parameter. It will not let you uncheck the parameters check box. Consequently, the only effect of specifying a value for *This Individual* at this stage, is to provide the default value which will appear in the **Query Parameters Dialog** when you next run the query.

Descendants of a Particular Individual

Suppose you regularly work with a query consisting of the descendants of a particular person, and want to be able to run this query without having to select that person's name from a list in the **Query Parameters Dialog**.

Let us suppose that the person's record id is 278.

Steps

1. Create your new custom query and give it a suitable name.
2. Select the *Rows* tab, and within that choose the *General* filter tab.
3. Set **Condition** to *Add If....*
4. Set **Expression** to '=RecordId()'.
5. Set **Operator** to *equals.*
6. Set **Value** to '278'.
7. Click on the **Add** button to add the filter.
8. Now choose the **Relations** filter tab
9. Set **Condition** to *Add If....*

10. Set **Relationship** to *Descendant*.
11. Set **Of** to Anyone in the Current Result Set.
12. Click on the **Add** button to add the filter.

Although this query can be run for any file, it is not likely to be at all useful for any file except the one that contains the person whose descendants you want to be able to find easily, who has record id 278. So you should add a note to this effect, as a reminder to yourself, in the **Description** field in the General tab.

An alternative approach to the one shown here would be to create a Named List which contained the person whose descendants you wished to see, and no-one else. Then the first filter, instead of using a record id, could simply add everyone in the specified Named List. For more on Named Lists, see Chapter 16.

15 Compare, Merge, Split, Copy and Export GEDCOM Files

If you wish to merge someone else's genealogy research into yours, you need to get the research in the form of a GEDCOM file (unless you want to manually type it all in yourself). All good genealogy software allows data to be exported in the form of a GEDCOM file, and genealogy information downloaded from the Internet will typically be in this format anyway. In this chapter we will look at how you can compare another genealogy file with the data in your current GEDCOM file, and optionally merge it in.

We will also look briefly at the opposite requirement – how you can *split* a GEDCOM file, using Family Historian's **Split Tree Helper dialog**. And along the way, we will also look at techniques for copying GEDCOM files, and at the **Export GEDCOM File** dialog.

3 Kinds of Merge Compare

Family Historian supports three kinds of Merging and Comparing. These are:

- File Merge/Compare
- Basic Record Merge/Compare
- Branch Merge/Compare

File Merge/Compare is when you compare and (optionally) merge two entire files.

Basic Record Merge/Compare is when you compare and (optionally) merge two records of the same type (for example, two Individual records or two Source records).

Branch Merge/Compare is an extension of Basic Record Merge/Compare for Individual or Family records. It sometimes happens that you discover that two records in your file turn out to be records for the same Individual. But it may further emerge that not only are they duplicated, but so too are their parents, children, spouses and other relatives. Branch Merge/Compare helps you locate entire branches of duplicated records, compare all records in each record, and merge them all in one step.

Can't Undo File Merge

You can undo a *Basic Record Merge* or a *Branch Merge*, just like you undo any other data change, by clicking on **Undo** on the **Edit** menu; but you can't undo a *File Merge*. For this reason, it's a good idea to always make a backup of your project data before doing a *File Merge*. That way, if you make a mistake, you can always get back to where you were before you did it.

Basic Record Merge/Compare and *Branch Merge/Compare* are both initiated by selecting one or two records that you wish to merge, and clicking on **Merge/Compare Records** on the **Edit** menu. For more information about them, see the Help within Family Historian. The remainder of this chapter deals exclusively with *File Merge/Compare*.

File Merge/Compare

With *File Merge/Compare*, Family Historian's **Merge/Compare Dialog** can be used to compare any two GEDCOM files (remember, that even if you are working on a Family Historian *project*, your data is in fact still stored in a GEDCOM file). Neither of the files being compared need have been created using Family Historian. Having compared the two files, you can, if you wish, use Family Historian to merge them. Once you have learned how to interpret the information Family Historian provides to you, you will be able to see exactly what the outcome of the merge process will be before Family Historian does it.

Why is File Merge/ Compare Needed?

Why do we need a file merge/compare facility? Isn't a record merge/compare feature enough? No it isn't.

Without a File Merge facility, records must be merged, one pair at a time. To do this yourself would be very time-consuming if you had a large number of records. But it's the wrong approach anyway. If X and Y are father and son in one file, and A and B are father and son in the other, the question of whether Y is the same person as B has to be answered at the same time as deciding whether X is the same as A. Being asked to decide these questions, one pair at a time, is like being asked to sign a contract one clause at a time. You don't want to have to commit to giving the other person your car before you know whether they in return are going to agree to give you your asking price – it's an all-or-nothing thing. The same is true of decisions about merging records.

If you don't have a full file merge/compare facility, the only alternative to you merging them one record at a time yourself, is to trust your genealogy application to do it for you – that is, you or the program simply insert all records from one file into another, and then you have to trust your genealogy program to automatically detect duplicates and merge them for you. This is still record-at-a-time merging – the only difference is that the genealogy program is doing it instead of you. It is a very risky strategy, as it could take years to detect errors that have been introduced in this way (if indeed you ever can detect them). Such an approach is not likely to appeal to anyone who values their data.

The Family Historian Solution

With Family Historian's file merge/compare feature you get to see the whole picture, make all the decisions, and see what you will get before you have to commit yourself to anything. Crucial to this solution is that Family Historian allows you not just to merge two files, but – before you do so – to compare them side by side, so that you can see exactly where and how they differ. Not only that, the compare facility is designed so that it is very easy to spot which records have differences and which do not. Suppose you had 10,000 records in each file. Imagine that all the records except 20 are identical, of which 3 are unique to one file, and 3 to the other. Family Historian lets you effortlessly detect (and group together for easy scrutiny) the 20 records that have differences, and see exactly how they differ. You can see exactly what will happen to your file if you merge them, and override Family Historian's proposed strategy for merging them if you wish.

You Are In Control

You can use the **Merge/Compare Dialog** just for comparing two files. You don't have to merge anything. If you want to merge the files, there are four options open to you:

(1) Leave it all to Family Historian
(2) Let Family Historian do it for you, but only after you have made whatever changes you want to 'override' Family Historian's initial merge plan.
(3) Use Family Historian for comparing and merging, but only after you have done all the actual 'matching' yourself. In this option, the merge plan is entirely created by you.
(4) Use Family Historian solely for comparison purposes – you do all the data changes manually yourself . In this last option, you don't use Family Historian for merging at all.

In this chapter, we will look at options (1) , (2) and (3), and at how to use the Merge/Compare dialog. If you want to do option (4), the best solution is to copy the files to be compared and view them in one instance of Family Historian while using another instance of Family Historian to actually make the changes.

Tip: *Before using merging, or even comparing, two GEDCOM files it is a good idea to ensure that both files are in a good state. Sometimes GEDCOM files created by other applications can contain errors. If you have not already done so, you are recommended to open each file in Family Historian at least once, run checks for errors if recommended to do so, and run the Validate command on the File menu. You are also recommended to ensure that each file has been saved using Family Historian at least once.*

Merging Projects
The discussion in this file is couched entirely in terms of how to merge one GEDCOM file into another, and we will demonstrate how to do this using two standalone GEDCOM files – that is, GEDCOM files which are not part of a Family Historian project. But bear in mind that, within a project, your genealogy data is still stored in the form of a GEDCOM file. So everything that is said applies equally well if either or both of the GEDCOM files being merged are part of a Family Historian project.

Preparation
To illustrate how merge and compare work, we need two GEDCOM files that have records in common, records which are identical, records which are similar but different, and records which appear only in one of each of the files and not in the other. For this, we will use two pre-prepared tutorial files.

Open First Tutorial File
From the **Project Window**, click on the **More Tasks** button, and then in the dropdown menu click on **Samples**, and finally **Tutorial – Chapter 15a**. The file opens and Cameron Peabody is displayed as the focus person in the Focus Window.

The *Direction* of a Merge
When files are merged, there is always a 'direction' to the merge – that is, a new file which you select is always merged into the current file. *All* the changes are made to the current file. The new file is never changed in any way by a merge.

The **Merge/Compare Dialog** lets you see both how the two files differ, and what would happen to the current file if you merged the new file into it. It is up to you whether you then go on to do this merge.

Open the Merge/ Compare Dialog
Open the **Merge/Compare Dialog** to compare the two files.

Steps

1. Click on **Merge/Compare...** on the **File** menu. If this is the first time you have used Merge/Compare, an advisory message will appear. Read it and click **OK**.
2. A "Select File" dialog appears. You need to look in the *Shared Documents* area, and then within that, look in the ***Calico Pie*** folder, then ***Family Historian***, then ***Tutorial Files***. When you have found this folder, select the file "Tutorial – Chapter 15b". If you can't find it, try using your Windows search facilities to do a search on your hard disk for "Tutorial – Chapter 15b" and make a note of the folder location when you find it.[31]
3. Having found it and selected it, click on **Open**. A "Record Matching Options" dialog box appears. Confirm that "Suggest candidate matches for merging" is ticked and click **OK**.
4. The **Merge/Compare Dialog** appears (see Figure 68 below).

The files in this case are both small. If the files had both been large, it could take a little while for the **Merge/Compare Dialog** to appear. This is because Family Historian has to analyse the two files and work out which records match – and within these records, which fields match – before opening the dialog. It uses a

---

[31] If you still can't find it, do this: Cancel out of the "Select File" dialog and close the current file (click **Close** on the **File** menu). From the **Project Window**, click on **More Tasks**, and then **Samples**, and finally **Tutorial – Chapter 15b** to open the file. Then click on **File** > **Gedcom File Tasks** > **Save a Gedcom File Copy**. Save the file anywhere convenient but make a careful note of where you put it. Then repeat the instructions from "Open First Tutorial File" onwards, but instead of looking for "Tutorial File – Chapter 15b" in the Shared Documents area, select the copy you just made.

sophisticated algorithm for record matching, and with large files, it can be a slow process.

At this point, of course, no changes of any kind have yet been made. So far Family Historian has merely compared the 2 files. If you were to click on **Cancel** now, to close the **Merge/Compare Dialog**, no changes of any kind would have been made to either file.

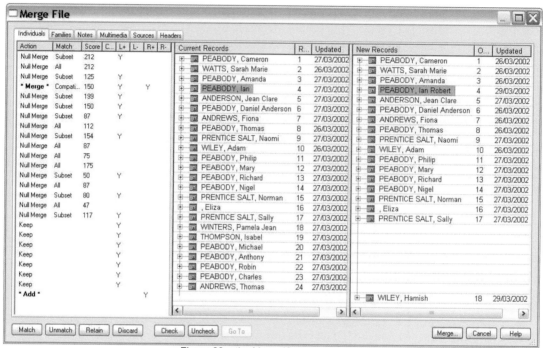

Figure 68 – the Merge/Compare Dialog

The Merge/ Compare Dialog

The **Merge/Compare Dialog** can be resized (like many dialogs in Family Historian). Click on its Maximize ⬜ button to make it full-screen now.

Remember also that you can resize any column by clicking-and-dragging on the line between column headings. Resize columns now so that you can clearly see the record names.

The dialog has some similarities to the **Records Window**. Like the Records Window, it has tabs – one for each record type. However, there is no facility to hide record types. The dialog will display a tab for a record type if and only if that record type occurs in at least one of the two files being compared. If there are no Note records in either file, for example, there will be no Note record tab in the **Merge/Compare Dialog**.

The Three Panes

Each tab of the **Merge/Compare Dialog** has 3 panes. These are (in order):

- the Information Pane
- the Current File Pane
- the New File Pane

Records in the Current File Pane are labelled 'Current Records'. Those in the New File Pane are labelled 'New Records'.

If you scroll any of these panes vertically, or expand any of the records in the Current or New File panes, you will find that they all move together. You should think of each row as extending across all 3 panes.

Matched Records

Each row displays a record (or field, if you 'expand' the record) in either the Current File Pane, the New File Pane or both. The records in the Current File Pane belong to the current file. The records in the New File Pane belong to the file you selected to compare with the current one.

If a row displays a record in one pane only, this means that the record is considered to have no equivalent in the other file. If, however, a given row displays a record in both the Current Pane and in the New Pane, this means that the 2 records have been 'matched' and are considered to be equivalents. Records in the same row will be merged, if you opt to execute a merge.

So far then we can see that Family Historian has matched most of the records; but there are 7 Individual records in the current file that have no equivalent in the 'new' file; and there is one Individual record in the new file (for Hamish Wiley) which has no equivalent in the current file.

Matched and Unmatched Fields

You can view the contents of a record by clicking on the expansion button next to it, to 'expand' it. Where you have a match between 2 records, some or all of the fields belonging to the records may also match. Again, fields on the same row are deemed to be equivalents and will be merged. Fields which occur in one pane only, are deemed to have no equivalent in the matching record.

Find the records for Ian Peabody. The one in the Current File Pane is lined up in the same row as the one in the New File Pane, which means that Family Historian has matched them. Expand either of these records. When you do so, both records expand together. Notice that the *Name* fields in each record are on different lines, because they do not match. Also, there is a *Birth* field in the new file record, that doesn't exist in the current file record. And there is a *Multimedia* Object field in the current file record which doesn't exist in the new file record.

If you were to merge the records now, Ian Peabody would acquire an additional name field (in which his name is recorded as 'Ian Robert /Peabody/'. It would also acquire a *Birth* field, and its associated *Date* field.

Retained Data and Discarded Data

Records or fields which only appear in one file or the other are said to be either *retained* or *discarded*. If a record or field has been flagged to be discarded, its name, and all of its fields/sub-fields, will display 'struckout' (that is, like this: ~~struckout~~). When Family Historian compares the two files (which it does while opening the **Merge/Compare Dialog**), it will always assume that all records should be retained. The only exception to this is that the header record for the new file is always flagged to be discarded.

You can override Family Historian to flag *any* records (except Header records), or any fields, from either file, as needing to be discarded.

The Information Pane

The Information Pane on the left provides information both for comparison purposes and for merge purposes. The *Action* column gives information about would happen if the files were merged. The *Chk* column is a special case that we will discuss later. All the other columns provide information about how the records compare with one another (or not as the case may be).

The Score Column

The **Score** column is only applicable to matches between records. When Family Historian compares 2 records it assigns them a match score to calculate the likelihood of a match. It will match any 2 records that have a match score higher than zero, unless either of them has a higher score when matched against another record. If you force Family Historian to match 2 records that it did not match itself (and we will look at how you do that shortly), you should not be surprised to see negative values appearing in the Score column.

Family Historian is not Infallible

There is no way that Family Historian can guarantee that its matches are correct. It may fail to match 2 individual records that should be matched because (you just happen to know) although quite different, they are about the same person. It may incorrectly match 2 individual records that look practically identical, but actually are about 2 different people. Family Historian uses a sophisticated matching method and checks not just the records themselves, but also takes into account other records that they are linked to (such as grandparents, in the case of individual records). Records which have few links to other records, or none, are particularly hard to match.

The Match Score is a very useful indication of how reliable a particular match is. In principle, if it matters, you should carefully check *all* of Family Historian's matches (and make sure it hasn't failed to match some it should). However, although no matches are guaranteed, you should always be especially vigilant in carefully checking any matches with a score less than 100. In our example, there are 7 records with a score of under 100, which merit close attention. In fact, in this case, all 7 are valid matches.

Sorting on the *Match* column is a useful way of grouping together all the records that have been matched. It also makes it very easy to find all records which have a low match score.

The Match Column

The **Match** column is only applicable to records or fields which have been matched. It gives information about the match. Possible values for this column are shown in the table below:

Note: A 'field branch' is a convenient name for a field and all of its sub-fields.

Match Column	Meaning
All	The records, and all of their fields, have been matched. When applied to 2 fields, it means that the entire field branches have been matched.
Subset	The new record or field branch is a subset of the current one.
Discards	Implies that at some level within the record, at least one field on one side or the other, has been flagged to be discarded (see the discussion of the **Discard** button below). Intuitively, 'Discards' implies that there are conflicts between the matching records or field branches.
Compatible	There are differences between the Current record or field and the New one (including some fields on the New side, which are not present on the Current side); but no fields have been flagged to be discarded on either side.

L+, L-, R+, R-

The L and R columns are either blank, or contain 'Y'. 'L' stands for 'Left' – i.e. the current file pane. 'R' stands for 'Right' – i.e. the new file pane.

'Y' in the L+ column means that the record or field branch is not discarded, and is or contains data that is only to be found in the current file.

'Y' in the R+ column means that the record or field branch is not discarded, and is or contains data that is only to be found in the new file.

'Y' in the L- column means that the record or field branch belongs to the current file and has either been discarded, or contains a field branch that has been discarded.

'Y' in the R- column means that the record or field branch belongs to the new file and has either been discarded, or contains a field branch that has been discarded.

Once you have got used to the L and R columns, you will find that you can use them

170

to easily and quickly see exactly where and in what way 2 records or field branches differ.

The Chk Column

This column is entirely for the convenience of the user. If you select a record and click on the **Checked** or **Unchecked** buttons, it will set or clear this flag. That way, you can methodically check each record if you wish to (to make sure that it has been matched correctly, or correctly left unmatched), and use this flag to remind yourself which records you have checked and which you haven't. If any records are unchecked when you click on **Merge...**, you will get a warning message to that effect, which you can safely ignore if you wish to.

All Columns are Sortable

The *Chk* column is particularly useful because you can sort on any column in any pane of the **Merge/Compare Dialog**, by just clicking on the column header. This is often a very useful thing to do – but it would be hard to keep track of which records you had checked if you didn't have the Chk flag to mark them.

The Action Column

The Information Pane's *Action* column gives information about what will happen if you choose to merge the new file into the current file at this point. As we have seen, any records or field branches which have been matched will be merged. But what does this 'merge' really mean? If the 2 records are identical, or if the new one is a subset of the current one, it may mean that nothing at all happens to the current record or field branch. This is labelled in the *Action* column as a 'Null Merge'. It is still counted as a 'merge', even though the current record or field branch is not updated in any way as a result of it.

A value beginning with an asterisk, indicates an action which will affect the current file. If it is for a record, it will be in **bold**. For example, Ian Peabody has '* **Merge** *' opposite his matched records. This is because merging these records will result in a new *Name* field being added, and a new *Birth* field (and Date subfield).

If you sort on the *Action* column, you can see all the rows that begin with an asterisk, in bold, grouped together. We have already seen '* **Merge** *'. '* **Add** *' means that a record will be added to the current file. '* **Delete** *' means that a record will be deleted from the current file.

Unmatched records in the current file which are to be retained are simply marked as 'Keep'. Unmatched records in the new file, which have been flagged as discarded (that is, to be ignored if and when the merge occurs) are marked as 'Discard'. Neither of these options are in bold, or start with an asterisk, because neither of them will result in changes to the current file.

For more information on this, see the Help.

Override Family Historian

We saw earlier that by default, Family Historian proposes to keep both versions of Ian Peabody's name. Ian Peabody will end up with 2 very similar *Name* fields if you execute the merge. This might not be what you want. Let us suppose that you happen to know that the new field is correct, and that Ian Peabody's full name is indeed, Ian Robert Peabody. Rather than being left with 2 very similar versions of his name, you might decide that you only want one – the new one.

The *Discard* Button

The easiest way to ensure that you are left with the field you want, is to click on the field you don't want, and flag it to be discarded. Do this now. Click on the **Name** field in Ian Peabody's record in the current file (left column of the Current File Pane), and click on the **Discard** button. When you do this, the field name and the field value are both displayed as 'struckout' (see Figure 69 below). This means that if you were to merge the files now, the **Name** field in the *current* file would be discarded. Effectively it would have been replaced by the Name field from the new file.

Of course you didn't have to do this. You could choose to discard the *Name* field from either file, or you could discard both of them, or you could leave things as they are and retain both of them.

The **Discard** button can also be used to flag whole records from either file as "to be discarded".

If you flag a record or a field as "to be discarded", when it is currently shown as matched, it will be automatically unmatched at the same time. The record or field that it had been matched with will continue to be retained.

The *Retain* Button
The **Retain** button is the opposite of the **Discard** button. If you change your mind having flagged a field (or a record) as "to be discarded", simply select it and click on **Retain**.

The *Match* and *Unmatch* Buttons
If you think that Family Historian has matched 2 records or 2 fields that it should not have matched, select either or both of them, and click on the **Unmatch** button. The 2 records or fields will cease to display in a single row, and will be moved onto 2 separate rows.

If you think that Family Historian has failed to match 2 records or 2 fields that should be matched, select both of them and click on the **Match** button. The 2 records or fields will now appear in the same row.

*Tip: To select 2 records or fields in different panes, click on the first one to select it. Then press and hold the **Ctrl** key, and click on the second to select it without unselecting the first one.*

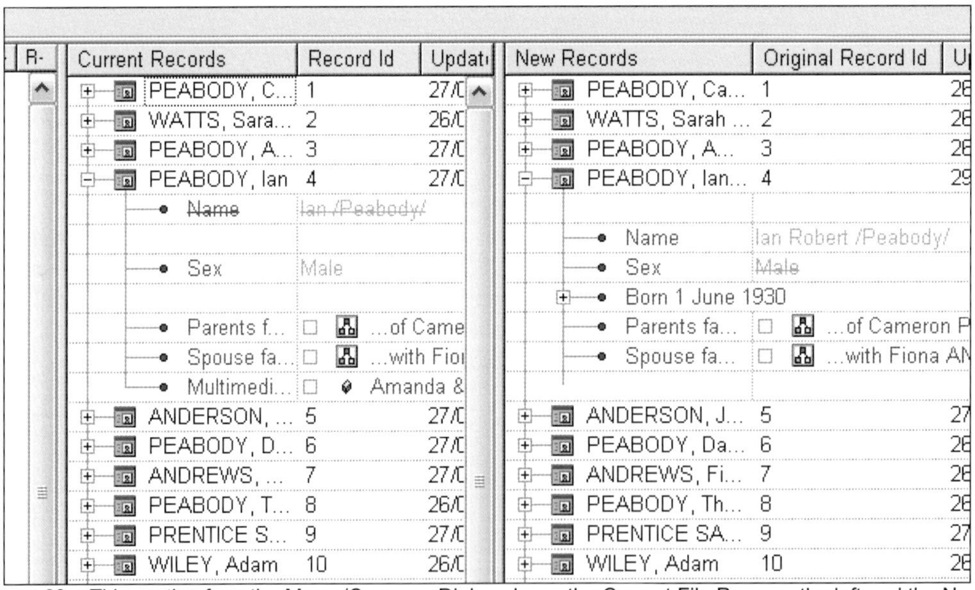

R-	Current Records	Record Id	Updati	New Records	Original Record Id	U
	⊞ 🔳 PEABODY, C...	1	27/0	⊞ 🔳 PEABODY, Ca...	1	28
	⊞ 🔳 WATTS, Sara...	2	26/0	⊞ 🔳 WATTS, Sarah ...	2	28
	⊞ 🔳 PEABODY, A...	3	27/0	⊞ 🔳 PEABODY, A...	3	28
	⊟ 🔳 PEABODY, Ian	4	27/0	⊟ 🔳 PEABODY, Ian...	4	29
	├─• Name	Ian /Peabody/				
				├─• Name	Ian Robert /Peabody/	
	├─• Sex	Male		├─• Sex	Male	
				⊞─• Born 1 June 1930		
	├─• Parents f... ☐ 🔳	...of Came		├─• Parents fa... ☐ 🔳	...of Cameron P	
	├─• Spouse fa... ☐ 🔳	...with Fio		├─• Spouse fa... ☐ 🔳	...with Fiona AN	
	└─• Multimedi... ☐ ♦	Amanda &				
	⊞ 🔳 ANDERSON, ...	5	27/0	⊞ 🔳 ANDERSON, J...	5	27
	⊞ 🔳 PEABODY, D...	6	27/0	⊞ 🔳 PEABODY, Da...	6	28
	⊞ 🔳 ANDREWS, ...	7	27/0	⊞ 🔳 ANDREWS, Fi...	7	28
	⊞ 🔳 PEABODY, T...	8	26/0	⊞ 🔳 PEABODY, Th...	8	28
	⊞ 🔳 PRENTICE S...	9	27/0	⊞ 🔳 PRENTICE SA...	9	27
	⊞ 🔳 WILEY, Adam	10	26/0	⊞ 🔳 WILEY, Adam	10	28

Figure 69 – This section from the Merge/Compare Dialog shows the Current File Pane on the left and the New File Pane on the right. Ian Peabody's Name field in the current file has been flagged to be discarded.

Restrictions
You cannot match fields in records if the records themselves are not matched. You cannot match fields if their 'parent' fields are not matched. You cannot match fields of different types – for example, you cannot match a *Birth* field with a *Death* field or a *Date* field with a *Name* field.

You cannot match individual records if they both have sexes and these are different.

Only the Merge Button Executes Changes

The **Discard**, **Retain**, **Match** and **Unmatch** buttons do not change any data in the current file. All they do is affect the way that Family Historian will merge the 2 files if you subsequently ask it to do so by clicking on the **Merge** button.

If you end up by clicking **Cancel**, no changes will be made to the current file, irrespective of what you have done with the **Discard**, **Retain**, **Match** and **Unmatch** buttons. Sometimes you may see references to the **Discard** button being used to 'discard' data. This is just a slightly loose way of saying that the **Discard** button has been used to flag data as "to be discarded" – i.e. to be discarded when (and if) the **Merge** button is pressed to execute a merge.

Multiple Selection

Neither the Current File Pane nor the New File Pane support multiple selection. However the Information Pane does. If you wish to retain, discard or unmatch a large number of records at a time, you can select them all in the information pane. The **Retain**, **Discard** and **Unmatch** buttons will all accept selections, including multiple selections, in the Information Pane. See the Help for more on this.

Discarding New Data vs. Discarding Old Data

Although we use the same word, 'discard', when we talk of discarding records and fields from either the current file or the new file, the significance in practice of the 2 actions, is very different. If you flag a field or a record in the current file as 'discarded', you are effectively ensuring that that field or record will be deleted when the merge occurs. If, on the other hand, you flag a field or record from the *new* file as 'discarded', this merely means that the field or record will not be added to the current file.

Conversely, *retaining* a field or record that belongs to the new file, is a more significant action than simply retaining a field or record that belongs to the current file, because the former implies that a new field or record will be added to the current file; whereas the latter merely implies that an existing field or record will be left as it is.

Matching Non-Identical Fields

What happens if you match non-identical fields? Suppose, for example, that instead of discarding one of Ian Peabody's *Name* fields, you matched them? If this were to happen you would get 2 slightly different fields on the same line. How would they be merged?

The short answer is that the value of the field from the current file would be preserved, and the value of the field from the new file would be discarded. So, if you matched the 2 *Name* fields for Ian Peabody, he would end up with an unchanged name – i.e. 'Ian /Peabody/'. The 'Ian Robert /Peabody/' version would have been discarded.

Does that not imply that there is no difference between matching fields, and simply discarding the field from the new file? Where a new file field has no sub-fields, as is the case with *Name* in this example, this is true – there is no difference. There would however be a difference if the field in the new file did have sub-fields.

Field Values are Never Merged

When we talk of merging 2 fields, what this actually means is that *the entire field branch*, including all descendant sub-fields on each side, is merged. Individual field *values,* however, are never merged. Where you have 2 field values on the same row, the new field value in the New File Pane is always discarded, and the current field value in the Current File Pane is always retained. This is why you will see that the new field value, in these cases, is displayed with a line through it ('~~struckout~~') to show that this value will be discarded.

The only way that you can override this is to unmatch the fields. You cannot leave 2 fields matched, and force Family Historian to use the New File Pane value instead of the Current File Pane value.

Adding, Deleting and Ignoring

What this shows is that merging is actually a simpler business than it might at first sight appear. Merging, if left up to Family Historian, is basically just a matter of adding new records, and new fields (and sub-fields). By clicking on the **Discard** button, you can additionally ensure that some records, fields or sub-fields are *deleted* in the current file, or simply *ignored* in the new file. And that is it. To repeat – there is no actual updating of individual field values at all.

Summary

We said at the start of this chapter, that once you had learned how to interpret the information that Family Historian shows you, you can see what the outcome of a merge will be before it has started. We can summarise what we have learned as follows:

- Any record or field branch in the struckout font in the Current File Pane represents data that will be *deleted* from the current file.
- Any record or field branch in the struckout font in the New File Pane represents data that will be *ignored* during the merge.
- Any unmatched record or field branch (not struckout) in the Current File pane represents data that will be retained in the current file (i.e. left unchanged in the current file).
- Any unmatched record or field branch (not struckout) in the New File pane represents data that will be added to the current file.
- Any matched record or field branch represents data that will be *merged* into the current file – but a merge may be a 'Null Merge' that doesn't actually change anything. Also, where 2 fields are matched, the field values are never merged. The field value from the current file is retained and the field value from the new file is discarded.

Check *All* Record Types

So far we have only looked at the *Individuals* tab of the **Merge/Compare Dialog**. Now click on all the other tabs in turn. The **Check** and **Uncheck** buttons work with all records of all types.

In this particular case, apart from one Family record, there are no significant changes to records other than Individual records. However, the issues we have discussed apply to all records – not just Individual records. So you should always be careful to check all tabs, to make sure that the merge, when executed, will do what you want it to do.

Execute Merge

Now click on the **Merge** button. When you do this, a warning dialog will appear, to warn you that not all records have been flagged as 'checked'. This warning is entirely for your own benefit. If you had not wished or intended to check every record you should ignore it.

It is a useful reminder, however, that the issues we have discussed apply to all record types, not just to Individual records; and that you should remember to check records of all types – not just Individuals.

For now though, click on **OK** to proceed with the merge and ignore the warning. Now a **Merge Options** dialog appears (see Figure 70 below).

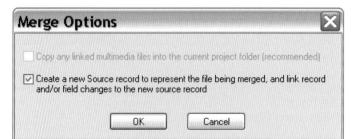

Figure 70 – The Merge Options dialog. The first option is greyed because, in the example, there is no current project.

Copy Linked Multimedia   If you were merging a file into a project, the first option would be ungreyed and you would be offered the chance to copy any linked multimedia into the current project folder. However, in this case, we are merging two standalone GEDCOM files, which is why that option is greyed in Figure 70.

Create Source Record to Represent File Being Merged   The Merge Options dialog also gives you the opportunity to create a source record to represent the new file being merged into the current one. If you opt to do this, a **Source Details for Merge Dialog** will appear offering you various options about how to do this.

You will be able, if you wish, to add a source citation for all the new data being merged into the current file, to link it to the new source record. You can add source citation links at either the record or field level. You can even specify whether you want data that is identical to the data you already have, to be linked to the new source record because it *confirms* that the data you already have is correct. You might well wish to use this option if the new file was created quite independently of the current file. But if the new file merely represented someone's corrections to the current file, it would not be appropriate to assume that any data which was the same had necessarily been confirmed.

For more information about this, see the Help for the **Source Details for Merge Dialog.**

For now, untick this option and click **OK**. At this point, the merge takes place. When it has completed, a **Merge Results Dialog** is displayed which shows the number of updates of various kinds that have taken place to records of all types. Confirm that these figures tally with what you expected, and click **Close** to close the dialog.

Save Changes   Finally, click on the Save button [Save] on the main application toolbar, to save changes.

Splitting Files   Splitting files is the opposite problem to merging them. The standard way to split a file in Family Historian is to copy it, and then delete all the records you don't want from the copy, which becomes the split off file. You can make two copies if you wish to, and make sure that you delete from one file all and only the records you didn't delete from the other – thereby partitioning your file into two. You can repeat this exercise to split the copies again, as many times as you like.

Why might you want to split a file? You might decide, for organisational reasons, that it makes sense to split off one side of the family into a separate file, perhaps.

Save a GEDCOM File Copy   There are numerous ways of copying files. You don't have to use Family Historian for this. All versions of Windows come with an Accessories program called Windows Explorer, which can be used to copy files. If you are already using Family Historian however, it is probably more convenient to use it. One very easy way to create a copy of your current GEDCOM file is to click on **Save a GEDCOM File Copy**, which is on the **GEDCOM File Tasks** submenu on the **File** menu. When you do this, the current GEDCOM file will be copied, and you will be asked if you wish to view the copied file. If you choose to do so, the file will be opened in a new instance of Family Historian.

The Split Tree Helper Dialog   Family Historian provides a dialog, called the **Split Tree Helper** dialog (see Figure 71 below) to help with the process of splitting family tree files. The **Split Tree Helper** dialog's full name is *Split Tree Helper: Delete Unwanted Data*. Although designed in the first instance to help with splitting family tree files, what the Split Tree Helper dialog actually does is delete records and fields. You don't have to use it as part of a file-splitting process. You can use it at any time, if you want to delete

175

a large number of records or fields.

It is very easy using the **Split Tree Helper** dialog to delete a large number of records from a file, or even all of them. So care should obviously be exercised when using this dialog. If your intention is to use it to delete records and fields from a copy of your main file, you should take care and make quite sure that you are using it on the copy, and not on the main file itself. It is a good idea to take backups before using this dialog, to protect yourself in case of errors.

For more on the **Split Tree Helper Dialog**, see the Help.

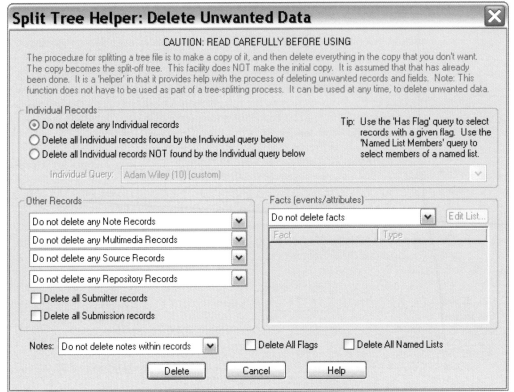

Figure 71 – The *Split Tree Helper* dialog

Export GEDCOM File   Splitting your family tree file is not something people want to do very often. A more common requirement is that you want to send a file, containing some part of your research, to someone else – and you don't want to send them all of it. You could use the techniques already discussed to do this. You could use **Save a GEDCOM File Copy** to make a copy of your main file, and then use the **Split Tree Helper Dialog** to remove from it any data that you did not wish to include. But there is a simpler method. The **Export GEDCOM File** dialog may provide all the features you need in one step. It allows you to specify which Individual records you wish to export, and to control other aspects of the export. See Figure 72 below.

To open the **Export GEDCOM File** dialog, click on the **File** menu, then **Import/Export**, then **Export**, and finally **GEDCOM File...**

If the Export GEDCOM File dialog doesn't do everything you need, you can still use the **Split Tree Helper** dialog on the exported file, for fine-tuning and to remove yet further details, if you wish to.

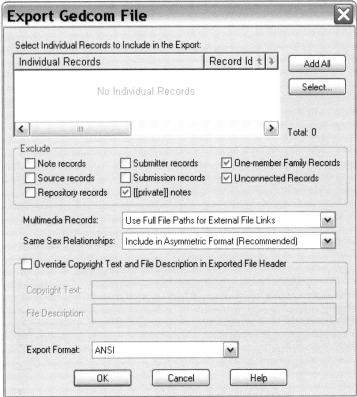

Figure 72 – The *Export Gedcom File* dialog

16 Named Lists and Record Flags

Like Queries, which we looked at in earlier chapters, *Named Lists* and *Record Flags* both also have a useful role to play within Family Historian. This short chapter briefly describes what they are for, and how to use them.

What are Named Lists For?

It is often useful to be able to put together and keep lists of records. Here are just some lists you might want to keep:

- a bookmark list as a shortcut to frequently accessed records
- a list of work-in-progress records
- a list of possible duplicate records you wish to check
- a list of records where Family Historian re-sequenced the fields, and you asked it to create a list of updated records for you to double-check
- a To-Do list of records that you plan to work on when you visit a particular record office (with notes about what you plan to do)
- a list of records you want to delete
- a list of records that you wish to edit, grouped together for ease of access
- a list of records you have selected for a report
- a list of records you wish to send to someone
- a list of pictures (Multimedia records) waiting to be linked to other records
- a list of famous or infamous people
- a list of relatives to invite to a reunion
- a temporary list to be used in conjunction with queries, to allow you to effectively create more complex queries[32]

In short, Named Lists can be used in a variety of different ways, and for a variety of different purposes.

What are Record Flags For?

With some issues, you don't want to keep a list as such – you want to put a little mark on a person's record itself. For example, suppose your cousin tells you that he does not wish to appear in a website you are creating. In that case, rather than adding him to a list of people who must not appear, a better approach is to set a flag on his record itself to show this. This is, in fact, what the 'Private' flag is for.

Here are just a few things that you might want to use a record flag to record:

- that a person doesn't want information about them to be published
- that a person is a another genealogist
- that a person is alive (the 'Living' flag)
- that a person is a twin (or triplet)
- that a person is famous or infamous
- that a person is known to you personally
- that a person has an occupation that you are keeping track of
- that you wish this person to be displayed in a special way in diagrams

When Should You Use Which?

You may notice that there is some overlap between the list of things that you might use a Named List for, and the list of things you might use a Record Flag. For many purposes, it may not matter which you use. You will discover that you can populate

---

[32] You can create arbitrarily complex queries without using Named Lists. Using Named Lists in this way, as a kind of temporary 'memory' (like the Memory buttons on a calculator) is just one option.

Named Lists based on Record Flags, and you can set Record Flags based on Named Lists; so it is easy to change your mind at any stage anyway.

In general, you should use Record Flags if you are likely to want the subject matter to determine the appearance of boxes in diagrams, or text within boxes in diagrams. For example, if your family contains a number of sailors, and you are interested in the nautical history of your family, you could set a 'Sailor' record flag for each relative who is a sailor. You could then arrange, say, for a little 'Ship' icon to appear beneath boxes in diagrams where the box owner is a sailor.

For the purpose of excluding a person from reports or generated websites or CDs, you must use the built-in 'Privacy' flag. You can also use the built-in 'Living' flag to restrict how much information is output; or you can use another flag of your own. But you must use a record flag for this.

Record Flags can only be set on *Individual* records; whereas Named Lists can contain lists of records of any type (even a mixture of types if you wish).

Where the issue is not about diagrams or privacy or record type, you should decide which to use on the basis of which feels most convenient.

Named Lists Pane

We will start by looking at Named Lists. Named Lists are kept in the ***Named List Pane*** which is a hideable area on the right hand side of the **Records Window**. Click on the appropriate icon on the Navigation Bar to view the Records Window now. The Records Window has its own toolbar, which is only available when the Records Window is active. There are only three buttons on this toolbar and they all relate to Named Lists. The first button is the **Named Lists Pane** button . Click on this now, if it's not already clicked, to show the Named List Pane. Figure 73 shows an example of what the Records Window can look like when the Named List pane is visible. In the example shown, eleven records have been added to the *Bookmarks* list.

List Item Notes

The Named Lists Pane has 3 panels. The top panel is the complete list of *Named Lists* in the current file. The middle panel shows the items in the Named List selected in the top panel. And the bottom panel shows a note associated with whichever list item is selected in the middle panel, if any.

The vertical partition lines between the Named List pane and the rest of the Records Window, and the horizontal partition lines between all 3 panels within the Named List pane, can all be moved. Move your cursor over any of these partition lines and click-and-drag to reposition them.

Every list can hold records of any type. Every item in every list can have a note associated with it. This note is not stored in the item's record. It is associated with the list, and is deleted when the item is removed from the list.

Add to Current List

To add one or more records from the Records Window to a Named List, you just need to select the list in the topmost panel of the Named Lists Pane, and then select which record or records you wish to add, and click on the **Add To Current List** button. You can add as many records at a time as you want. To select multiple records in the Records Window, you can use any of the normal Windows techniques for multiple selection. For example, you can click-and-drag on an unused part of the window to 'lasso' the records you want with a stretchy box; or click on one record, then press-and-hold the **Shift** key and click on another, to select all records in a range.

New Named List

To create a new Named List, click on the **New Named List** button and enter the name of the new list.

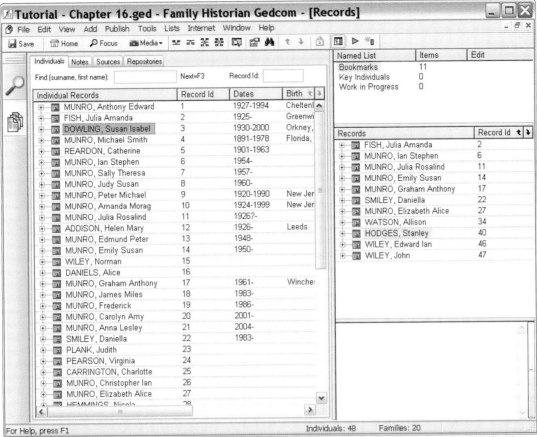

Figure 73 – The Records Window with the Named List Pane showing. Eleven records have been added to the Bookmarks List.

Remove Item From List To remove one or more items from a Named List, select the items in the middle panel of the Named Lists pane, and press the **Delete** key. When items are removed from a list in this way, the actual records are not deleted. If the item has a list item note (the kind that display in the bottom panel) that will be deleted.

Auto-Create Named Lists Some lists are so convenient that you may want them to be automatically created for you whenever you open a project (or standalone GEDCOM file), if the project or file doesn't already have such a list. You may always wish to have a *Bookmark* list, for example, even if empty, so that you can easily add records to it whenever you want to. You can specify the names of up to 6 auto-create Named Lists in the **Preferences Dialog**, which is accessible from the **Tools** menu.

Add to Named List Although **Add To Current List** is easy to use and convenient, it is only available to you in the **Records Window**. If you want to add records to a Named List from other windows, you should use the **Add to Named List** command on the **Edit** menu. This also works with multiple selection.

For convenience, you can also add all the selected items in the **Selector Dialog** – used with reports (see next chapter) and in other contexts – to a Named List too. And you can add the result set produced by a query to a Named List.

Named Lists and Queries Named Lists and Queries are designed to work well together. You can take the output from any query and add all the records associated with each row in the result set to a Named List, using **Add Row Records to Named List** which is located on the Query Menu (the Query Menu is the menu that drops down when you click on the **Query Menu** button on the **Query Window** toolbar). This command is only available when you have run a query and are viewing the result set in the Result Set tab of the Query Window.

Alternatively, you can do the opposite and remove from a given list, all the records in a query result set, using the **Remove Row Records From Named List** command, located on the same menu.

You can also select a range of cells in any result set and click on **Add Selected Cell Records to Named List** also on the Query menu, to add all records in the selected range to a Named List.

You can use a Named List as a filter within a query. In the simplest case, you can simply add to the result set, the records in the list. This could be useful if you want to display a Named List using the column formatting of a query.

The *Named List Members* query simply returns all the Individuals who are members of a Named List that you specify when you run the query. This means that you can effectively use a Named List in any context where a query can be used. For example, the **Split Tree Helper** dialog does not let you specify the records to delete using a Named List, but you can specify them using a query. But by using the Named List Members query you can get round this.

It could also happen that you want to create a complex query, but your filtering requirements are too complex to be implemented using simple filtering conditions. One way round this problem, for those who are familiar with such things, is to use functions with logical operators to create arbitrarily complex expressions (look up 'Functions' in the Help Index for more on this strategy). But if that doesn't appeal, a simple solution may be to break down your query requirements into multiple steps, and use a Named List to store the intermediary results, as you progress through the steps.

By using Queries and Named Lists together in multiple steps, you should be able to achieve any kind of filtering, however complex, and end up with the result set you require.

Differences between Queries and Named Lists

Although they work well together, Named Lists and Queries are actually very different. Queries do not store any data (and hence have no overhead associated with them). They store criteria for retrieving data (and displaying it) when required. But they do not store the actual data. Named Lists are stored lists of data. Also, whereas a Query is kept in a separate file and is not part of a Family Historian (GEDCOM) file, a Named List *is* stored in your Family Historian file.

You can reference a Named List using a query, and run that query in files which do not have the Named List. This is not a problem. For query purposes, it will be treated as if it were there, but empty.

Another difference between Queries and Named Lists, is that a Query result set only contains records of one type. But a Named List can store records of any type.

Merge Named Lists

There is no command as such for merging Named Lists. Nor is there a command for extracting the overlap between 2 Named Lists, or for removing the contents of one Named List from another. But you should be able to achieve all of these tasks, and other similar tasks, by using List filters in queries. To merge 2 Named Lists, for example, simply create a query that has 2 List filters and adds records to the result set if they belong to either list. The result set can then be saved as a Named List, using the **Add Result Set Records to Named List** command on the Query menu.

Delete Named List

To delete a Named List, select the list in the **Named Lists Pane** and use the **Delete Named List** command on the **Lists** menu. None of the records in the deleted list will be deleted, but any list item notes for that list will be deleted.

Empty Named List To empty a Named List without deleting it, select the list in the **Named Lists Pane** and use the **Empty Named List** command on the **Lists** menu. All items will be removed from the list. None of the actual records will be deleted, but any list item notes for that list will be deleted.

Delete All Records in a Named List It may sometimes happen that you want to delete a number of records. Although the Records Window will let you delete records one at time, it won't let you delete multiple records, even though you can select them.

One way to delete multiple records is to create a list of records you want to delete. You might call this list "*Delete Pending*". You can easily add multiple records to this list. Then select the list in the **Named Lists Pane** and click on the **Delete All Records in a Named List** command, on the **Lists** menu. This time, the actual records will be deleted. You will be required to confirm that you understand that records will be deleted, when you do this.

List Reports There is a *List Report* that can be reached from the **Publish** menu (under **Miscellaneous Reports**) that will print out a list of items in a given Named List, together with any notes associated with any of the items. Reports are covered in Chapter 17.

Keep Current List Order Items in a Named List have a fixed order. This is the order that items in the list are displayed in, unless you click on a column heading to change their sort order. There are two buttons, **Move Up** ⬆ and **Move Down** ⬇, at the right end of the column headings for the middle panel of the **Named List Pane**. You can use these to move items around in a list. If you do so, the new order is not automatically preserved. If you want the displayed order to be preserved as the new order for the list, you must click on the **Keep Current List Order** command on the **Lists** menu.

Named List Properties As well as a name, each Named List can have a note attached to it (this is in addition to the note that can be attached to each item in the list). To change either the name or the note, click on **Named List Properties** on the **Lists** menu. List Notes are printed at the top of List Reports (see above).

If you wish to edit records in a Named List, using 'low-level editing' (the kind of editing that you can do in the Records Window or in the *All* tab of the Property Box), check the **Record Editing Enabled** flag.

Record Flags Dialog We will now turn to Record Flags. Key to working with Record Flags is the **Record Flags** dialog which is accessed from the **Edit** menu (see Figure 74 below). To open this dialog you must first select one or more Individual records. The dialog will show you, for all the selected records, which flags they have. It states at the top how many records are selected. A checked box means that all of the selected records have the flag (e.g. 'Private'). An unchecked box means that none of the selected records have the flag (e.g. 'Twin' and 'Genealogist' in the example). Finally, if some do and some don't, the box will display in an intermediary state (e.g. 'Living' in the example).

If you tick a flag and press **OK** you set that flag for all the selected records. If you untick it and press **OK** you will clear that flag on all selected records.

Create New Record Flags You can create as many new record flags as you want. To create a new one, simply click on the 'New' button in the Record Flags dialog and give the new flag a name.

You can also create a new record flag using 'low-level editing' in the Records Window, by right-clicking on any record that you wish to have the new flag, and clicking on **Set Flag** and then **<New Flag>** in the dropdown menu that appears. Again, you have to give the new flag a name.

Once you have created a new flag, it will appear in lists of flags, and you can set it on other Individual records.

Figure 74 - The *Record Flags* dialog,
accessible from the Edit menu

Delete Record Flags

As we have seen, you can clear a record flag for a particular record, by using the Record Flags dialog. But what if you want to delete an entire record flag?

There are two parts to this. To clear a particular flag on all records in the current project, you need to use the **Work with Lists and Flags** dialog (see Figure 75 below). That won't, of itself, prevent a record flag you created appearing in lists of record flags though. To stop that, you must again use the **Work with Lists and Flags** dialog. You need to select the flag in question and click on the **Flag Status** button. The **Record Flag Status** dialog appears. Untick "Always include this record flag in flag lists" in this dialog, and press **OK**.

If you do both of the above, the next time you open your project, you should find that the unwanted record flag has gone.

Standard Record Flags

There are only two standard record flags: the *Private* record flag and the *Living* record flag. These flags are primarily used to protect Individuals' privacy when creating websites, CDs & DVDs, reports or books.

Viewing Record Flags

To see which record flags a given record has, you can either use the Record Flags dialog, or you can expand the record in the Records Window, or the *All* tab of the Property Box. If any flags have been set, they will be listed in the last field of the record.

Low-level Editing

You can use low-level editing in the Records Window, and in the *All* tab of the Property Box, to set or clear records. To set a flag, simply click on the record and select an item from the **Set Flag** submenu. To clear a flag, simply select the flag (you will have to expand the *Flags* item) and click on the **Delete** key. If you select the 'Flags' label and hit **Delete** you will delete all flags for that record. A record with no flags will have no item labelled 'Flags'.

Flags and Named Lists

We mentioned earlier that you can set Named Lists based on flags, and vice versa. The limitation on this is that Named Lists can contain records of any type, whereas flags can only be set on Individual records.

To move data between Named Lists and Flags, use the **Work with Named Lists and Flags** command on the **Tools** menu. This opens the **Work with Lists and Flags** dialog (see Figure 75 below).

To use this dialog, select the Named List and Flag that you wish to use, and choose the task you want. Then click **Perform Action**.

You can use this dialog not just to set flags based on lists, or lists based on flags, but also to clear all instances of a given flag (as mentioned earlier), and to empty a given list.

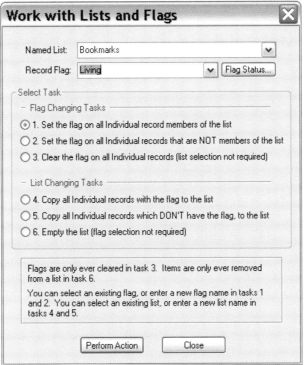

Figure 75 – The Work with Lists and Flags Dialog

Flags and Queries
You can use flags in queries just as you can use any other field – either as a column, or as a field whose value you want to test in a filter. You can also take the output from any query and use it to set or clear a flag on all the records in the result set, using **Set Flag on Row Records** and **Clear Flag on Row Records**. These commands are located on the Query Menu (the Query Menu is the menu that drops down when you click on the **Query Menu** button ⊞ on the **Query Window** toolbar). The commands are only available when you have run a query and are viewing the result set in the Result Set tab of the Query Window.

Add Record Window Column
You can set a column in the Records Window to show either Named List membership, or a flag state. Right-click on any Record Window column heading and choose **Configure Columns** from the menu that appears.

In the left column, select the Named List (in quotes) or record flag in question, and click the ⊡ button to add the item as a column.

The same technique can be used to configure columns for Named Lists too – that is, for the middle panel of the Named Lists Pane.

17   Reports

Reports and Query Reports

Family Historian is installed with 40 standard queries. As we saw in Chapter 13, each query can be printed as a report. In addition, you can create your own custom queries, all of which can be printed as reports too. In Query Reports, the data is laid out in tables of rows and columns.

Query reports are relatively simple. Family Historian can generate much more sophisticated reports in which data is presented in a variety of complex and interesting layouts. It is these other kinds of report that we will be looking at in this chapter. However, do not forget about query reports. For some purposes they may be just what you need.

Henceforth, when we talk about 'reports', we shall always mean these other kinds of reports. When we wish to talk about reports based on queries, we will always refer to them as 'query reports'. The two kinds of reports are handled quite differently in Family Historian.

Open Tutorial File

To illustrate some of the things you can do with Family Historian reports, we shall use a tutorial file and look at two standard reports. From the **Project Window**, click on the **More Tasks** button, and then in the dropdown menu click on **Samples**, and finally **Tutorial – Chapter 17**. The file opens and Anthony Munro is displayed as the focus person in the Focus Window.

The Publishing Tools Finder

As well as reports and query reports, Family Historian can also create books, charts & diagrams, family tree CDs & DVDs, and websites. The **Publishing Tools Finder** (the first menu command on the **Publish** menu) is there to help you find the right tool for your needs – see Figure 76 below. Select a publication type from the list on the left of the Finder, and the available tools in that category will be shown in the middle panel. The right panel gives a description of the currently selected tool, and tells you where its menu can be found for quick access. You can of course also open the tool from within the Finder itself.

The Finder is a useful guide to the tools available to you, and you can use it to help you find a particular type of report (or for other purposes). However, it isn't essential. All reports are also listed on the Publish menu – either on the Publish menu itself, or on submenus in various categories.

The Family Group Sheet

We will look first at the Family Group Sheet.

Steps

1. Click on Family Group Sheet on the Publish menu.
2. A dialog appears with the caption "Select Records". This is the **Select Records** dialog (see Figure 78 below). Like many dialogs in Family Historian, you can resize it if it is too small, and even maximize it if you wish to. The list on the right is the *Selection List*. If there are any records there already, click the ⧉ button to get rid of them. Then select *Michael Smith Munro* in the list and click on the ⧉ button. When you do this Family records for all of Michael Smith Munro's marriages (in this case one only, to Catherine Reardon) are added to the *Selection List* on the right hand side. Click **OK**.
3. The *Reports Window* appears and displays the *Family Group Sheet* for the Family of Michael Munro and Catherine Reardon – see Figure 77 below.
4. The **Reports Window** has a grey side panel to the right of the report area, and

two vertical scrollbars. One of these is just to the left of the side panel. The other is on the right side of the side panel. Family Historian can display two pages side-by-side, but it never displays more than one page vertically. The leftmost of the two vertical scrollbars allows you to scroll up and down within the current page (or two pages if you're showing two). The rightmost scrollbar also scrolls up and down within the current page, but will scroll across pages too. Click on this 'outer' scrollbar now to browse down through the entire report.

If you are using the default options for the *Family Group Sheet* you should see that there is a picture of the whole family at the top of the report. The topmost section of the report gives a brief overview of the family. Thereafter there is a section for each member of the family, starting with the parents. You should see that to the right of the text, there is a picture displayed of each family member's face. Notice that the face picture is taken from the family picture at the top.

The picture is quite grainy. This is because the original photo was only about 2" wide; so blown-up detail is blurry. If your pictures are sharp (and preferably not too small if you are scanning them) you should not be able to get them to appear as sharp and clear as you want.

Source citations are listed at the end of the report. If there were pictures, such as scans of documents, associated with sources, or even with individual source citations, you would be able to display those to the right of the text in the source citation listing.

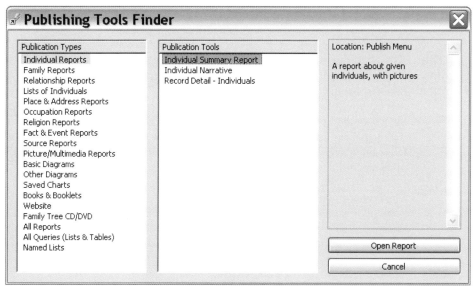

Figure 76 – The Publication Tools Finder

The Individual Summary Report

Now look at an example of an *Individual Summary Report*.

Steps

1. Click on Individual Summary Report on the Publish menu.
2. The **Select Records** dialog appears again. Click on the ⟫ button to add all records to the *Selection List* and press **OK**.
3. A new **Reports Window** opens to display the *Individual Summary Report* for all the records you selected. Click on the outer scrollbar to scroll down through the report. Notice that although there are no pictures for Susan Dowling and Julia Fish, each of them has a picture of Anthony Munro showing him as a spouse.

4. Find the entry for Anthony Edward Munro (using the rightmost scrollbar – or the arrows to the right of the current page number, at the top of the grey side panel). His entry illustrates various features of this report. As well as a picture of Anthony Munro, there is also a sizeable list of events and attributes, with additional information showing about some of the events and attributes. There is a section for each of his two marriages, a note about Anthony Munro headed "Individual Note", and a separate note about each of his marriages. There is also a list of source citations for his entry.

5. Now browse down to Michael Smith Munro's entry. Notice that as well as a photograph of him, there is also a photograph of his family with Catherine Reardon, and separate photographs of his spouse and children. The photographs of individuals show the date of the picture and the person's age at the time.

We will now look in more detail at the various components of the **Reports Window**.

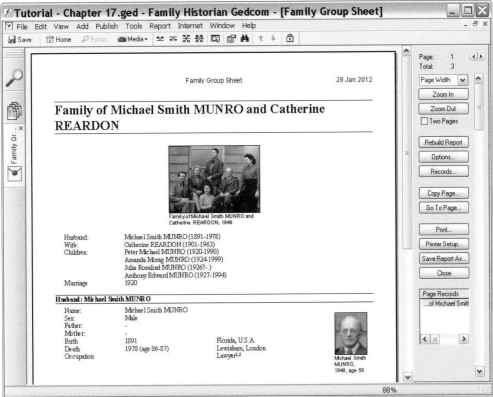

Figure 77 – the Reports Window showing a Family Group Sheet.

Select Records Dialog
As we have seen, when you wish to print a report, you choose the report from the **Publish** menu (or open it using the *Publication Tools Finder*). Family Historian then displays the *Select Records* dialog (see Figure 78 below). The only exception to this is the List report which uses the **Select Named List** dialog (see Figure 80 below). You can normally display the report for one record, or multiple records, whichever you prefer. [33]

When the **Select Records** dialog is displayed, you select the records you want and press the **OK** button. If you are planning to print a report with a great many records, you don't have to select them all now. You might prefer to keep the report small while you look at it initially, because you may want to make a number of changes to the layout. You may find it more convenient to do that with a small

---

[33] The *How Related* report is an exception to this. You have to select two Individual records – and no more than two – for that report.

number of sample records than with a large number.

When the **Reports Window** is displayed, you can click on the **Records** button at any time to change the records selected for the report (the equivalent of this for the List Report is you click on the **List** button to choose a different list).

Features of the Select Records Dialog

As has already been mentioned, the right hand side of the **Select Records** dialog lists the records you want to appear in the report. This is called the **Selection List** (although it is not labelled as such). If you click on the ![button] button, all records selected on the left hand side will be copied to the Selection List. If you click on the ![button] button, all the records listed on the left hand side will be copied to the Selection List. If you click on the ![button] button, all selected records in the Selection List will be removed from the list; and if you click on the ![button] button it will be emptied.

You can add ancestors, descendants and spouses by clicking on the **Add Relatives** button. If you have more complex requirements, you can use a query – by clicking on **Add Using Query**. More rarely it may be useful to be able to remove from the Selection List, all records that match a given query. You can do this by clicking on **Remove Using Query**.

The left hand side of the Select Records dialog normally has 2 tabs: one for records of the required type, and one for Named Lists. When selecting records for a Family Report, however, there are 3 tabs: one for Individuals, one for Families, and one for Named Lists. In this case, if you click ![button] when an Individual record is selected, the Family records for each of that individual's marriages (if any) are added to the Selection List.

You can use the Named List tab to add items from a Named List, or the entire Named List, to the Selection List. Although all Named Lists are shown, you will only be able to add records of the required type for the report. You will be warned if none of the selected records are of the required type.

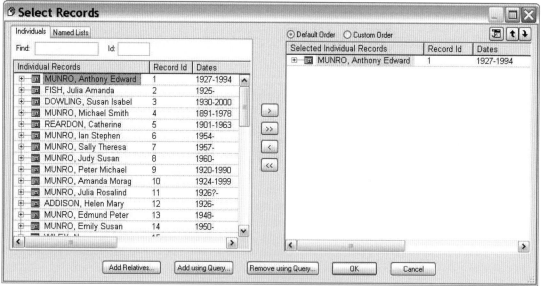

Figure 78 – the *Select Records* dialog

Add to Named List

You can preserve the contents of a **Selection List** as a Named List if you wish to by clicking on the **Add All to Named List** command, which appears when you click on the Menu toolbar button ![button] in the top right corner of the dialog. Alternatively, you can use the **Add Selection to Named List** command.

The Reports Window When you press **OK** on the **Select Records** dialog, the **Reports Window** opens and displays the report you have selected.

The **Reports Window** is another of Family Historian's *subwindows*.[34] As we have already seen, you can have as many subwindows open at a time as you like, and you never need to close them. Each open subwindow will get an icon in the Navigation Bar, and you can click on these to switch between subwindows at any time. There is no need to close the **Reports Window** if for example you want to open a diagram, or run a query, or even open another report in another Reports Window. The Navigation Bar icon for the Reports Window is shown on the left.

Tip: To view the Help for the Reports Window, press the F1 key when viewing the Reports Window. You can do this with all Family Historian subwindows, not just the Reports Window.

The Report Menu Some subwindows have their own menu which only appears when that window is active. The Diagrams Window has its own **Diagram** menu. The Multimedia Window has its own **Multimedia** menu. The Reports Window also has its own menu, which is only there when the Reports Window is active. This is the **Report** menu.

The Reports Window Side Panel On the right hand side of the **Reports Window**, there is a grey *Side Panel* with a number of buttons on it (see Figure 79 right). The exact number of buttons displayed varies depending on the size of the window. If you resize the window you will find that some appear or disappear as the window changes size. If you use a small screen resolution on your computer, you may not see all of the buttons that it can show even when your window is full size. However, the same commands are all also available from either the **Report** menu or (in the case of the **Print** and **Print Setup** commands) from the **File** menu.

The current page (or pages if you are showing two) is shown at the top of the Side Panel, as well as the total number of pages in the report. To the right of the current page are two small buttons for stepping forwards and backwards through pages of the report – useful if you want to jump from one page to the next without having to scroll up and down.

Just below the page information is a list where you can specify the zoom level (100%, 200%, 50% etc). If you select *Page Width* (the default), Family Historian will change the zoom so that you can always see a full page width, whatever the window size – or two page widths if you are showing 2 pages at once. Likewise, *Whole Page* lets you see a whole page at a time.

Check **Two Pages** if you want to see two pages at a time. Odd-numbered pages are always shown on the right, as this is standard practice in publishing.

Figure 79 – the Reports Window Side Panel

The Side Panel Buttons The Side Panel buttons are mostly self-explanatory. **Zoom In** and **Zoom Out** behave as you would expect. **Copy Page** copies the current report page to the clipboard in a choice of formats – you can then paste it into another program such as a word-processor. **Go To Page** jumps you to a particular page in the report. **Print**

---

[34] Subwindows were introduced in Chapter 1.

and **Print Setup** behave as you would expect. There is no difference between these button commands and the **Print** and **Print Setup** commands on the **File** menu.

Using the Mouse Wheel

If your mouse has a wheel, you will find that you can use it with most of the main Family Historian windows. However, if you use the mouse wheel with the *Reports Window* you will find that the wheel does different things depending on where the arrow is positioned. If the arrow is over the report page you will scroll up and down within that page. If the arrow is over the outermost scrollbar on the right-hand side, you will scroll up and down within the whole report - not just within a page, but across pages. And finally, if the mouse is over the two small buttons ◄|► to the right of the **Page** field, it will scroll forwards and backwards through the report, jumping from page to page, but keeping to the same relative position within each page.

Save Report as PDF File

When you click on the **Save Report As** button (see , a dropdown menu appears giving you the choice of formats to save the report in. The first of these is PDF File. If you want to send a report to someone else, PDF file is probably the best format to use, as the report will look just like it does in Family Historian when they view it.

Save Report as Web Page

If you save a report as a web page, it will be saved in HTML format, in a folder that you specify. All the files necessary to represent the web page will be copied to this folder. Pictures are included in web pages, but if your report has an index, that is not included. This is because an index makes no sense for a single web page (every item on the index if there were one, would be on page 1).

Save Report as Word-Processor Document

If you save a report as a word-processor document, it will be saved in Rich Text Format (RTF). This format is supported by most good word-processors. Microsoft Word, for example, supports it. Having saved the report in this format, you can then open it in MS Word (or another word-processor) and make any further changes that you want. This may also be a useful format to save a report in if you wish to send it to someone else.

When you save a report as a Word-processor document, pictures and their captions are also saved. However, they may not be laid out in the same way relative to the text as they are when you view the report in Family Historian.

If your report has an index, this will be included. But you are recommended to open the document and 'refresh' the Index in the new context, so that the index page values are correct. In Microsoft Word, for example, you would right-click anywhere on the index and click on **Update Field** in the dropdown menu that appears.

Save Report as Text File

Saving a report as a text file is rarely likely to be useful, unless you don't have a word-processor that supports Rich Text Format. Pictures are not saved in text format (by definition, text format just contains text), and nor is the index if there is one.

Styles in HTML and Rich Text Format

As already mentioned, the report should look exactly the same in PDF format as it looks in Family Historian, but the same is not true of the other formats. Although it is not possible to guarantee that every aspect of a report will be reproduced perfectly in these other formats, Family Historian tries to ensure that the HTML and Rich Text Format versions are as close as possible to the report that you see. There can however be differences. We have already mentioned that the positioning of pictures relative to the text can be different in Rich Text Format. Also, if the report contains additional graphics of any kind (such as the connecting lines in *Ancestor Outline* reports or in *Descendant Outline* reports) these will not be saved to these formats.

Family Historian uses *heading styles* and other style-based formatting (see the **Format** tab of the **Report Options** dialog), and these are incorporated into the equivalent style formats in both the HTML and RTF formats. What this means is that if you need to change the look of a Family Historian report, using a word-processor or an HTML editor, you should find that it is easy and convenient to do so.[35]

Save as Custom Report Type
As well as saving a report as a file, you can also save it as a custom report *type*. This is the last item on the **Save Report As** dropdown menu. Any report, including other custom reports, can be used as your template, and can be saved as a new custom report type.

Although you can do this with any report, some reports make more flexible templates than others. The *Individual Summary Report* and *Family Group Sheet* are both reports which make very good templates for other reports. In *Create a Custom Hobby Report* below, we will walk through an example of how you might create a custom report.

Custom reports are listed on the **Custom Reports** submenu, which can be found on the main **Publish** menu.

The Records Button
Clicking on the Side Panel **Records** button (see Figure 79 above) brings up the **Select Records dialog** (see Figure 78 above). You can see which records are selected for the report, in which order. You can change the records selected, and/or their order, at any time.

The List Button
The **List** button is shown instead of the **Records** button if you are running the *List Report*. It brings up the **List Selector Dialog** so that you can select which Named List you wish to see in the report (see Figure 80 below).

Figure 80 – The *Select Named List* Dialog

Report Options
The **Options** button brings up the **Report Options** dialog (see Figure 81 below). The options available are extensive and vary considerably between reports. The best source of information about the options in the **Report Options** dialog is the Help (click on the **Help** button when the **Report Options** dialog is displayed.

The standard tabs and their role are described in the table below:

---

[35] If you don't use HTML editors or word-processors, or you do but don't make use of the style-based formatting that they offer, you may not understand what *style-based formatting* means. Styles are a powerful and useful feature of word-processors (and HTML), but beyond the scope of this document. For more information about them see your word-processor's documentation or Help.

Report Options Tab	Description
Contents/Main	Specify the data content of the report. The contents of this tab vary considerably between reports.
Pictures	Specify what pictures you want in the report and how you want them laid out. The available picture options also vary considerably between reports.
Sources	Do want source citations? If so, how do you want them to be handled?
Index	Do you want the report to have an index? If so, what information do you want indexed, and how do you want the index laid out?
Format	Specify the appearance and style of all the different kinds of heading (font to use, font size and colour, etc), as well as the text to use for headings, and also the fonts to use for non-heading text.
Page Layout	Specify details of the page orientation and margins, as well as header and footer details. On this page you can also specify dimensions of columns, paragraph and tab indentations, and header and footer depth. You can specify the starting page number for the report here, and also whether you want each record to start on a new page.
Privacy	This tab allows you to control, and even hide altogether, information about individuals who wish to remain private – either entirely, or to some degree – and who might otherwise be mentioned in a report. You are recommended to click the Help button to read the Help pages describing the precise function of the options on this tab.

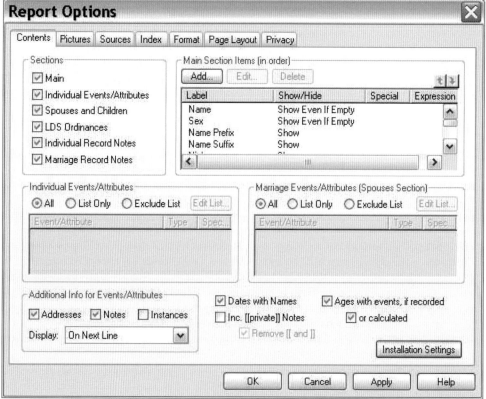

Figure 81 – The Report Options Dialog. The options available, and even the dialog tabs, vary depending on the report type.

Page Records

At the bottom of the the Reports Window Side Panel (see Figure 79 above), the **Page Records** list is a list of records displayed in the current page. It doesn't include every record that is referred to anywhere in the current page. It only includes records that have an entry of their own (or part of one) on the current page. The **Page Records** list is a useful way of getting quick access to the data underlying the report that you are looking at. Select any record in the list, and click on the

Property Box button [image] on the main toolbar (or just double-click on the item) to bring up the **Property Box**, to view the record details for the record in question.

Reports are Dynamic

When looking at the Diagram Window in earlier chapters, we saw that you can change almost any aspect of a diagram, or the data underlying a diagram, 'on the fly' and it will immediately update to reflect the change. The same is also true of reports. While viewing a report in the **Reports Window**, you can do any of the following and the **Reports Window** will immediately update itself to reflect the change:

- Change the page layout (margins, portrait/landscape etc).
- Change the style and formatting of the report
- Change options which determine the content displayed for each record
- Change the records selected for the report or the order in which they appear
- Change the actual data underlying the report, that it is reporting on (but see *Rebuild Report* below)

You use the **Report Options** dialog to do the first three. You use the **Select Records** dialog (click on the **Records** button) to change the records selected for the report. And you use any technique you like to change the actual data underlying the report.

See What You Are Doing as You Do It

The intention of the Family Historian design for the Reports Window is that you should be able to see what you are doing as you do it. You can see the implications of each decision as you make it. A good way of working is to find a good sample page that illustrates the aspects of the report that you want to change. Then open the **Report Options** dialog and make the changes. By using the **Apply** button, you can make small changes, and check the effects of each one as you make them (just move the **Report Options** dialog to one side if it covers the **Reports Window** so that you can see what the effect was). This way of working is similar to the way that diagrams work in Family Historian. It is illustrated below in the section *Create a Custom Hobby Report* below.

Rebuild Report

The ability to change the data underlying a report, while you are viewing the report, is another useful feature. Suppose you notice that a name has been misspelled. In simple cases, you can simply double-click on the appropriate record in the **Records on this Page** list and correct the mistake in the **Property Box**. If the record in question does not have an entry on the current page, you may have slightly more work to do to find the record to change. If necessary switch to other windows by clicking on their icon in the Navigation Bar. In any case, you can find the record and change it, *without* closing the **Reports Window** and losing the context of your work.

When you make a change to data underlying a report, the **Reports Window** will immediately update itself to reflect the change. However, when it does so, for performance reasons it does not rebuild the entire report. It will simply redisplay the information for affected records within the area of the report that had previously been allocated to them. Some changes may mean that a record's entry now requires more or less space than it did before. This can mean that gaps appear between this record entry and the next. It can also mean that one record entry suddenly overlaps another and you get a mess where two sets of text compete for the same space. This is not an error but a deliberate policy decision. The ability to see changes immediately reflected in a report is too useful to be dispensed with. But equally, it would take too long to rebuild every report after every change. The policy adopted is a compromise.

When you come to print a report, or save it to a file, or copy a page, Family Historian will not let you do this if the data underlying it has changed, and the report has not been rebuilt. In this situation, you will be prompted to click on the **Rebuild Report** button. When the report is rebuilt, the correct space to allocate to each entry is recalculated in the light of the new data, and any unwanted gaps between entries, or overlapping entries, are sorted out.

Of course you don't have to wait until prompted to do so, to rebuild a report. You can do this at any time. If you can see that a change has left the report looking a mess, click on the **Rebuild Report** button to sort it out immediately.

Create a Custom Hobby Report

We will now walk through an example of how you might create a custom report. From the **Project Window**, click on **More Tasks**, and then **Samples**, and finally **Tutorial – Chapter 17**.

In this example, we will assume you want a report on Individuals' hobbies. 'Hobby' is not actually a standard attribute. It was used as an example of how to add a custom attribute in Chapter 6.

Steps

1. Click on **Individual Summary Report** on the **Publish** menu. Select Julia Munro and click ◄ to add her to the **Selection List**. Make sure she is the only item in the **Selection List** (if there are any others, select them and click on the ◄ button to remove them). Now click **OK**. The Individual Summary Report for Julia Munro is displayed in the Reports Window.
2. Click on **Save Report As** in the Reports Window Side Panel (see Figure 79 above) and then **Custom Report Type**. Enter Custom Report Name as "Hobbies". Press **OK**. Notice that although nothing appears to have changed, the main window caption now ends "[Hobbies]" and the Navigation Bar icon for the Reports Window also shows the text "Hobbies".
3. Click on *Whole Page* in the list just above the **Zoom In** button. This isn't of course necessary but it may make it easier to see what you are doing. If the text is too small to be read at this zoom level, you may prefer to switch back to *Page Width*, or choose another zoom level.
4. Click on the **Options** button to bring up the **Report Options** dialog. In the **Contents** tab, uncheck all items in the *Sections* area, except for *Individual Events/Attributes*. Click **Apply**. Notice that most of the information in the report has disappeared.
5. In the *Individual Events/Attributes* area, click on *List Only*. What had been a grey list, becomes a white one with "Empty List" showing in light grey text. Double-click on the list (anywhere in the white area). A dialog comes up with the caption "Edit List of Individual Events and Attributes".
6. Click on the **Add Custom Event/Attribute** button. Another dialog appears with the caption "Add Custom Event/Attribute for Individual".
7. Click on *Attribute* as the item type, and enter 'Hobby' as the **Attribute Name**. Click **OK**.
8. The "Edit List of Individual Events and Attributes" dialog should now be showing *Hobby* as the sole item in its Selection List. Click **OK** to close this dialog.
9. Click **Apply** in the **Report Options Dialog**. All rows of data about Events and Attributes disappear except data relating to *Hobby*.
10. Let us assume that you don't want any pictures in your Hobby report. Click now on the **Pictures** tab in the **Report Options** dialog and set all **Max Pics** values to 0. Click **Apply**. The picture of Julia Munro disappears.
11. Let us assume that we don't want source information. Click on the **Sources** tab

and uncheck **Show Source Citations**. All the other fields on this tab become greyed.

12. At this point there is still a heading for "Individual Events and Attributes" in the report. We don't want this so click on the **Format** tab and double-click on the text "Ind. Events & Attrs" item in the list of headings (the bottom list). A dialog appears entitled "Heading Details". Change **Hide/Show Headings** to *Hide*. Press **OK**.

13. In the **Report Options** dialog, click on **Apply**. The "Individual Events and Attributes" heading disappears.

14. In the Empty Section Text field type "<No hobbies>". This text will appear for Individuals who have no hobbies.

15. Click on the **Page Layout** tab and uncheck **Start Records on New Page**. In our report, there is not likely to be much information for each Individual so we don't want to give each of them a whole page.

16. If we wanted to get rid of the *Additional Information* about each person's hobbies, we could do this by unchecking **Inc. Event/Attr Notes** and **Inc. Event/Attr Addresses** in the **Contents** tab. But presumably we do want this information, so leave those checked and press the **OK** button to close the **Report Options** dialog.

17. Now, to test our report, click on the **Records** button and select all the records in the file. Browse through the report and confirm that Julia Munro is the only one who has any hobbies listed.

18. Finally close the **Reports Window** (click on the **Close** button). Click on the **Publish** menu and confirm that **Hobbies** is now listed under **Custom Reports** and behaves as you would expect when you click on it.

The custom report we created is actually a relatively simple one. You can create more complex custom reports by adding custom fields using *Data References*. The *Main Section Items* area of the **Contents** tab for the *Individual Summary Report*, allows you to do this, for example. See the Help for more details.

Trouble-shooting Layout Issues

Family Historian reports can be printed on any paper size that your printer supports, portrait or landscape. So what happens, if you choose to print on very small paper (A5 say), and there simply isn't room for the information to print? The answer is that it won't get printed (or displayed). In such a situation, you can adjust the layout so that the report will print nicely; but it is up to you to do it. Family Historian will not automatically reposition everything for you. If you want to print a report on small paper, you should think seriously about adjusting any or all of the following:

- the font size for all of the text, including fonts for headers and footers
- the margin sizes
- the column indents, paragraph indents and tab width
- the size of pictures
- the gaps around pictures

It can happen, even on standard page sizes, like A4, that some text does not get printed because there is no room for it. Here's an example of how this can occur:

Sometimes within reports Family Historian will display items of data lined up in columns. For example, with events and attributes in the *Individual Summary Report*, the event/attribute labels always line up, and so too do the event/attribute *dates* (2nd column) and *places* (3rd column). You can control how much room is left for each of the *label*, *date* and *place*, by adjusting the **Column Indent** values on the **Page Layout** tab of the **Report Options Dialog**. Now suppose that your paper is setup to print on A4 in portrait mode. That means the paper size is 210mm wide (slightly less than 8.5"). If side margins are 0.5" each, that leaves 7.5" of usable space. Column Indents are measured from the start of the usable area. Suppose the 3rd indent was set at 5" and you had a picture that was 2" wide displaying to its right. Allowing for gaps round pictures, (0.15" on either side by default) you would only have 0.2" to display the *place* information.

In a situation like that, Family Historian will print as many characters as it can (if any) squeezed into the line – not many in this case. It will not 'wrap' the text onto further lines, because if it did, it would produce a very large column of data containing only a couple of characters per line.

The solution to this problem is to adjust the column indents or the picture size or both. If need be, you might also adjust the font size.

Sometimes in a report, it may not always be obvious whether the layout is based on column indent (and if so, which one) or on page indent or tab width. The best solution in this case is simply to experiment by adjusting the values and see what moves. Remember you can always reset all values back to their installation defaults, by clicking on the **Installation Settings** button, so it does no harm to experiment.

One possible requirement is to print a report with a very wide margin, to leave room to make notes. If you do this, check whether you need to adjust column indents and other values, to leave room for the data. If you find some report settings that you want sometimes, but not always, you might like to consider saving what you've done as a custom report, so that you can reuse it whenever you want to, without having to repeat the process of adjusting the data layout.

List of Standard Reports

For a complete list of reports, together with a description of what each one does, open the Publication Tools Finder (see Figure 76 above) and choose 'All Reports' in the left column. Then select each listed report in turn in the middle panel (use the down arrow to move quickly from one to the next) to view a description of each selected report in the right panel.

Narrative Reports

We will conclude this chapter by looking briefly at narrative reports in general, and the *Descendants by Generation* report in particular.

Narrative reports are reports which use ordinary English sentences to provide information about people - as if telling a story. Family Historian has three narrative reports:

- Descendants by Generation
- Ancestors by Generation
- Individual Narrative

Sentence Templates

The sentences used are generated by Family Historian from the basic information provided about each person. You can see what kind of sentence Family Historian will generate for any given event or attribute by looking at the *Facts* tab of the **Property Box**. At the bottom of the dialog is a **Sentence** box in which Family Historian displays the sentence (or something very close to it) that will be generated in a narrative report, for the currently selected event or attribute.

In order to generate these sentences, Family Historian uses a sentence template for each different type of event or attribute, whether standard or custom. You can modify the contents of these sentence templates. To do so, click on **Work with Fact Sets** on the **Tools** menu. This opens the **Event/Attribute List** dialog. Select the fact type (event or attribute) you wish to modify and click on the **Properties** button which in turn opens the **Fact Definition** dialog. Click on the **Help** button to learn how to modify the sentence template to get the results you want.

As well as modifying sentence templates for an entire fact type, you can also modify them for any given instance of a fact type (that is, any given event or attribute) by clicking in the **Sentence** field in the **Facts** tab of the Property Box, and making whatever changes you require. Press the **F1** key while viewing the **Facts** tab of the Property Box to view the Help for this tab, including help with the **Sentence** field, and how to modify it.

The Descendants by Generation Report

Now open the *Descendants by Generation* report to try it out, using Michael Munro as the report subject. You will find that you can control the number of generations displayed, and other aspects of the report in **Report Options**. Click on the **Help** button within the *Report Options* dialog to learn what the various options are for.

The first person in the *Descendants by Generation* report is always listed as number 1. All of their descendants are also given a number, in sequence. Their first child is numbered 2, the next 3, and so on.

You will notice that where you can see a list of a person's children, some of the children will have a '+' before their descendant number, as in this example:

+5   Anthony Edward Munro (1927-1994)

The '+' means that more information is provided about this person somewhere else in the report (usually in the next generation, below). It means that the person has a section of their own, devoted to them.

If a person does not have a section of their own, there will be no '+' before their descendant number; and such information as is held about them (typically not much) is displayed after their name in the list itself, in italics.

Within the **Main** section of **Report Options**, the **One Section Per Descendant** field is checked by default. If you uncheck this field, Family Historian will not automatically give each descendant their own section. Instead it will use the following rules for determining whether a descendant gets a section of their own or not:

If the person is in the last generation of the report (if you asked for 6 generations, say, and this is the 6th generation), they will not get a section of their own. Otherwise, they get a section of their own if they have one or more spouse families (that is, they have either a spouse, or children, or both), or if they have 5 events or attributes or more, or if they have a picture that would display given the current options for this report, or if they have a record note that would display given the current options for this report.

18 Books & Booklets

What is the best way of presenting your research to family members or anyone who might be interested? We have already seen how you can create charts and reports. Wouldn't it be nice if you could bundle up a number of reports, perhaps with some extra text that you write yourself and some relevant charts, and give the whole thing a title page, table-of-contents (each report could be a chapter, say), and an index at the back? This is essentially what Family Historian's Book functionality lets you do. Whether you call it a 'book', a 'pamphlet', or a 'booklet', is just a question of scale and ambition. The method is the same in each case.

You can create as many books as you like for each project. And you can work on them and improve them over time. If you add or change your records in any way, the books will remain in step with your work, and automatically update themselves appropriately. If, for example, you correct a person's name or dates, when you next view the sections on them in any of your books, you will find that the names and dates have been automatically corrected.[36]

Open Sample Project   In this chapter we will look at how you can work with books using the Family Historian Sample Project. We need to use a project for this, because books can only be created or opened in the context of a project. If you have a standalone GEDCOM file and you wish to create a book to show the information in it, you will first need to create a project and import the GEDCOM file into it.[37]

The Family Historian Sample Project should be listed as a project in the list of Family Historian Projects in the Projects Window. If it isn't there, click on the **More Tasks** button and then on the **Samples** submenu, click on **Reset Sample Project**. You should find that the Family Historian Sample Project is now listed. Select it and click **Open Project** to open it. When you do this, the project opens and Ian Munro is displayed as the focus person in the Focus Window.

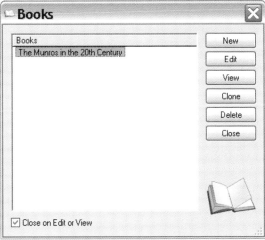

Figure 82 – The Books Dialog

---

[36] This doesn't apply to any 'free text' that you have added yourself as chapters or book sections.
[37] See the section "Projects and Files" in the Introduction if you are unclear about the difference between projects and standalone GEDCOM files.

The Books Dialog   Click now on **Books** on the **Publish** menu. The **Books Dialog** opens (see Figure 82 above). When you first do this in a new project that you have created yourself, the list will be empty. But one book has already been created in the sample project – called "The Munros in the 20th Century". Select that book and click the **View** button. When you do that, the Books Dialog will close and the book will be displayed in the Book Window (see Figure 83 below).

The Book Window   The Book Window is another subwindow. It is very similar to the Report Window. Like the Report Window, it has a side panel to the right, and most of the buttons are the same as, or very similar to, the Report Window Side Panel buttons. Whereas the Reports Window has a **Report** menu which only appears when the Reports Window is active, the Book Window has a **Book** menu which only appears when the Book Window is active.

By default books are displayed showing two pages at a time. The first page is always displayed on the right, leaving the left side blank. This is so that you can see what the book would like when printed. Scroll up and down to view all pages of the book "The Munros in the 20th Century". You should see that there is a short page with acknowledgements and a copyright statement, followed by the Contents page. As you can see from that, there are four chapters, followed by an index. A fan chart has been added to chapter 3 (on page 7), and a descendant diagram has been added to chapter 4 (on pages 10 -11).

Setting the Page Size and Orientation   The book "The Munros in the 20th Century" was designed to be printed on A4-sized paper. Confirm that the paper size is A4 by clicking now on **Print Setup** on the **File** menu. You can choose any paper size you want for a book, portrait or landscape. You can change the page size at any stage, and the book will reformat itself appropriately. However, leave the page size as A4, portrait.

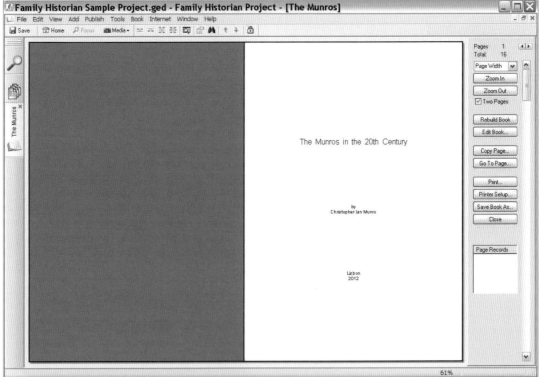

Figure 83 – The Book Window, displaying the book "The Munros in the 20th Century"

Choosing a Printer   Before closing the Print Setup dialog, take note of the printer: "Family Historian PDF". This isn't a real printer. It is a 'virtual' printer that is installed when Family Historian is installed. If you print to this 'printer' a PDF file will be generated. You can of course use any printer you want. For now, however, leave the printer as "Family Historian PDF" and close the Print Setup Dialog.

The Edit Book Dialog

Now click on the **Edit Book** button in the side panel on the right side. When you do this, the **Edit Book Dialog** appears showing the book contents (see Figure 84 below). The caption of the book is "Edit Book:" followed by the name of the book being edited. In this case it is "The Munros in the 20th Century".

The list of items that make up the book (the "Current Book Items") is displayed on the right-hand side. Each item in the Current Book Items list has at least one page. That isn't necessarily true in all books, but it is in this one. Select each item in turn and click the **Go To Page** button ☑ on the toolbar below the list. When you do this, the dialog doesn't close, but the page for the selected item (the starting page if it has more than one) will be displayed in the Book Window. If nothing happens when you click the button for some items, it is probably because the starting page for that item is already showing in the Book Window. If you want to see unambiguously which page is the starting page for a given item, untick "Two Pages" in the Side Panel on the right-hand side of the Book Window.

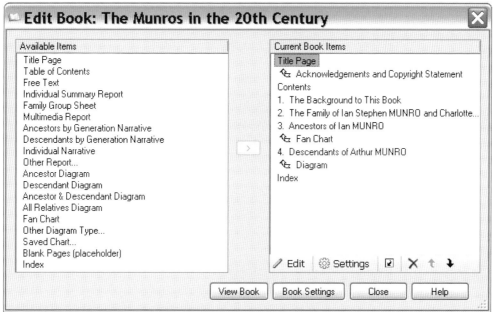

Figure 84 – The Edit Book Dialog, displaying the contents of the book "The Munros in the 20th Century"

Dialogs You Don't Have To Close

You will no doubt be aware that most dialog boxes are designed so that you can't do anything elsewhere in the application until you have closed the dialog – usually by pressing an OK or Cancel button. Dialogs that work like this are called 'modal' dialogs. But some dialog boxes, like the Property Box, aren't like that. These dialog boxes – called 'modeless dialogs' – are designed to work in conjunction with other windows, and you never have to close them. Both the **Edit Book Dialog** (Figure 84 above) and the **Books Dialog** (Figure 82 above) are modeless dialogs. To confirm this, click on the scrollbar to scroll up and down the Book Window, or tick/untick the "Two Pages" button in the Side Bar – without first closing the **Edit Book Dialog**. Now – still without closing the Edit Book Dialog – click the Close button in the Side Panel of the Book Window. The Book Window closes but the Edit Book Dialog remains open.

Performance Tip

Not only is there no problem about having the Edit Book Dialog open when the Book Window is closed, it is often a good idea. You will use the Edit Book Dialog to manage all aspects of the contents and layout of books. Some of the changes you may want to make could be much slower if the Book Window is open. So if the

Book Window is open and you notice the performance is slow when you are editing, try closing it. You can re-open it at any time, either from the **Books Dialog** or from the **Edit Book Dialog**.

Create a Book

We will now walk through an example of how to create a book. The book we will create will be an exact copy of "The Munros in the 20th Century". That way, you will have an example to compare against, so you can see if you have done it correctly. It doesn't really matter if either the **Edit Book Dialog** or the **Book Window** are open at this point, but start by closing them anyway.

Steps

1. Click on the **Books** menu command on the **Publish** menu. The **Books Dialog** opens once again (see Figure 82 above).
2. Click on the **New** button on the Books Dialog. The **Create Book Dialog** appears.
3. Enter the name of the new book as 'Test' and press the **Create** button. The **Edit Book Dialog** appears with the caption "Edit Book: Test". The Current Book Items list on the right-hand side is empty.
4. Select 'Title Page' in the 'Available Items' list on the left side and click on the Add Item button ⬚ to add it. When you do this the **Title Page Dialog** appears. Change the **Main** title to 'The Munros in the 20th Century'. In the **Author** section, set **Line 1** to 'by' and set **Line 2** to 'Christopher Ian Munro'. In the **Publication Details** section, set **Line 1** to 'Lisbon' and set **Line 2** to '2012'. Press **OK** to save and close the dialog.
5. Select 'Table of Contents' in the 'Available Items' list on the left side and click on the Add Item button ⬚ to add it. No other dialog appears. It is simply added to the 'Current Book Items' list.
6. Select 'Family Group Sheet' in the 'Available Items' list on the left side and click on the Add Item button ⬚ to add it. The **Select Record Dialog** appears. Click on 'Munro, Ian Stephen' in the list on the left side, and click on the Add button ⬚ to add all his family records to the list on the right side. Confirm that the list on the right side has one family record only: "...of Ian Stephen MUNRO and Charlotte CARRINGTON". You may have to resize the window and/or columns to see the full name. If there are any other records in the list on the right side, select them and click the Remove button ⬚ to get rid of them. Then press the **OK** button.
7. Select 'Ancestors by Generation Narrative' in the 'Available Items' list on the left side and click on the Add Item button ⬚ to add it. The **Select Record Dialog** appears again. Click on 'Munro, Ian Stephen' in the list on the left side, and click on the Add button ⬚ to add his Individual record to the list on the right side if it isn't already there. Confirm that the list on the right side has one Individual record only: 'MUNRO, Ian Stephen'. If there are any other records in the list on the right side, select them and click the Remove button ⬚ to get rid of them. Then press the **OK** button.
8. Select 'Descendants by Generation Narrative' in the 'Available Items' list on the left side and click on the Add Item button ⬚ to add it. The **Select Record Dialog** appears again. Click on 'Munro, Arthur Michael' in the list on the left side, and click on the Add button ⬚ to add his Individual record to the list on the right side if it isn't already there. Confirm that the list on the right side has one Individual record only: 'MUNRO, Arthur Michael'. If there are any other records in the list on the right side, select them and click the Remove button ⬚ to get rid of them. Then press the **OK** button.
9. Finally, select 'Index' in the 'Available Items' list on the left side and click on the Add Item button ⬚ to add it. No other dialog appears. It is simply added to the 'Current Book Items' list.

At this point, the Edit Book Dialog should look like Figure 85 below. Click on the

View Book button to view it in the Book Window. Close the Edit Book Dialog and the Books Dialog, or move them to one side, to get them out of the way, and scroll up and down the Book Window to view all the pages. Clearly it is not finished yet, but we've made a good start.

Tip: If you move the mouse over the scrollbar, or over the buttons in the top right corner ◀ ▶*, you can use your mouse wheel to scroll forwards and backwards through the book. This works on the Reports Window too.*

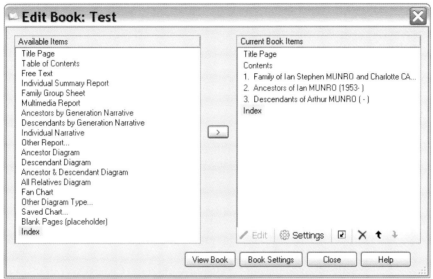

Figure 85 – The Edit Book Dialog, with three chapters added

Set Page Size and Printer Details

As we saw earlier, you can change page size and printer details whenever you want. But as we will be wanting to compare our book with the pre-installed one, it will be helpful to set page and printer sizes straight away.

Steps

1. Open a **Book Window** to view the 'Test' book we are creating, if there isn't already one open.
2. Click on **Print Setup** on the **File** menu. The **Print Setup Dialog** opens.
3. Make sure that the Paper Size is *A4* and that the Orientation is *Portrait*. They may already have these values, but if they don't, select them now.
4. Select 'Family Historian PDF' as the Printer and press **OK**.

Why choose that printer? It isn't essential, but it will be useful if we want our book to look exactly like the pre-installed one. The precise layout of text in books (and reports and diagrams) is affected by the printer. What you see is what you will get when the book is printed. And that can vary very slightly between printers. By choosing the same printer as the one the pre-installed book uses (as well as the same page size and page orientation) we can be sure that our book will look exactly the same.

View Two Books at the Same Time

You can have more than one Book Window open at the same time. Click on **Books** on the **Publish** menu to open the **Books Dialog**. You should see two books listed there: the new one 'Test', and the old one 'The Munros in the 20th Century". Temporarily untick **Close on Edit or View** at the bottom of the **Books Dialog**, and then select each book in turn and press the **View** button to display that book in the Books Window. Then tick **Close on Edit or View** once again, and close the **Books Dialog**.

You can switch between the two book windows by clicking on their respective icons on the Navigation Bar. Chapter 3 in the pre-installed book corresponds to Chapter 2 in the 'Test' one. But notice that, even apart from the fact that the chapter numbering is different, the chapter title is slightly different. The title in the 'Test' version has "(1953-)" on the end whereas the pre-installed book doesn't. Even more significant is that there are more generations on display in the pre-installed version. We have a little more work to do to make these chapters consistent.

Modify Chapter Settings

Make sure that you are viewing the 'Test' book in the Book Window. Then click **Edit Book** on the Side Panel to open the Edit Book Dialog. Its caption should read: "Edit Book: Test" and it should look like Figure 85 above.

Steps

1. Select the item "1. Family of Ian Stephen MUNRO and Charlotte..." and click on the **Settings** button on the toolbar below. The **Item Settings Dialog** opens (see Figure 86 below). If the caption says "Book Settings" you pressed the wrong button! We will look at book settings latter, but for now it is item settings that we're concerned with. So take care not to confuse the two buttons. The tabs and options available on the Item Settings Dialog will vary considerably depending on the type of item selected. In this case, the item we have selected is a chapter based on the Family Group Sheet report; so the tabs and options are ones that are suitable for a report of that type.
2. The heading for this chapter is currently "Family of Ian Stephen MUNRO and Charlotte CARRINGTON". But the pre-installed version has a 'The' on the front of it. Notice that at this point, the background of the heading box is yellow. Add the word 'The' on the front so that the heading now reads: "The Family of Ian Stephen MUNRO and Charlotte CARRINGTON". When you do this the background changes from yellow to white. The yellow background hints at a capability that advanced users can take advantage of if they wish. Ordinary users can simply ignore it, and we will in this book.[38] Leave other values unchanged and press the OK button to close the Item Settings Dialog.
3. Now select the item "Ancestors of Ian MUNRO (1953-)" and press the **Settings** button on the toolbar below. The **Item Settings Dialog** opens again. Change the Heading to read simply "Ancestors of Ian MUNRO" (that is, remove the year information on the end). Again, the box background changes from yellow to white when you do this. Now click on the 'Main' tab and change the number of Generations to 6. Leave other settings unchanged and press the **OK** button to close the Item Settings Dialog.
4. Select the item "Descendants of Arthur MUNRO (-)" and press the **Settings** button on the toolbar below. The **Item Settings Dialog** opens again. Change the Heading to read simply "Descendants of Arthur MUNRO" (that is, remove the "(-)" on the end). Again, the box background changes from yellow to white when you do this. Leave other settings unchanged and press the **OK** button to close the Item Settings Dialog.

Add Free Text Page

We will now add an acknowledgements page with a copyright statement.

Steps

1. Open the **Edit Book Dialog** if it isn't already open. Make sure that is showing the contents of the 'Test' book. Its caption should read: "Edit Book: Test". It doesn't matter whether or not the Book Window is open at this point.
2. Select 'Free Text' in the list labelled "Available Items", on the left side of the

---

[38] The yellow background indicates that the text is auto-generated – which means that if the names change, the heading will automatically update itself. Headings with white backgrounds do not automatically update themselves when the data changes. If you want to learn how to modify headings while preserving their generated status, or to create new auto-generated headings, click on the Help button, where it is all explained in detail.

Edit Book Dialog, and press the Add Item button [›] to add it to the list of Current Book Items. When you do this, a new text window opens with the caption "Enter Text". Type the following into the text window: 'Many thanks to everyone who helped me with my research.' Then press the ENTER key twice to add two line breaks, and add the line: 'Copyright (c) Christopher Munro, 2012. All rights reserved.' Finally press the OK button to close the dialog. Now the **Item Settings Dialog** appears. Change the 'Heading' to 'Acknowledgements and Copyright Statement'. Change the 'Format' to 'No heading'. Leave the 'Start on' value as 'New Page' and press OK to close the Item Settings Dialog.

3. In the Edit Book Dialog, our new free text item has been added just above the index. Make sure that it selected and click on the up arrow button [↑] on the toolbar, until it appears between Title Page and the Contents in the list of Current Book Items.

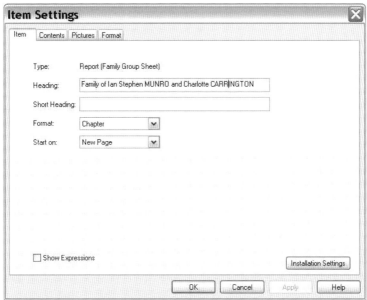

Figure 86 – The Item Settings Dialog for a Family Group Sheet report

Item Settings   All book items have settings – that is to say, if you select any item in the Current Book Items list, the **Settings** button will always be ungreyed, and you can click on it to edit that item's settings. The same is not true however of the **Edit** button. This button is only available for certain types of item.

Add Free Text Chapter   We will now add a free text chapter – that is to say, a chapter in which the text is provided entirely by you, and isn't auto-generated at all. Actually, as this is just an exercise, the text in this 'chapter' will consist of a single sentence only. But you can, of course, have as much text as you want in a free text item.

Steps

1. Select 'Free Text' in the list labelled "Available Items", on the left side of the Edit Book Dialog, and press the Add Item button [›] to add it to the list of Current Book Items. When you do this, a new text window opens with the caption "Enter Text". Type the following into the text window: 'My father was very close to his grandfather, Michael Smith Munro, and often told me stories about him.' Press the OK button to close the dialog. Now the **Item Settings Dialog** appears. Change the 'Heading' to 'The Background to This Book'. Leave the 'Format' as 'Chapter' (we want this item to be a chapter in its own right), leave the 'Start on' value as 'New Page', and press OK to close the Item

Settings Dialog.

2. In the Edit Book Dialog, our new free text item has been added just above the index as "4. The Background to This Book". Make sure that it selected and click on the up arrow button ⬆ on the toolbar to move it, until it appears just after Contents in the list of Current Book Items. Notice that all chapters are automatically renumbered when their order changes. At this point, the Edit Book Dialog should look like Figure 87 below.

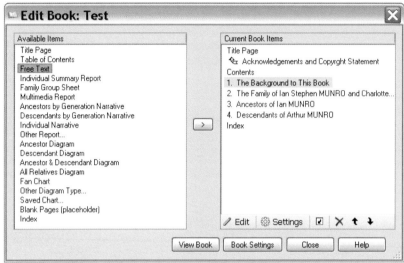

Figure 87 – The Edit Book Dialog with the new Free Text chapter

Add Fan Chart The pre-installed version of the book has a fan chart at the end of the chapter 3. We will add that now.

Steps

1. Open the Edit Book Dialog for the 'Test' book, if it isn't already open. Select 'Fan Chart' in the list labelled "Available Items", on the left side of the Edit Book Dialog, and press the Add Item button to add it to the list of Current Book Items. When you do this, the Fan Chart Dialog opens. Choose Ian Munro as **Root Person**, set **Chart Type** to 'Half', set **Generations** to 5, set **Contents** to 'Ahnentafel & Dates', set **Colour** to '7 Colours', and set **Gen Depth** to 1 inch (2.54 cms). Press **OK**. The **Select Chart Pages dialog** opens looking like Figure 88 below.

2. The Select Chart Pages allows you to do a number of things: scale your diagram to any size, position it where you want on one page or over a number of pages, and select which pages of the diagram you wish to appear in the book. Set the scale to 59%. You can either type that into the Scale box or move the slider till the value is 59%.

3. Now check **Position on Page** in the **Mouse Action** area in the bottom left of the dialog box. Then move the mouse over the diagram, and click-and-drag until the fan chart is centred on one page.

4. Check **Select Page** once again. When this option is checked, you click on a page to select it or de-select it. Only selected pages will appear in the book. Click on the one and only page a few times to select and deselect it. Finally select it (so that it has a blue border).

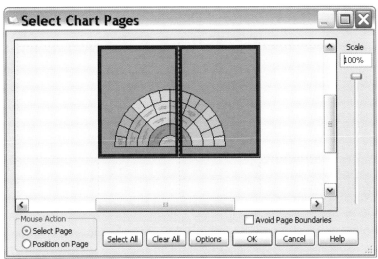

Figure 88 – The Select Chart Pages dialog before changes

5. The fan chart currently has a grey background. But we don't want it to have any background in the book; so click on the **Options** button to open the **Diagram Options Dialog**. Choose the **Print** tab, and untick **Print Background**. Press **OK** to close the Diagram Options Dialog.

6. At this point the **Select Chart Page Dialog** should look like Figure 89 below. Press OK to close the dialog.

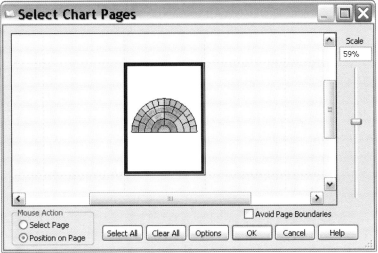

Figure 89 – The Select Chart Pages dialog after changes

7. Within the Edit Book Dialog, the fan chart has been inserted as a chapter: "5. Fan Chart". Select it and click the Up arrow ⬆ to move it up one, so that it comes immediately after "3. Ancestors of Ian Munro".

8. We don't want the fan chart to be a chapter in its own right. We want to add it to the previous chapter; so select it and click the **Settings** button. Leave **Heading** as 'Fan Chart', and change **Format** to 'No Heading'. Press **OK**.

9. Finally, to view the Fan Chart, select it in the list and click on the **Go to Page** button on the toolbar. The Book Window is opened and jumps immediately to the Fan Chart page.

Add Diagram Our example book is nearly finished. It is only missing one item. The pre-installed version of the book has a Descendant Diagram at the end of Chapter fan chart at the end of the chapter 3. We will add that now.

You can add any kind of diagram, even including custom diagrams, to a book (just as you can add any kind of report, even including custom reports). In this example, we will add a previously saved chart.

Steps

1. Open the **Edit Book Dialog** for the 'Test' book, if it isn't already open. Select 'Saved Chart' in the list labelled "Available Items", on the left side of the Edit Book Dialog, and press the Add Item button ⟩. When you do this, a dialog appears with a list of Saved Charts. In fact there is only one: "Descendants of A.M.Munro". Select this chart and click on the **OK** button. The **Select Chart Pages Dialog** appears. At this point the chart may appear on as many as 8 pages. Drag the Scale slider until the Scale is at 40%.
2. Tick **Avoid Page Boundaries**[39] to ensure that no boxes overlap page boundaries. Then select **Position on Page** and click-and-drag on the diagram until it nicely straddles two pages (see Figure 90 below).
3. Again, we don't want the background of this diagram appearing in the book; so to prevent that, press the **Options** button to open the **Diagram Options Dialog**. On the **Print** tab, untick **Print Background** and press **OK** to close the **Diagram Options Dialog**.
4. Make sure both pages are selected (a quick way to do this is to click on the **Select All** button). Then click **OK** to close the **Select Chart Pages** dialog.

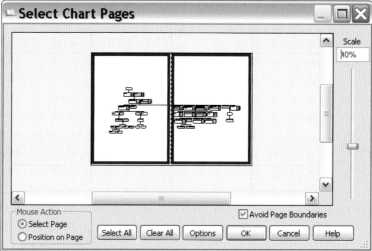

Figure 90 – The Select Chart Pages dialog with the Descendant diagram

5. In the Edit Book Dialog, the new diagrams has been added as another chapter: "5. Descendants of A.M. Munro". We need to change that. We don't want the descendants diagram to be a chapter on its own. We want to add it to the end of the previous chapter. So select the item and click on **Settings** on the toolbar. In the **Item Settings Dialog**, **Heading** should read 'Descendants of A.M. Munro'. Change this to 'Diagram'. Change **Format** to 'No heading' and press **OK**.

At this point, the book you have created should be exactly like the pre-installed one and the **Edit Book Dialog** should look like Figure 84 above. Scroll through the book you created in the Book Window now, and confirm that it looks as it should.

Diagram
Headings

In our example book, we didn't want either the fan chart or the diagram to be a chapter in their own right – but they could be if you wanted them to. Also, we

---

[39] The Avoid Page Boundaries option only affects tree boxes. It has no effect on fan charts.

didn't want either of them to have a heading in the book – which is why we chose 'No heading' as the **Format** option for both. If you want a chart or diagram to have a heading, there are two ways of doing it. You can either type the heading you want to use into the **Heading** field of the **Item Settings Dialog**, and pick a suitable format level (anything but 'No heading'). Or you can save your diagram as a saved chart in the Diagram Window, and add your own custom-designed heading to the chart itself, using text boxes and rectangles and all the features available to you on the Shapes toolbar in the Diagram Window. If you take this approach, you will want to choose the 'No heading' format option in Diagram Settings.

Saving Book in PDF Format

When you have finished your book, if you want it to be properly printed and bound, you can take it to your local print shop, or use an online printing website. Chances are good that either the print shop or the printing website will want you to provide the book to them in the form of a PDF file. To save your book in PDF format, click on the **Save Book As** button on the Side Panel of the Book Window when viewing the book, and choose 'PDF File'.

Saving Book as a Word-Processor Document

The alternative to saving your book as a PDF file is to save it as a word-processor document. This can be a good option if you want to make further changes to your book in your word-processor. To do this, click on **Save Book As** on the Side Panel of the Book Window when viewing your book, and choose 'Word-Processor Document (RTF)'.

When you save your book as a word-processor document, the pagination will inevitably change. That means that the page references in the table of contents, and in the Index, will be inaccurate. However this should not be a problem as Family Historian saves both the table of contents, and the index, as word-processor *fields* – that is, as 'smart' word-processor items that can automatically update themselves to show the correct values. To make them show the correct values, you just need to *update* them. How you update fields will depend on what kind of word-processor you use. In Microsoft Word, for example, you just need to right-click on the table of contents or index, and select **Update Field** from the dropdown menu that appears.

19 More Wizards and Tools

Family Historian contains numerous tools and wizards to help you do various tasks. We have already looked at several of them during the course of this book. For example, we looked at the **Publishing Tools Finder** in Chapter 17. We looked at **Gedcom File Export**, **Split Tree Helper** and **Merge/Compare** (record, branch and file) in Chapter 15. And we looked at the **Work with External File Links** tool in Chapter 5. This final chapter will look at some other useful 'wizards' and tools that we haven't yet encountered.

Create Website Wizard

You can easily create a website using your family tree data. The **Create Website Wizard** walks you through the whole process in 8 simple steps. To start the wizard, click on **Create a Website** on the **Publish** menu. When you finish, Family Historian will have created all the files for your website in a folder that you specify.

At each step of the wizard click on the **Help** button for detailed context-sensitive help explaining what the options mean and what you need to do. Once the website files have been created, you can click on a button entitled "Learn How to Put Your Website on the Internet".

You can only use the **Create Website** tool in the context of a Family Historian project.

Make CD/DVD Wizard

Creating a family tree CD or DVD is just as easy – and indeed is very similar. The **Make CD/DVD Wizard** is largely the same as the Create Website Wizard. To start it, click on **Make a Family Tree CD/DVD** on the **Publish** menu. The **Make CD/DVD Wizard** creates all the files you need for your family tree CD or DVD. To burn these files onto a CD or DVD you will need a CD/DVD writer and CD/DVD burning software. CD/DVD burning software will most likely be included with your CD/DVD writer; but if it isn't, you can use the burning capability built into Windows.

As with the **Create Website Wizard**, click on **Help** at each step for detailed help as you go along.

The reason that creating a family tree CD/DVD is so similar to creating a website, is that the same technologies will be used in each case. If you give someone a copy of your family tree CD or DVD, they will use their web-browser to view it, and to explore the CD or DVD.

Their web-browser should start automatically when they put the CD or DVD into their CD/DVD drive; but if that isn't working for some reason, tell them to start their web-browser and use its **Open** menu command to open the start page (normally, index.html) in the **data** folder on the CD or DVD, or the **start.html** page in the root folder of the CD or DVD.

The How Related Tool

To open the **How Related** tool, click on **How Related** on the **Tools** menu (see Figure 91 below). Use it to find out how any two people are related. People can be related in more than one way – for example, your spouse may also be your cousin. The **How Related** tool can optionally show up to nine ways that two people are related. If they are not *directly* related Family Historian will show how they are *indirectly* related to one another, through some third person, if they are.

You may want to copy the relationship information into another document. To do this, select the text in the box, and press **Ctrl-C** (that is, press-and-hold the **Ctrl** key while pressing the **C** key). That copies the text. To paste it into another context, position the cursor where you want the text to go and press **Ctrl-V**.

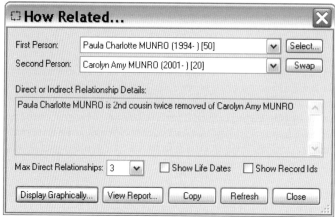

Figure 91 – The How Related tool

Display Graphically If you want to see exactly in what way two people are related (for example, Paula Munro and Carolyn Munro in the example in Figure 91 above) click on the **Display Graphically** button. If you already have a Diagram Window open, and if it is possible to show how the two people are related in that Diagram Window, Family Historian will ask you if you want to use the current diagram. If you answer No, or if there is no suitable diagram to use, a new diagram will be opened. The exact relationship is marked on the diagram using a *route* (see Figure 92 below). We encountered routes earlier in Chapter 10. You can manipulate to them, change their appearance, delete them, add boxes to them or remove boxes from them, using the Family Connection Mapper. See Chapter 10 for more on this.

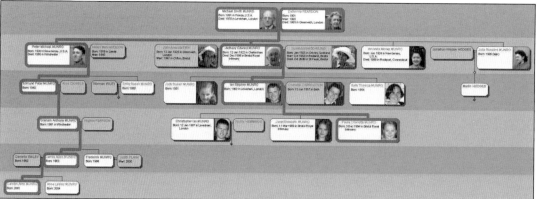

Figure 92 – Graphical Display of a Relationship

The How Related Report Instead of, or as well as, viewing a relationships graphically in a diagram, you can also click on the **View Report** button in the **How Related** tool, to see a report describing in detail how the two people are related. The **How Related** tool is another example of a *modeless* dialog. A modeless dialog, as we saw earlier, is one that you don't need to close. You can access other parts of the program without closing it first.

Internet Search To start the **Internet Search** tool, click on **Search the Internet** on the **Internet** menu. You will need access to the Internet.

There are a great many websites round the world with databases that you can search, containing important genealogical data. The list shown here does not attempt to be comprehensive. It is a highly selective list of just some important research sites. With each site, click on its entry in the list to see a brief description of what it offers, in a box below the list.

With some sites, you can type name details (and possibly a start and end year) into the Internet Search dialog, and click **Search Now** to start the search from within Family Historian. Click on **Only show sites that can be searched from here** to filter out sites that cannot be searched in this way.

With all sites, click on **Go To Site** to direct your browser to the site.

Autosave

It was briefly mentioned in Chapter 1, but in case you missed it – Family Historian has an autosave facility. You can get it to automatically save changes every few minutes if you wish. This can be set either in the Project Window (click the **More Tasks** button) or in **Preferences** (see the **Tools** menu).

Backup and Restore

It has also been mentioned before, but remembering to backup your data is very important. You can backup a Family Historian data file using the **Backup** command on the **Backup/Restore** submenu off the **File** menu. You will also be prompted to backup your file at the end of every session in which you have made any changes to your data (unless you opt not to be prompted). Family Historian supports 3 kinds of backup: Full, Medium and Small:

Small Backup: This is the smallest and quickest backup option. In this option, only the GEDCOM file itself is backed up. This is the only Backup type which can be used if you are editing a standalone GEDCOM file.

Medium Backup: The most important project files are backed up, but not the entire project folder – only a subset of it. Specifically, the project file and the project data subfolder are backed up. The project data subfolder contains the GEDCOM file which Family Historian uses to store all your data records, and it also contains all multimedia files which you opted to copy into the Project folder, and potentially other files too – such as some settings files and log files.

Full: The entire project folder is backed up. If you have made use of the optional 'Public' subfolder to store output of any kind, this too will be backed up. 'Full' is potentially the largest, slowest and most comprehensive backup. But even with this backup option, any multimedia files which you chose to not copy into the project folder will not be backed up.

By default, when you opt to do a backup at the end of a session, you will be given a choice of which kind of backup to do. If you always do the same kind of backup at this point, you can configure this in Preferences, in the Backup tab, and save yourself effectively being asked an unnecessary question. Or if you don't wish to be prompted to backup at all, you can specify this too.

Some people back up at the end of every session into another folder on the same hard disk. This isn't necessarily a bad idea. It's easy to do, so you're more likely to do it. After all, one of the best reasons to backup is to protect you against your own errors – and having backup copies of your file on the same hard disk should help with that. But remember that hard disks can fail too, and it's not an uncommon thing to happen. If yours does fail, all backup files on the same hard disk will be lost along with everything else. And you won't get any warning that it's about to happen. So whether or not you do some backups onto the same hard disk, you should definitely also periodically do other backups onto some other medium – such as a CD.

Think about what the implications would be if your hard disk suddenly failed now. If you could live with losing a week's work, you can presumably afford to backup onto another medium only once a week. If you couldn't face losing even a day's work (perhaps because the data came from an interview which you won't be able to repeat) backup onto another medium at the end of each day. If your genealogy research is your life's work and *really* precious, think about giving a copy to a trusted friend to keep in case you're burgled or the house burns down. There are also internet backup services. You never need to lose data if you're careful.

You should have a policy on backing up, and you should back up regularly. And at least some of those regular backups should be onto a completely different medium so that if your hard disk fails, they aren't lost too. When you backup onto another medium, such as a CD, be sure to label it carefully, and have a place where you keep backups, so they don't get lost.

To restore from a backup, use the **Restore** command on the **File** menu within Family Historian.

Plugins   Support for plugins was added in version 5. A plugin is an extension to the main program, which adds new features. For example, the 'core' program has no mapping tool for showing events on maps, and no timeline reports; but at time of writing there are already some plugins in the **Family Historian Plugin Store** that add support for mapping, and one that adds support for timelines.

To run a plugin, you must first install it. If, for example, you download a plugin file to your desktop, you can simply double-click on it to install it. Once installed, you can run it from the Plugins Dialog (see Figure 93 below). To open the **Plugins Dialog**, click **Plugins** on the **Tools** menu. To run a plugin, just select it and click on the **Run** button. Plugins are powerful programs in their own right, so it is important that you know and trust the source of the plugin, and you know what it does, before you run it.

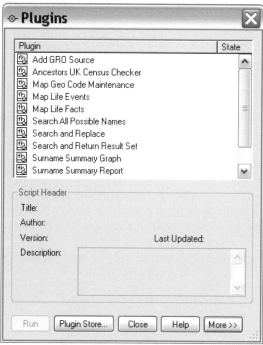

Figure 93 – The Plugins Dialog

The Plugin Store

A good place to look for free plugins is the Family Historian Plugin Store. To access the store, just click on the **Plugin Store** button on the **Plugins Dialog**. This will open your web-browser to take you to the Plugin Store area of the Family Historian website. You can browse all plugins in the store, read about them, and download and install them. New plugins can be added to the store at any time, so don't forget to check for new ones periodically.[40] You can also provide feedback on plugins by rating them, and view ratings given by others.

Add Plugins to the Tools Menu

Some plugins are so useful that you may find yourself using them frequently. In which case, you may want to add them to the **Tools** menu, for quicker and more convenient access. To add a plugin to the **Tools** menu, open the **Plugins Dialog** and press the **More** button to see extended options. Select the plugin in question, and check **Add to Tools Menu**.

Write Your Own Plugins

Writing plugins is not hard for anyone who has any experience of writing scripts in scripting languages, or of simple programming. All the tools you need – including a combined editor and debugger – are provided for you by Family Historian, together with all the documentation you need. To learn how to write plugins, click on the **More** button within the **Plugins Dialog**, and then click on the **How to Write Plugins** button.

Plugins as Scripting Tool

Anyone can write a plugin to add new features to Family Historian. If you write a plugin that others might find useful, we encourage you to submit it to the Family Historian Plugin Store. However, you may sometimes just want to write a script to make a very specific one-off change to your data. You can use the Family Historian plugin editor/debugger to do this.

Troubleshooting

If Family Historian does not appear to be working correctly, the two most likely explanations are that there is something wrong with your family tree data file (that is, your GEDCOM file) or there is something wrong with your installation.

Family Historian should never cause any data corruption in your GEDCOM file; but it is possible that corruption could have arisen if the file, or part of it, was created by another genealogy application. In any case, the first thing to do is to run the **Validate** command on the **File** menu. This can not only detect whether or not the GEDCOM file is corrupt, it can often automatically fix the problem. It will produce a report when it does this and you should keep a copy of this report if it has fixed corrupt data, because any such corrections will usually involve simply removing the bad data. If a bad link, such as a corrupt parent-child link, has been removed, you will probably want to reinstate it with a valid one. But it will be up to you to do that from within the program. Family Historian will not do that automatically. You need to keep the report, so that you know which links to reinstate.

If there is something wrong with your installation, you should uninstall and reinstall. To uninstall, start the **Control Panel** (accessible from the Start menu) and run the Control Panel applet that is responsible for uninstalling programs (it may be called **Add or Remove Programs** or **Programs and Features** or something similar – it varies depending on your version of Windows). Select *Family Historian* and uninstall it.

When you reinstall it, re-apply your original method of installation. Remember to reapply any upgrades.

---

[40] If you subscribe to Family Historian Bulletins you will receive periodic notifications of new plugins, amongst other news of interest to Family Historian users. See the Family Historian website (www.family-historian.co.uk) to learn more about Family Historian bulletins.

Index

Free Services for Family Historian Users

Free Upgrades

Minor upgrades are usually free and can be downloaded, when available, from
http://www.family-historian.co.uk/downloads

Family Historian Bulletins

If you would like to be notified of upgrades (including free upgrades) and new releases of Family Historian, you should subscribe to our Bulletin Service. You should expect to receive only a few such bulletins each year. To subscribe send an email to bulletins@family-historian.co.uk with the single word 'subscribe' as the subject header. You will be able to unsubscribe whenever you want to by sending an email to the same email address with 'unsubscribe' as the subject header. We will not make your email address available to anyone else.

The Family Historian Users Mailing List

The Family Historian Users Mailing List is a free forum where Family Historian users can discuss aspects of the program, new and inexperienced users can post questions and ask advice, and experienced users can share their knowledge and give tips.
See http://www.family-historian.co.uk/support for instructions on how to join.

The Family Historian User Group Website

The Family Historian User Group Website is an independent website, set up and run by Family Historian users, for Family Historian users. It also is free. It has news, forums, links, downloads, articles, a newsletter, wish list, chat rooms and more. Downloads include utility programs, installable extensions to Family Historian and video demos. The website is located at http://www.fhug.org.uk

Further Supplies

Further copies of this manual or the software or future upgrades are available from:
http://www.my-history.co.uk